Ethics of the Fantastic Four

Ethics of the Fantastic Four

Mark D. White

Published by Ockham Publishing in the United Kingdom in 2025

ISBN: 978-1-83919-640-9

Cover by Ockham Publishing

www.ockham-publishing.com

Acknowledgments

I would like to thank the *fantastic* Rob Johnson and Sarah Hembrow at Ockham for their support during the development and preparation of this *fourth* volume in the series. (See what we did there?)

I thank my own Fantastic Four—Lauren Hale, Carol Borden, Anita Leirfall, and William Irwin—for their continued encouragement, which I needed more than ever this time around.

I thank all the creators who have told the stories of the Fantastic Four over the years, including John Byrne, Tom DeFalco, Jonathan Hickman, Karl Kesel, Dwayne McDuffie, Carlos Pacheco, George Pérez, Paul Ryan, J. Michael Straczynski, Mark Waid, Mike Wieringo, and most of all, Stan Lee and Jack Kirby, to whom I dedicate this book with my eternal gratitude.

Contents

Introduction

Everybody knows them. They are Marvel Comics' First Family, featured in the World's Greatest Comics Magazine, which launched the modern Marvel Universe in 1961 thanks to the creative genius of Stan Lee and Jack Kirby. Besides the four themselves, the Fantastic Four comic also introduced the world to Black Panther, Silver Surfer, Galactus, the Watcher, the Inhumans, and most notoriously, Doctor Doom. In addition to their countless appearances in Marvel Comics, they are the stars of (to date) five feature films and four animated series, with countless toys and action figures capturing their classic images.

Their origin story is as well as known as rocketing to Earth from a doomed planet, being bitten by a radioactive spider, or witnessing your parents' senseless murder. Four brave space travelers are bombarded by cosmic rays that change each of them in different ways. Reed Richards, whose brilliant mind could wrap around any scientific puzzle, gained the ability to stretch his body over incredible distances and into strange shapes. Susan Storm, whose initial shyness masked her inner strength, could now become invisible at will, and later learned she could turn other things invisible as well as project powerful force fields. Johnny Storm, the classic impetuous teenager, found that personality trait embodied in flames that encompassed his body and enabled him to fly. Finally, Benjamin Grimm, the wise-cracking football star and ace pilot, is covered with rocks and endowed with physical strength that matches his stalwart perseverance. Still stunned by their transformations, they immediately agree to use their powers for the good of humanity as... the *Fantastic Four!*

Over the last sixty-plus years, these four heroes have faced every challenge imaginable—and many of them unimaginable, except to the brilliant minds of the writers and artists who brought them to life for the benefit of the rest of us. Although many of their adventures take place on a cosmic scale, involving the survival of the entire universe if not multiverse, their personal struggles are just as engaging. Whether it's Reed and Sue's path to marriage and becoming parents to Franklin and Valeria, Johnny's quest to find true love and purpose in life, or Ben's struggle to come to terms with his "monstrous" appearance and accept the love of Alicia Masters, it is the personal lives and relationships of the Fantastic Four that bring their stories down to Earth and make them relatable (which set the standard for every Marvel Comic to come).

In this book, I'll explore many of the ethical issues that the Fantastic Four have struggled with in their time together, ranging from the moral dilemmas that threaten the entire populations of worlds and universes to the more down-to-earth ways they deal with each other and those around them.

The first chapter introduces the basic ethical nature of the members of the Fantastic Four by surveying the three main systems of moral philosophy that I'll reference throughout the book: virtue ethics, utilitarianism, and deontology. The next four chapters take a deeper look at a specific issue relevant to each member, starting with Reed Richards (Mister Fantastic) and his planet-sized sense of responsibility, followed by Susan Storm-Richards (the Invisible Woman) and the various ways that she embodies strength. Then we turn to Johnny Storm (the Human Torch) and how he deals with the inherent danger of his powers, concluding the tour with Ben Grimm (the Thing) and his struggle with self-loathing, especially in his relationship with blind sculptress Alicia Masters.

The final three chapters extend our philosophical exploration to other essential parts of the Fantastic Four's world. In the sixth chapter, I look at one of the most ethically contentious storylines in the history of the Marvel Universe, the first superhero Civil War, which raised fascinating issues of privacy, security, and autonomy that divided the heroes of the Marvel Universe—including the Fantastic Four. The seventh chapter takes us from Earth to the farthest reaches of space as we try to figure out the moral agency and status of Galactus the Devourer and consider the complicity and responsibility of his herald, the Silver Surfer, in satisfying his hunger by destroying inhabited worlds throughout the universe.

We conclude the book with an examination of the person who would be very upset to learn that his chapter did not come before Reed's: Victor von Doom, otherwise known as Doctor Doom, ruler of Latveria and archfoe of the Fantastic Four. After reviewing Victor's early life and the circumstances that transformed him into one of the most feared individuals in the world, we'll dive into his obsession over his appearance and the deep insecurity it reflects, his competition with "the accursed Richards," and his presumption to be a man of honor despite what his behavior shows.

Although it only scratches the surface of the philosophical wonders inherent in the decades of stories of the Fantastic Four, I hope this book provides fans of the comics, animated series, and movies with new ways to think about the characters and stories they love. For those new to the adventures of Marvel Comics' first family, I hope this book gives you insight into why they are beloved by so many people around the world (even in Latveria, if they dare). And let's not forget that there's some fantastically fascinating filo—sorry, *philosophy*—in these pages as well!

So find a cozy chair in the Baxter Building, have H.E.R.B.I.E. bring you a refreshing drink, and let's get started…

Chapter 1
Overview of the Fantastic Four and Moral Philosophy

In this first chapter, we are going to use some general observations about the Fantastic Four, both as a group and individually, to introduce the three main schools of ethics that we'll use throughout this book: virtue ethics, utilitarianism, and deontology. Even if we don't mention them by name every time an ethical topic is introduced and discussed in later chapters, these are the concepts of moral philosophy that ground everything we talk about in this book (and most debates about ethics outside of it).

The Virtues of the Fantastic Four

Near the end of the first year of the World's Greatest Comic Magazine, we meet William "Willie" Lumpkin, the team's loyal and faithful mail carrier.[1] Over many years of service, Willie gets to know all the members of the team well, so it is to him that we give the honor of providing an ethical evaluation of the Fantastic Four. "Good people," he told a television crew for a tribute special for the team. "A real family."[2] We could leave it there—and make this a *very* short book—but instead we'll go a little deeper. We will start with Willie's statement that the Fantastic Four are "good people," because it is in the spirit of the first school of ethics we discuss: virtue ethics.

Virtue ethics is the oldest of the three major schools of ethics, going back to the ancient Greeks, among whom Aristotle is the best-known exponent.[3] When Willie calls the team "good people," he is following the virtue ethics tradition of evaluating the moral quality of a person, rather than the things they do (or fail to do). We'll see later that the other prominent school of ethics, utilitarianism and deontology, both look at actions, such as helping, lying, or killing, and say whether they're good or bad, right or wrong, permitted or prohibited. But virtue ethics looks at the person performing the actions instead and says whether or not they are "good people."

What does it mean to say someone is "good" in terms of virtue ethics? They must possess character traits, or *virtues*, that lead them to ethical actions that contribute to positive outcomes. Honesty is one common example of a virtue: if a person possesses the character trait of honesty, they are more likely to behave honestly in situations where it is morally required, especially if there is some incentive *not* to behave honestly. The honest person does not need to be perfectly honest, but they would behave honestly more often than the dishonest person, as well as in circumstances that would tempt the less honest person more.

There is an important way Aristotle narrows down what exactly it means to have a virtue such as honesty: the *golden mean*. Every virtue is found at the middle point between two extremes, which themselves would be *vices*. For example, honesty lies between deception at one extreme and forthrightness at the other. While it is obviously bad to practice deceit, which represents a deficiency of honesty, it is just as bad, albeit for different reasons, to be completely forthright, which represents an excess of honesty. In terms of the latter, think of that one person you know who enjoys being blunt, who just "calls it like I see it," with no regard for anyone's feelings.

In addition to recognizing the golden mean, a truly honest person must also use practical wisdom or *judgment* to decide how honest to be in particular situations. As Aristotle wrote, virtues must be put into practice "at the right times, with reference to the right objects, towards the right people, with the right motive, and in the right way."[4] Understood in this way, virtuous behavior is very sensitive to context and circumstances, and the virtuous person needs to adapt to the relevant aspects of a situation. It's not so complicated, though: Most of us do this whenever a situation calling for honesty also rubs up against other concerns, some of which may be other virtues themselves, like sensitivity. We don't want to be the person who blurts out the truth and then defends the harm done with "I was just being honest"—there is more to ethics and virtue than honesty alone.

An example may help at this point. Although it is not emphasized as much his other virtues, Reed Richards is a fairly honest person (as are the other three, of course). There are many instances in which he chooses not to be completely honest, but for a good reason that is not rooted in his own self-interest. Many of these cases deal with his repeated attempts to cure Ben of his rocky condition, so he can live once again as a flesh-and-blood man and be with his true love, Alicia Masters. After one such attempt, Ben does revert back to normal but at the cost of his memories, to the point where he doesn't even recognize Alicia. Reed quickly changes him back while saying, "It's what he would want! Being Ben Grimm would be meaningless without his memory...without his love for Alicia!" Later, Reed tells Ben that he failed altogether, and when Sue asks him why he lied, he says he wanted to save him the disappointment. Johnny calls him "a great pal" to Ben, impressed that he would "let him think you were a complete flop, in order to soften the blow for him."[5]

In this case, Reed decided not to be completely honest—he did, after all, succeed in restoring himself to normal, but with complications he knew Ben could not accept—but he did so in the interest of another virtue, compassion. This is another way that *judgment* is essential to the proper exercise of the virtues, balancing the pull of several important virtues at once. Reed could have told Ben the complete truth, but he anticipated that Ben would react badly in the thought that he may never be cured without losing his memories. So Reed weighed the importance of both honesty and compassion in this particular situation, and he chose to act out of compassion—as many of us do when we tell white lies to spare a friend's feelings, or withhold the details of a gruesome death from the deceased person's survivors.

The complexity of ethical decision-making based on virtues is well illustrated in the comics when Kosmos and Kubik, two sentient versions of the all-powerful Cosmic Cube, want to know why Earth is given special status among the higher powers of the universe. They decide to start with the Fantastic Four and the question: "why did the cosmic hand of fate touch these four seemingly insignificant mortals?"[6] To this end, Kosmos and Kubik run what Johnny calls later "some kind of alien test of character": they take away what they consider to be each member's "dominant character trait—that singular element of their psycho-genetic programming which directs their every action." They identify these traits as "Mister Fantastic's superhuman intellect—the Invisible Woman's vast capacity for compassion—the tremendous courage of the Thing—and the Human Torch's innate aggressiveness." After they "extract" what they consider to be the Four's essential traits, they observe how they react to artificial crises.

Before we discuss their results, we need to say a few words about their proposed experiment. The idea that character traits would "direct their every action" is an oversimplification of how virtue ethics works—as we saw above, and which Kosmos and Kubik will discover for themselves— but it has a long history in both philosophy and psychology (where it goes under the name *dispositional theory*).[7] More important for our purposes, even if the character traits they identify with each of the four were accurate in terms of predicting and explaining their behavior, they are not all traits we would associate with virtue itself. Compassion and courage are definitely virtues, but intellect and aggressiveness are not. Intellect is a valuable tool, but can be used for good or bad, as the Fantastic Four's more brilliant foes, such as Doctor Doom and the Mad Thinker, prove in their every appearance. Aggressiveness (or impetuousness) would be the vice associated with a deficiency of patience or restraint, with the extreme on the other end being something like passivity, such as the Watchers' self-imposed rule of noninterference (which they seem to break as often as they adhere to it).

When Kosmos and Kubik put the Fantastic Four through their paces, they discover that, in the absence of their "dominant character traits," other traits compensate and enable each member to defeat the obstacles put in their way. They conclude that the four are "exceptional beings" whose "versatility is almost without limit," although this has less to do with their powers and more to do with the human capacity for nuanced behavior and judgment. As Kubik observes:

> the usually brutish Thing demonstrated a rare capacity for compassion; while the Invisible Woman displayed courage far beyond her usual inclination—which itself is well above normal! And Mister Fantastic revealed a core of aggressiveness which is normally subliminated [sic] into intellectual pursuits; while the Human

9

Torch demonstrated a powerful intellect, which his usually aggressive nature typically leaves him without the patience to use.

Note that their "previously-unsuspected secondary traits," as Kubik calls them, are primary traits of other team members: basically, Sue and Ben swap compassion and courage, while Johnny and Reed swap aggressiveness and intellect. (If you're surprised Johnny has any intellect, be sure to read chapter 4!) Aside from the fact that these are not all virtues in the moral sense, it does show that human beings tend to possess many of the same virtues, and the differences in their individual moral behavior emerge from the unique ways they prioritize and balance them differently in specific circumstances.[8]

Much later, humanity as a whole faces a similar test, this time from a Celestial, another all-powerful cosmic being, in an event called "Judgment Day."[9] While the Avengers, X-Men, and the Eternals banded together to confront the Celestial, the Fantastic Four deal with events on the periphery, with Reed contemplating the Celestial's task while Sue handles an attack on the Baxter Building. Reed comes to realize that "the Celestial isn't here to test our strength… but to learn who we truly are."[10] In other words, the Celestial is investigating *moral character*, which includes the virtues a person possesses, how they balance them when they conflict, and how they act on them in morally fraught situations.

When Reed reflects on the other members of the team—or family, as in "my ordinary, extraordinary family"—he thinks that Sue's greatest superpower is "that she always makes people feel seen," by which he means her compassion, her attention to other people's well-being or suffering, and protectiveness of those she cares about (as we'll see in chapter 3). "If Sue is my true north," he continues, "then Ben Grimm is my bedrock of friendship and loyalty," although the virtue of Ben's that is most often emphasized in the comics is perseverance, his quality of never giving up, no matter how tired or hurt he is, when someone needs him. Finally,

Reed thinks that "Johnny Storm reminds us all to live life in a blaze of glory," which may imply the virtue of joyfulness or lightheartedness, which contrasts starkly with the inherent danger posed by his powers (as well as his impetuousness, which is definitely a vice). More important than this, however, is his willingness to sacrifice himself for others, although as we discuss in chapter 4 this has its roots in his feelings of being less worthy than the others (a trait Ben shares as well, as we'll talk about in chapter 5).

Reed doesn't discuss himself, of course, so we have to rely on others. For example, one time that Reed was believed to be dead, Johnny says that he was "the most decent, self-sacrificing man I have ever known! He had a reverence for life—an insatiable curiosity," the last one being perhaps the quality that sets him most apart from the rest (as we will see in the next section).[11] Soon afterwards, the Inhuman named Triton tells Johnny that Reed "had a spirit and courage second to none" and that when things are at their worst and "any other man would have long since surrendered to despair," Reed does not.[12] Many of the character traits mentioned by Johnny and Triton, and echoed by many others over the years, are virtues associated with leadership, such as the ability to inspire others to greatness, the humility to emphasize others' achievements and qualities above your own, and the optimism needed to keep trying to find solutions to problems. This last one may be the most impressive, considering the challenges the team has faced over the years, but Reed refuses to give up looking for ways to create a better world, not only for his family but for humanity as a whole (and beyond). Even the first time Galactus comes to Earth and things seems hopeless, Reed tells Sue that "there's always a chance, darling... so long as we're alive!"[13]

Although the specific traits he identified for each member stand out, Reed also realizes that, for the most part, they share core heroic virtues.

At the end of his reflection inspired by the Celestial's judgment, he combines many of them when he thinks that "the real strength of my family—my ordinary, extraordinary family" is that "every single day, they face down the impossible to protect those around them…and every single day… they find the courage to persevere." He adds a touch of his trademark optimism when he stands with the other three and says to the heavens, "no matter what the universe throws at us…as long as we're together…our family will always find a solution."[14]

What Is the Fantastic Four…For?

At the end of their origin in their very first issue, the Fantastic Four establishes its purpose going forward. After each member experiences their new abilities—even if not the full extent of them, especially in Sue's case—Reed proclaims that "together we have more power than any humans have ever possessed!" Ben interrupts, saying, "You don't have to make a speech, big shot! We understand! We've gotta use that power to help mankind, right?" Reed agrees, and the team's mission is set, if still vague: to use their powers in the service of others.

This basic purpose is reiterated many times over the years, sometimes with additions noting the nature of the "team." One time, after they defeat Doctor Doom, Reed apparently forgets their original mission statement and wonders if, with their main adversary gone, the team might be dissolved. After calling him "the most stubborn jackass I've ever known," Sue reminds him that "we're not merely a team…we're a family…and families stay together through thick and thin." Later, Reed remembers what he said after their fateful accident, and reiterates "our reason for existence. We've been given extraordinary abilities—and not to use them to benefit mankind…would be to waste what we have, in the most foolish manner imaginable!" As we would expect, Sue adds, "as I've been saying—we're a family…we work together…we stay together the way a family is meant to be."[15]

From Reed's reflections noted above, we know that he appreciates Sue's "addendum," but this doesn't change the essential purpose of the team: helping people to be better off. In terms of moral philosophy, this is consistent with *utilitarianism*, the school of ethics that judges actions by the degree to which they increase overall well-being. The best-known statement of utilitarianism is due to Jeremy Bentham, who advocated for a "principle of utility" that "approves or disapproves of every action according to the tendency it appears to have to increase or lessen—i.e. to promote or oppose—the happiness of the person or group whose interest is in question."[16] A more familiar way to summarize utilitarianism is that it promotes actions that create "the greatest benefit to the greatest number," or that maximize the total amount of well-being or happiness in society. Johnny puts it even more simply when he tells an interviewer that, while he likes the fame and the excitement of being a member of the Fantastic Four, "mostly it's about doing good, corny as that sounds."[17]

Promoting "the good" is perhaps the simplest statement of utilitarianism possible while still capturing its essence. Utilitarians want to do things to benefit mankind, and if there is more than one option available to them, they do the thing that creates the most benefit possible. The Fantastic Four are not strictly utilitarians, because they never commit to creating the *most* utility or well-being—and this is not a criticism, because few are as strict as this demands.[18] "Merely" devoting your life to helping others is admirable enough without being expected to help others in the absolute best way possible! So the question facing the Fantastic Four is: how exactly should they use their powers to help mankind?

13

The most obvious answer is: to be superheroes! After all, this is what most individuals with superpowers do: use their abilities, skills, and talents to benefit others by saving lives, fighting crime, and battling wrongdoers, whether they be supervillains, world conquerors, or invaders from other galaxies. All of these activities are generally utilitarian in spirit, making the lives of ordinary people safer and more secure. They do, however, increase well-being *negatively* in the sense that they focus on preventing harm more than directly providing benefit. But if we remember that overall (or net) well-being is the difference between the good and bad effects on one's life, it is no less helpful to reduce the bad effects than to promote the good ones.

For his part, Ben loves the traditional superhero role. Once, when frustrated by the team's increasingly complicated business affairs, Ben says it "seems ta me bein' a superhero shouldn't be a whole lot more'n punchin' out the occasional bad guy."[19] When Reed later reminds him that "there are other ways to aid humanity than simply battling super-powered malcontents," Ben responds, "Aah, gimme a good malcontent any day."[20] But even the ever-lovin', blue-eyed idol o' millions realizes that superheroics doesn't capture the main way the Fantastic Four does good. On a late night talk show, Ben tells his host (who looks very much like Conan O'Brien) how the team works: "Reed wants to know stuff, and he'll go anywhere to learn. We come with him ta keep his pointy head out of trouble. Sometimes while we're there, we'll meet people getting a raw deal, so we fix it. That's what we do."[21]

Although their mission can be defined generally as using their abilities to help mankind, the way they put that mission into action, or the specific way they promote the good, is as Ben put it: explorers first, superheroes second. As a junior public relations agent who is charged with shadowing the team reports back to his company,

These guys aren't super heroes. Not really. They don't fight crime. They don't go on patrol. They don't have a Bat-signal. They're astronauts. They're envoys. Adventurers. Explorers. Sure, Galactus comes to town, they'll step up. Trouble finds them, they'll kick its ass. But that's not the job. It just comes with.[22]

Earlier, he wrote in his notes about what Ben said later to "Conan":

It's that kind of help that allows Richards to focus on scientific breakthroughs that…well, not to overstate, but that could possibly pioneer the future of the human race. My god…does his family realize how much they contribute to that? Is that why they do what they do?

When Ben asks why he thought they did it, the PR guy says, "Because you're super heroes…?", and Ben just walks away laughing.[23]

The public relations agent really should have known better, because when he got the assignment, his boss described the Fantastic Four as "pioneers of science…they are the world's first imaginauts, if you will."[24] Later, when introducing Ben at a fancy event commemorating a new science grant in the team's honor, the emcee recounts the team origin before saying,

They became the Fantastic Four. They became super heroes. But to describe them as just heroes is wrong. They were adventurers. Explorers. The Fantastic Four discovered new worlds, new universes—pushing the human race to the furthest limits of science and technology.[25]

Perhaps their role as superheroes isn't even that important. After the destruction of the entire Marvel Universe—multiverse, really—Reed, Sue, and the kids of their Future Foundation, including Franklin and Valeria, join with the Molecule Man to rebuild the multiverse. (If that's not helping, nothing is!) When Franklin asks his father, "are we not super heroes

15

anymore?", Reed tells him, "It's doing good that counts, not necessarily how you do it. And what we're doing right now matters—it might be the most important thing ever—and the best part is I get to do it with all of you. So, no…no super heroes for a while, just science."[26]

After the entire family is reunited, they take turns describing the team, managing to bring all the aspects of the Fantastic Four together. Johnny surveys other people's names for them: "We've been called 'super heroes,' 'adventurers,' 'imaginauts'… That last one isn't even a word. I looked it up." Reed goes a little deeper, saying that "we're a band of explorers. All working together as one. Using our great gifts to find and celebrate the new and unexpected," and Sue adds, "It's simpler than that. Me. The man I love. My brother. Our best friend. We *are* adventurers. And we're on the greatest adventure of all. Being part of a family."[27]

Will they ever be finished? I doubt people will stop needing help, or that villains or conquerors will give up trying to do evil or take over the world. And there will never be an end to the wonders of the multiverse to be explored and the knowledge to be gained, both for its sake as well as the good it can do for people across the universes. When the team visits heaven, Ben's brother Daniel, who died when Ben was young, says "the big guy" invites them to stay, having earned eternal reward in paradise and, as Reed points out, "in the province of ultimate knowledge." He asks Daniel, just to be sure: "The solutions to every mystery of the universe will be at our fingertips? Every answer conceivable ours simply for the asking?" Daniel says yes, but Reed turns it down, saying they're honored, "but we're not yet done exploring. What gives this family its purpose and its joy isn't the destination…it's the journey." That answer gets them in the door to meet God, who looks an awful lot like Jack Kirby and tells Reed, "You know never to stop asking 'why.' That was the test."[28] The Fantastic Four will never run out of ways to use their abilities to help others, in whatever way they chose to do it—for which we should be very grateful, as readers if not direct beneficiaries of their good works!

Doin' the Right Thing

While the utilitarian purpose of the Fantastic Four, and Reed's guidance of them toward this purpose—in terms of scientific discovery and innovation as well as sheer heroism—are admirable and noble, there are other valid moral concerns that need to be observed in the process. As an interviewer mentions to Sue, after the superhero Civil War in which Reed pushed some ethical boundaries in his support of superhero registration and created a significant rift between him and Sue, "Some people say you're Reed Richards's compass. That without you, he flounders."[29] Sue chooses not to respond, but after what they went through during the ideological battle over privacy, security, and autonomy (which we discuss at length in chapter 6), one suspects she does not disagree, at least in principle.

To see how Sue acts as a "compass" for Reed, we need to introduce *deontology*, the third major school of moral philosophy. Like utilitarianism, deontology evaluates the morality of actions, but rather than judging them to be good or bad, or better or worse, it proclaims them to be right or wrong when held up to some important moral principle or ideal.

It is the principled nature of deontology that allows us to be a "check" on utilitarianism's pursuit of the greatest good. For example, Reed has a habit of keeping his plans from the rest of the team or outright lying about them—not out of a malicious or deceitful streak, but out of a sincere belief that they don't need to know, they are better off not knowing, or they can wait to know later. In other words, Reed may think it benefits both the plan itself and the other members of the team to withhold certain details from them, which makes his secrecy justified according to his general utilitarian goals of making people better off.

Deontology, however, takes a different view, maintaining that lying is wrong because it violates some more basic ethical ideal. For example, Immanuel Kant, the most widely influential deontological philosopher, argues that lying violates the respect we owe to other persons by using them as a tool for our purposes (even if those purposes themselves are well-intentioned).[30] Another well-known deontologist, W.D. Ross, maintains that lying violates duties not to harm and duties of fidelity (the implicit promise we make, especially to those close to us, to be truthful when we speak to them).[31] There are many formulations of deontology, but what they all share is a reliance on *principle* that takes priority over good outcomes or consequences.

We see this in the objections the rest of the Fantastic Four make to Reed when he withholds information from them. When Johnny and the others learn that Reed has a lab in the Antarctic where he conducts particularly dangerous experiments, Reed finds it "odd" that Johnny is even interested. But Johnny considers it "rude" that Reed kept it a secret, saying "you have this annoying habit, Reed...of never telling the rest of the team exactly what it is you're thinking."[32] Reed jokes that sometimes he isn't even aware of what he's thinking, but that just dodges the issue, which (as Johnny notes) does happen a lot (and is rude every time).

There are other ways Reed dismisses or minimizes the others for what he regards as good reasons. Later in the same story, Sue calls Reed out on making decisions for the team without consulting them—not the same issue as deception, but with the same effect of failing to fully respect the rest of the team. She argues that "personal decisions that affect all of us," such as, in this case, moving the team's home and headquarters, "are choices we make as a family." Reed apologizes, saying he got carried away and asking if it wasn't a good idea all the same. Franklin looks up at Sue and asks, "he doesn't get it, does he?" to which she replies, "not even."[33] To their minds, Reed does not fully appreciate the respect the other members of the family deserve, preferring to think he is better suited to make decisions without including or informing them—again, out of a sincere belief that it is better for them, but without giving them the benefit of asking them first.

Of course, there is more to the conflict between deontology and utilitarianism than lying, especially in superhero stories dealing with life and death—and in Fantastic Four stories, life and death are often on a global scale (or larger). Like most heroes, the members of the Fantastic Four abstain from killing as a rule, often based on the sanctity of life (as Sue says when she considers trying to kill Galactus).[34] This holds even when doing so may help them achieve another goal more easily or quickly—or even save more lives. After Ben defeats some nearly indestructible foes, he thinks to himself, "I wonder how many fights I'd have ended this fast if I wuzn't scared I might accidentally kill somebody?"[35] Here, Ben implies that he holds back his mightiest blows against lesser enemies so he merely incapacitates them without killing him, even though that means he can do less good in a given amount of time.

As admirable as this is, it is an example of preventing incidental death, whereas refusing to actively take a life as a means to furthering a mission can be more meaningful, especially when the benefits are significant. While Reed's mind was twisted by having worn Doctor Doom's armor too long, he orders Johnny to kill Doom, which Johnny only pretends to do. Sue lashes out at Reed, saying he was the one who told her that "having the power to kill, and even sometimes the right, requires a person of ethics and morality and civilization to try to find a better way." She says she could understand self-defense, "but this was murder!" The corrupted Reed replies that his responsibility makes "execution, for the common good, a regrettable but necessary sacrifice." After Reed goes on to explain his plan to enslave humanity "for their own good," even Doom criticizes Reed for maintaining that "your 'noble' ends so justify your acts that you cannot even see what an obscenity it is."[36]

Here, Doctor Doom—ironically, given his own penchant for justifying wrongful actions for the greater good, as we will see in chapter 8—invokes a common criticism of utilitarianism on the part of deontologists, namely that it allows immoral actions to be taken to advance overall welfare. Ben quotes the standard form of the objection more precisely when he questions the Silver Surfer for agreeing to serve as Galactus's herald after he was released from the task of warning civilizations of their impending doom. When the Surfer says that "sometimes to save lives, one must commit acts that in other contexts one would find reprehensible," Ben responds that what he's saying is that "the ends justify the means, huh?"[37]

The Surfer argues that sometimes the ends *do* justify the means, such as when Ben uses violence, which in isolation would be considered wrong, "to protect those who cannot protect themselves." When Ben says he sounds like Reed, who is more pragmatic about ethical matters and willing to accept moral compromises than the other members of the Fantastic Four, the Surfer praises him, saying "Reed is a wise man, willing to make hard choices. Like the choices you often make. Like the choice I have made."[38] As it happens, it is in response to one of Reed's hard choices concerning running Latveria in Doom's absence—during which time Ben felt his best friend was acting more like Doom than himself—that Ben urged the team to "not do the right thing the wrong way," another way to say that the ends, no matter how admirable or noble, do not (necessarily) justify immoral means of furthering them.[39]

This Tragic Choice, This Trolley Problem

What the Surfer is describing is what philosophers call a *tragic choice*, a decision in a morally fraught situation from which "it is impossible to emerge with clean hands."[40] Such dilemmas are common in superhero stories because they are inherently dramatic, forcing heroes to choose between saving one person or another, or saving one person at the cost of killing another. In such cases, there is no "right thing to do," because neither option is morally acceptable, whether it's letting one person or die or killing them. In a story in which the heroes are fighting and killing evil versions of themselves—when Johnny even burns the imposter of his sister alive while asking whether the team needs to change with the times and become more violent—Ben asks, "is any victory worth the price we're payin'?", fearing that, even if they prevail, they'll never be the same. This is the sense in which moral dilemmas leave the decision-maker with "dirty hands," which can weigh on them even if they feel they made the right (or less wrong) choice.[41]

The most well-known tragic choice in moral philosophy is *the trolley problem*. In the classic treatment, a runaway trolley with five passengers is barreling toward a broken track, and if it hits the broken track, the trolley will derail, killing the five passengers. A bystander is next to a switch, with which they can divert the trolley to another track, saving the five passengers, but also killing another person standing on the other track. The question is whether the bystander should pull the switch, saving the five passengers but killing the person on the other track.[42]

The trolley problem invokes many moral issues, but most obviously touches on the conflict between utilitarianism and deontology: Pulling the switch saves five lives at the cost of one, which would be the utilitarian choice, but also involves directly acting to kill one person, which would be judged wrong by most deontologists. There are countless variations to the basic trolley problem which have surprisingly significant effects on many people's intuition regarding the correct answer (whatever that may be). In one, instead of the one person standing on a different track, an overweight man is standing on a bridge over the main track, and if the bystander pushes him off, he will fall onto the track and stop the trolley before it crashes.[43] In a more different one, a surgeon is treating five patients who each need a transplant of a different organ, and she realizes that her (healthy) nurse happens to be a perfect match for all five. Should the surgeon kill her nurse to save the five patients?[44] Those who accept the hard choice of pulling the switch in the basic case are often more hesitant to "push the fat man off the bridge" or sacrifice the nurse, even though the number of lives saved and lost are the same.[45]

Given the intergalactic scale of the threats superheroes face, their trolley problems are often much bigger as well. When a captured queen of the Skrulls, a violent and imperialistic alien race of shapeshifters that often plague the Fantastic Four, mocks them for protecting a single life at the risk of the entire universe—and, based on this fact, wonders why the Skrulls never conquered the human race—Johnny answers, "probably because we *do* worry about one, single life, Queenie."[46] Speaking of the Skrulls, when they blame Reed for saving Galactus's life, after which he devoured the Skrull throneworld and killing all of his inhabitants, Reed responds that while he mourns their deaths, he defends not letting Galactus die, asking "who are we to make such a decision? To allow another living being—any living being—to die, when ours is the power to prevent it?"[47]

Trolley problems don't come much bigger than what Reed and the rest of the secretive Marvel Universe brain trust, known as the Illuminati, faced in the build-up to the recent iteration of the "Secret Wars." It begins when the Illuminati become aware of "incursions," the repeated collision of Earths from parallel dimensions, destroying both universes and leading to a complete breakdown of the multiverse.[48] Reed tells the others they have only eight hours until another Earth collides with theirs, and a debate begins about the ethics of acting to destroy another Earth and universe to save their own (and possibly the entire multiverse). Doctor Strange (or maybe Doctor Obvious) says that "the scale of this… is infinite, and the stakes…I fear the hard choices we will soon face, my friends."

Namor the Sub-Mariner—ruler of the seven seas who is also Reed's main rival for Sue's affections—just laughs, saying "the question you have to ask is, who here would kill to save their world?" Captain America puts his foot down, telling the others "I will not tolerate—I will not allow—any talk of the necessity of necessary evil. I have spent my life on that line and every time I've seen someone cross it, death and horror and shame was what followed." The Illuminati agree to use the all-powerful Infinity Gems to repel the next incursion without destroying the other world, but some have doubts. Speaking to the Black Panther before the incursion, Reed admits that if this doesn't work, "then we teach ourselves to do the unthinkable…We have to learn how to destroy a world."[49]

Their attempt does work, but the Infinity Gems are destroyed in the process, leaving the Illuminati with no way to prevent future incursions. Cap stands alone in arguing that they must find an alternative to destroying the next encroaching Earth, with Reed criticizing him for implying this isn't a hard choice for the rest of them just because they're willing to consider all the options, saying "it's, well, quite insulting." Cap tells them he knows how this goes: first they'll build a weapon while not planning to use it, then using it once but "never again," then deciding when they *will* use it again. "One by one, you'll convince yourselves. We're doing this for the right reasons. There's no other choice. It's the lesser of two evils."[50] Cap is insisting they find a way out of the tragic dilemma or trolley problem they're in, as superheroes often do, but the others have already accepted their hands will definitely not be clean this time.[51]

Eventually the Illuminati (without Captain America) prepare a device to destroy another Earth, and when one of its inhabitants says they don't have to do this, Reed acknowledges the tragic dilemma at the heart of the situation: "I wish that were true, but it isn't, is it? It does have to be one way or the other." Yet, he can't bring himself to activate it, saying,

> I know it's a necessary evil. I know I would be saving hundreds of trillions of lives at the cost of mere billions. I know there is no real shame in coming to that conclusion—in making that choice. But even with all things hanging in the balance…there is a line.

T'Challa, the Black Panther, takes the device next, urged on by the ghosts of his ancestors, but he can't use it either. When he tells Reed he tried, his old friend understands, saying that "when we got to the end ourselves, we found out that there were things we would not do…And you know…I am not ashamed of that. You shouldn't be either…it matters."[52]

Both Reed and T'Challa discover that, as much sense as destroying the other world—or "pulling the switch" to "divert the trolley"—makes in utilitarian terms, it still means acting directly to end lives, which they cannot abide. But Namor just laughs again, telling Reed and T'Challa that none of them matter, and the lines they refuse to cross "shame you. How dare any of you put yourself—your damned morals—above the lives of every living thing?"[53] Namor points out that refusing to kill, even if it will save many more lives, is to put their own moral sanctity above those lives they could save. As noble as it seems to proclaim that "I am not a murderer" or "I will not compromise myself by taking a life," it is not the same as maintaining that killing is wrong—these statements are

24

more about the person making them than the wrongfulness of the act itself, and they improperly center the person's virtue rather than the lives saved or sacrificed.

Namor then activates the device and destroys the other Earth and its universe. This leads to an argument among the members of the Illuminati, after which Reed concludes that "a terrible thing has been done…and the greater tragedy is that we are no closer to finding a way to stop this from happening again. And make no mistake…it cannot happen again."[54] When the next incursion comes, Reed asks T'Challa what they're going to do, and the Wakandan king responds, "I cannot be responsible for the destruction of another world, Reed. I simply cannot." When Reed agrees, T'Challa says, "then there's only one thing left to do. We die, Reed…and hopefully better than we lived."[55] But T'Challa and Reed are not just accepting their own deaths, which may seem noble, but those of their loved ones and friends and everyone in their universe, all for the sake of dying "better than we lived," which is a morbid and futile take on maintaining one's virtue.

It gets worse, because this situation differs from the standard trolley problem in one important respect (other than sheer scale): If nothing is done, both Earths and universes in an incursion are destroyed, and if the Illuminati destroy one Earth, then only one universe dies. In other words, there is no cost, because the other Earth and its universe are doomed either way (assuming no third option that can save both worlds, like they managed to do the first time). So Reed and T'Challa's refusal to act to destroy the other world has no effect on its fate, and it also dooms their own world and their loved ones to death, all in the hope of keeping their hands clean. This is quite a shift from Reed's earlier response to Captain America when the latter says, "You will lose yourself in this, Reed," and Reed responds, "You seem surprised that I would be willing to sacrifice myself for my family."[56]

If we're going to be critical of Reed for standing by his principles even when it leads to unimaginable suffering and death, we should ask ourselves this: Is there any way to justify moral compromise, such as what Namor engaged in when he set off the device that destroyed the other world and universe, based on tremendous cost of upholding our principles? After all, one of the purposes of the deontological concept of principle is to place limits on the pursuit of the greater good when doing so involves wrongdoing. If we are willing to compromise that purpose, does it violate the very purpose and meaning of principle?

According to the concept of *threshold deontology*, it does not, although it does recommend weakening it in exactly those cases in which the costs are too high. First introduced in the context of using torture to extract information from terrorists suspected of planting bombs that could kill millions, threshold deontology allows for the suspension of deontological principle if the costs of maintaining it exceed a "threshold" level of unacceptable harm.[57] This recognizes the brutal truth that, as important as moral principles are, they are not necessarily so important that tremendous costs should be suffered to preserve them—especially when those suffering have no role to play in the decision. Namor's feelings against killing may not be as strong as those of Reed or T'Challa, but even if they were, he realizes that he cannot condemn to death untold trillions of lives to support them.[58]

In a more recent trolley problem, Reed embodies the superheroic ideal by denying the tragic dilemma altogether.[59] The team finds itself in an altered timeline in which Earth never acquired a moon and life evolved completely differently, meaning the entire human race and its society never existed. Reed thinks of a way to reverse the change, but they realize that, by doing so, they would be dooming all of the inhabitants of the current timeline to bring back those of the previous one. Johnny objects—partly because he has fallen in love with an inhabitant of the new timeline—and calls what they're proposing genocide. Reed corrects him, saying "speciocide" or "omnicide" would be more accurate, and Johnny points out that even though he has to invent new words to describe what he's proposing, he's still considering it.

Reed mutters to himself, "it's an impossible choice," in which case there's only one thing to do: "To refuse…to choose from the available options. To find another way." And he does, devising a way to create a split in the multiverse so he can restore the previous timeline without destroying the new one, thereby avoiding the tragic dilemma altogether. (Johnny has to abandon his love, but that is often his fate, as we'll see in chapter 4.) This is a Fantastic-sized version of the more typical case in which a villain threatens a busload of schoolchildren on one side of the world and the hero's love interest on the other, and the hero still manages to save both. Superheroes are super in large part because they often find a way to overcome the tragic dilemma and escape with sparkling clean hands—and the fact that sometimes they cannot, such as in the case of the incursions, drives home the seriousness of such situations.

Now that we have the three major schools of ethics under our belts, we can go on to explore specific moral aspects of the individual members of the Fantastic Four in more depth, followed by other fascinating explorations of other characters and storylines. We begin with Mr. Fantastic himself and the incredible amount of responsibility he holds himself to as he leads the team on their mission of exploration and heroism.

[1] *Fantastic Four*, vol. 1, #11 (February 1963). Willie actually debuted in his own newspaper comic strip in 1960, written by Stan Lee and drawn by Dan DeCarlo, and was portrayed in the 2005 *Fantastic Four* film by none other than Lee himself.

[2] *Fantastic Four*, vol. 3, #543 (May 2007), "C'mon, Suzie, Don't Leave Us Hangin'."

[3] Aristotle's main work in this area in his *Nicomachean Ethics*, which dates from about 350 BCE, and is available online at https://classics.mit.edu/Aristotle/nicomachaen.html. For more on virtue ethics in general, see Craig A. Boyd and Kevin Timpe, *The Virtues: A Very Introduction* (Oxford: Oxford University Press, 2021) or Rosalind Hursthouse and Glen Pettigrove, "Virtue Ethics," in Edward N. Zalta & Uri Nodelman (eds.), *The Stanford Encyclopedia of Philosophy* (Fall 2023 Edition), at https://plato.stanford.edu/archives/fall2023/entries/ethics-virtue/.

[4] Aristotle, *Nicomachean Ethics*, Book II, Chapter 6.

[5] *Fantastic Four*, vol. 1, #32 (November 1964).

[6] *Fantastic Four*, vol. 1, #351 (April 1991), from which all the quotes from Kosmos and Kubik's inquiry hail.

[7] For a critique of dispositional theory, as well as versions of virtue ethics that rely on it, see John M. Doris, *Lack of Character: Personality and Moral Behavior* (Cambridge: Cambridge University Press, 2005).

[8] They all observe that "with each hardship they become wiser, their character stronger," an aspect of virtue and willpower that we explore more in reference to Sue in chapter 3.

[9] This event is collected in two trade paperbacks, *A.X.E.: Judgment Day* and *A.X.E.: Judgment Day Companion* (both published in 2023).

[10] *Fantastic Four*, vol. 6, #47 (November 2022); the quotes from the next paragraph are from this issue too.

[11] *Fantastic Four*, vol. 1, #382 (November 1993).

[12] *Fantastic Four*, vol. 1, #386 (March 1994).

[13] *Fantastic Four*, vol. 1, #49 (April 1966).

[14] *Fantastic Four*, vol. 6, #48 (December 2022).

[15] *Fantastic Four*, vol. 1, #201 (December 1978).

[16] Jeremy Bentham, *An Introduction to the Principles of Morals and Legislation* (1789), Chapter 1, Paragraph 2, available at://www.earlymoderntexts.com/assets/pdfs/bentham1780.pdf.

[17] *Fantastic Four*, vol. 3, #543, "C'mon, Suzie, Don't Leave Us Hangin'."

[18] One movement that does adhere to strict utilitarianism is Effective Altruism, which goes to significant lengths to ensure that their philanthropy not only does good but does the most good possible. For more on the controversy around the idea, see Jeff McMahan, "Philosophical Critiques of Effective Altruism," *The Philosophers' Magazine*, 73 (2016): 92-99.

[19] *Fantastic Four*, vol. 1, #251 (February 1983).

[20] *Marvel Two-in-One* #71 (January 1981).

[21] *Fantastic Four*, vol. 3, #543, "C'mon, Suzie, Don't Leave Us Hangin'."

[22] *Fantastic Four*, vol. 3, #60 (October 2002). How did he know what the Bat-signal is? The DC heroes do exist in media in the Marvel Universe: for instance, Ben says the 1989 film *Batman*, "about some bozo wearin' colored long johns…with a yellow target painted on his chest…hangin' out in a million dollar mansion with Kim Basinger" is "too unreal" for him (*Fantastic Four*, vol. 1, #334, December 1989).

[23] *Fantastic Four*, vol 3, #60.

[24] Ibid.

[25] *Marvel 2-in-One* #1 (February 2018).

[26] *Secret Wars*, vol. 2, #9 (March 2016).

[27] *Fantastic Four*, vol. 6, #1 (October 2018).

[28] *Fantastic Four*, vol. 3, #511 (May 2004).

[29] *Fantastic Four*, vol. 3, #543, "C'mon, Suzie, Don't Leave Us Hangin'."

[30] Kant's most essential work in ethics is his 1785 book *Groundwork for the Metaphysics of Morals* (Indianapolis, IN: Hackett Publishing, 1993 edition). A good way to start on Kant is through Roger J. Sullivan's book *An Introduction to Kant's Ethics* (Cambridge: Cambridge University Press, 1994).

[31] Ross's main work is his 1930 book *The Right and the Good* (Indianapolis, IN: Hackett Publishing, 1988 edition).

[32] *Fantastic Four*, vol. 3, #1 (January 1998).

[33] *Fantastic Four*, vol. 3, #2 (February 1998).

[34] *Fantastic Four*, vol. 1, #391 (August 1994).

[35] *Fantastic Four*, vol. 1, #250 (January 1983).

[36] *Fantastic Four*, vol. 3, #31 (July 2000). It may surprise you to know that Sue has plenty of experience with the opportunity to kill, as we will see in chapter 3.

[37] *Fantastic Four*, vol. 3, #545 (June 2007).

[38] Ibid. We discuss more about the Surfer's decision-making in chapter 7.

[39] *Fantastic Four*, vol. 3, #505 (December 2003).

[40] Rosaland Hursthouse, *On Virtue Ethics* (Oxford: Oxford University Press, 1999), p. 71.

[41] For more on such situations, see Lisa Tessman, *When Doing the Right Thing Is Impossible* (Oxford: Oxford University Press, 2017).

[42] The canonical presentations are in Philippa Foot, *Virtues and Vices* (Oxford: Oxford University Press, 2002), ch. 2, and Judith Jarvis Thompson, *Rights, Restitution, & Risk: Essays in Moral Theory* (Cambridge, MA: Harvard University Press, 1986), chs. 6 and 7. For more recent scholarly analysis (including commentary from Thomson and others), see F.M. Kamm, *The Trolley Problem Mysteries* (Oxford: Oxford University Press, 2016).

[43] See David Edmonds, *Would You Kill the Fat Man? The Trolley Problem and What Your Answer Tells Us about Right and Wrong* (Princeton, NJ: Princeton University Press, 2013), and Thomas Cathcart, *The Trolley Problem, or Would You Throw the Fat Guy Off the Bridge: A Philosophical Conundrum* (New York: Workman, 2013).

[44] This variant, "the transplant problem," is found in the Jarvis chapters cited above.

[45] One famous superhero, mentioned above, faces a version of the trolley problem whenever he has to decide whether to kill his most murderous foes, especially a particular clownish one; for more on this, see chapter 6 in my book *Batman and Ethics* (Hoboken, NJ: Wiley, 2018).

[46] *Fantastic Four Annual*, vol. 1, #19 (1985).

[47] *Fantastic Four*, vol. 1, #261 (December 1983). We discuss this situation more in the next chapter.

[48] This is all explained in more detail in *New Avengers*, vol. 3, #2 (March 2013).

[49] Ibid.

[50] *New Avengers*, vol. 3, #3 (April 2013).

[51] For what happens to Cap next and how his involvement with the incursions proceeds, see my book *The Virtues of Captain America: Modern-Day Lessons in Character from a World War II Superhero*, 2nd ed. (Hoboken, NJ: Wiley, 2024), pp. 98-101 and 149-150.

[52] *New Avengers*, vol. 3, #21 (September 2014). Incidentally, we were introduced to the Black Panther in *Fantastic Four*, vol. 1, #52 (July 1966).

[53] Ibid.

54 *New Avengers*, vol. 3, #22 (October 2014).

55 *New Avengers*, vol. 3, #23 (October 2014).

56 *New Avengers*, vol. 3, #3.

57 Threshold deontology was introduced by Michael S. Moore in his article "Torture and the Balance of Evils," *Israel Law Review* 23 (1989): 280–344; for a critique, see Larry Alexander, "Deontology at the Threshold," *San Diego Law Review* 37 (2000): 893–912.

58 Namor does not, in fact, oppose murder as strongly as Reed and T'Challa: in fact, Sue once has to stop him from killing a foe, telling him she hopes "we can find a better way," and that she cannot live with "the thought of you becoming like her," combining her concern with his virtue with her principle against killing (*Fantastic Four*, vol. 3, #32, August 2000).

59 The following situation and quotations come from *Fantastic Four*, vol. 7, #25 (November 2024).

Chapter 2
Reed Richards (Mister Fantastic)

Ever since the fateful accident that granted the Fantastic Four their powers, Reed Richards has led them on most of their adventures, whether exploring new worlds or dimensions or fighting for the safety and lives of innocent people everywhere. As one of the most intelligent people in the world, especially when it comes to science, Reed is well suited for this role. However, much of what drives him to take charge of the team is the responsibility he feels for them and the guilt he harbors over the space flight that altered their lives forever.

Are these feelings appropriate, though? It is certainly noble and admirable to take responsibility for one's actions and their consequences, but this must be limited by other factors, such as how much someone knows, how much they *could* know, and how much control they have over what happened. Even if one is justified in taking responsibility for something, this can be taken too far, which is very common among superheroes who can do so much but feel nonetheless that they should do even more. This can trigger feelings of intense guilt, a negative emotion that can ideally be used for good but can easily make things much worse for someone already burdened with too much responsibility.

With Great Power Comes Great Responsibility

The fateful trip that Reed Richards, Susan Storm, Johnny Storm, and Benjamin Grimm embarked on in the first issue of *Fantastic Four* changed all of their lives in very specific ways, but the powers they acquired may be the least interesting of them. In Reed's case, the accident gave him a new sense of responsibility—two, in fact.

On the positive side, Reed realized almost immediately what the accident meant for their futures. As we saw in the last chapter, after each of the four reveals their new abilities, Reed says, "Together we have more power than any humans have ever possessed!" Ben knows what's next, saying, "We've gotta use that power to help mankind, right?" Reed agrees, after which they all choose their superhero names and the narration proclaims them the Fantastic Four.[1] Years later, Reed reiterates this when he tells his son Franklin that "our abilities are a gift. But with the gift comes responsibility—to use our abilities to defend humanity and our world against harm."[2]

This describes responsibility in the positive sense of a duty or obligation—or, as another famous Ben said, "with great power comes great responsibility."[3] It isn't just his stretching ability that makes Reed feel responsible for helping the world, but also his "universally relevant intelligence," as Galactus once put it.[4] Later in the same issue in which he tells Franklin about responsibility, he tries to stop the sun from exploding, saying to himself that "there has to be an answer," not just for his family and friends, "but all the family and friends who share this blessed world. This rare and supremely precious island of life amidst the eternal cosmos. At the very least, I owe them my best effort. And I owe them success."[5] At one point, he goes as far as to tell Sue, "we're all responsible for what happens to everybody," an astonishingly broad statement of solidarity among humankind that does not obligate him specifically, and which he can hardly take literally, but nonetheless serves as an example of how he thinks about responsibility.[6]

Where does this outsized sense of responsibility come from? In one story, Reed examines alternate timelines to find one in which a particular disaster was avoided, and finds that, in all of them, collective action among the world's superheroes failed. The only way to prevent disaster was through decisive and singular action on the part of one person: Reed Richards. He asks himself, "Is this total arrogance? Or is it honesty meeting responsibility?" As much as he resists it, he is forced to admit there is

> only one person smart enough to solve all the problems and answer all the difficult questions. For too long I have hidden behind false humility and as a result ran from the things I was supposed to do. I am the most brilliant man in the known universe—my mind is a gift—and when problems present themselves, it falls to me—I have a responsibility—to solve them.[7]

Here we see he regards his intelligence as just as much "a gift" as the elastic powers he gained from the accident, and in the service of reciprocity, he believes that he must "pay forward" that gift by using it to help the world. As he tells Ben early on, "Fate has been good to us...We've been able to use power to help mankind...to fight evil and injustice!"[8]

Is Reed right, though? Do we have an obligation to use "gifts" in this way? Few philosophers would say there is any such obligation in a strict sense. Even though a gift is unearned, it is also normally unrequested, and the recipient doesn't "owe" anybody anything in exchange or gratitude for it. In a larger sense, though, if one does have altruistic or utilitarian sentiments that guide them to want to help others, and their "gift" enables them to do that in an especially effective way, that sentiment itself can generate an internal obligation, such as Reed feels. Deontology can also generate this type of obligation, although not in a strict, binding sense: Immanuel Kant wrote of *wide* or *positive duties*, attitudes that we should adopt to whatever extent we can, one of which was to cultivate our talents "inasmuch as they are given [us] for all sorts of possible purposes."[9] Soon after the episode above, Reed goes through a period of introspection and emerges with the goal to "solve everything," asking himself, in a more of a virtue-oriented mood, "what kind of man am I if I don't do everything I can to make that happen?"[10]

Although such a strong sense of responsibility to use his abilities to help others is noble, it can have negative consequences when taken too far—which Reed definitely does. We see this in the way he expects perfection from himself and characterizes anything less as an abject failure. At one point of discord amongst the team, Reed beats himself up: "All this work—the endless experiments—and what have I accomplished? I've lost my wife...my child...everything that matters to me. And for what? A frustrating series of failures. I've accomplished nothing. Nothing!"[11]

When the team discovers a Skrull—a member of the hostile race of shapeshifters from another world we mentioned in the last chapter—had been living among them for months, Reed rages to Sue, saying he should have known. "It's my responsibility to anticipate these problems...and to prepare appropriate defenses! I should have been prepared!" When she tells him he's only human and can't anticipate everything, he agrees, but then says he's "ultimately responsible for every ill that has ever befallen us since that fateful day," categorizing that as his original sin and asserting that "I can never...I must never forget that it was all due to my carelessness...my failure to anticipate and solve an obvious problem!"[12] As Sue later tells Johnny about Reed's guilt complex,

> we started saving the city. Then we were saving the country. Then the planet, the galaxy, the universe, the multiverse…It weighs on him, you know. He can't stop himself from figuring out how impossibly high the odds are, calculating exactly how close a last-second victory was to a full-blown catastrophe.[13]

Out of this drive to do everything, and do it perfectly, Reed often drives himself to the limits of human endurance. In one battle, after he is "traumatized—mentally as well as physically—by the psionic scythe of Huntara, an otherworldly barbarian," Reed leaves the hospital, where he is supposed to recovering, to try to cure their teammate Sharon Ventura, who had been transformed by Doctor Doom into a Thing similar to Ben. Johnny watches, thinking "Reed must be on the verge of exhaustion," and when Reed finally does collapse, the other three run to his side, reminding him of his doctors' orders. He only mutters, "I'll be fine…I'm sorry to cause such a fuss," drawing even more admiration from Johnny. But when Reed later sees Johnny's distress signal from bed, he starts to get dressed, telling Sue that "I'm a member of a team…a family…and they're counting on my help! I can't fail them…no matter what the consequences!"[14]

It does not fall solely on his teammates to reassure him that he isn't perfect. During the first "Secret Wars" event, Reed apologizes to Captain America—no stranger himself to feeling excessive responsibility—that "it took so long for me" to figure out an alien machine, and Cap assures him that no one else could have done it at all. When Reed next explains how he found a way to help the Enchantress, a villain from Thor's home of Asgard, Cap hails his compassion and says, "you give added meaning to the word hero, Richards!"[15] Even though we can imagine this praise

36

was appreciated, as is that from his family and teammates, it is not long before Reed is feeling responsible for other failures, whether actual or perceived.

It Happened One Night

Even more concerning than exhaustion is the tremendous guilt Reed carries due to his "failures" to live up to the demands of his exaggerated sense of responsibility. We'll see that even though his guilt stretches as far as his limbs, its main focus remains on the accident that changed the four forever, and especially its effects on his best friend, Ben Grimm.[16]

Reed's guilt over the accident is a constant theme throughout the Fantastic Four's history. In the second issue of the series, when discussing Ben's outbursts with Sue and Johnny, Reed urges patience and says "he's not really to blame! It's actually my fault that he is the way he is!" He then recounts their origin and asserts that "it was my fault that our flight to Mars failed and we nearly lost our lives when we crash-landed to Earth! … I can't punish the Thing when the fault is mine!"[17] As Hank Pym, a fellow hero and scientist, says years later on a television special commemorating the team's anniversary, it was "a freak accident. No one could have predicted it," and adds that "Reed argues with me about this, but he wants to take the blame for everything."[18]

The depth of Reed's guilt becomes clear in a revealing "story" he tells his infant daughter Valeria, in which he describes "a very arrogant man who did something very stupid," leading his friends to disaster because of his lack of preparation and anticipation for every contingency. "His guilt was unbearable…and deserved," he says, claiming that he destroyed their lives, and goes on to explain that he made them into celebrities with superhero names, costumes, "and a flying car," all in the hope of being "forgiven for taking their normal lives away."[19]

Reed also explains how he wanted to make sure the public didn't fear them, remembering how the original Human Torch, Jim Hammond, went from being seen as a public menace upon his introduction—in 1939's *Marvel Comics* #1, the *real* first issue of Marvel Comics back when the company was called Timely—to a hero alongside Captain America in the Invaders. "I can make the world see them for what they truly are," he later told an interviewer during a celebration of the team, "three of the best of bravest adventurers anyone could hope to meet."[20] Even when the team learns that the Overseer, the leader of alien race, was responsible for directing the cosmic rays toward their ship (in defense of what his world saw as a threat from Earth), Reed still feels responsible for putting his family at risk in the first place (and for failing to see even *that* remote possibility).[21]

Is Reed responsible for the accident, though? Before we assign moral responsibility, we need to address several factors of the situation.[22] The first is simple: was Reed a *cause* of the accident, and if so, how closely tied to it was he? The flight was his idea, as was the "crew" he assembled for it, so he was definitely involved in getting the four into space. But the cosmic rays played a more crucial role in the accident itself, and Reed had no control over them.[23] Holding him responsible for the accident based on his level of causal responsibility would be like holding the driver of a car responsible for being hit by a drunk driver: true, the accident would not have happened had the first car not been in the wrong place at the wrong time, but the *proximate* cause of the accident was the other driver.

In this case, the drunk driver would be not only causally responsible for the accident, but morally responsible as well, because their action alone was *wrongful*. Moral responsibility normally derives from a violation of a duty or obligation owed to somebody, such as not getting behind the wheel of a car after you've had too much to drink. According to the recent revelation about the source of the cosmic rays, the Overseer could be held morally responsible for the accident, and certainly would be from the Fantastic Four's point of view. Objectively, though, he considered his pre-emptive attack to be a justified act of self-defense against an invasion (which, if correct, would make Reed morally responsible for it).[24]

Let's set aside the Overseer's role in the cosmic rays and go back to the prevailing belief for most of the history of the team, which was that the rays were a freak accident that affected the people aboard the ship because the ship's shielding was not strong enough to withstand them. This latter aspect could be seen as one that Reed is causally responsible for, but is he morally responsible? He clearly had a responsibility to protect himself and the others, but the key here is that, to the best of his knowledge, he did.[25] Based on the information he had at the time, he installed the proper amount of shielding, but he could not anticipate the severity of the cosmic rays they encountered. When others tell him that he couldn't have predicted this, they are trying to absolve him of responsibility by assuring him that he simply had no way to know.

Moral responsibility holds us to do the best we can, given the limits of our ability and agency, and also the best information available to us. According to this understanding, Reed would not be held morally responsible for the accident. So why does he hold himself so responsible for it? Perhaps he believes he could have done something differently. Of course, he could have—it was possible to install more shielding—and he would have done so *if* there was some reason to believe more shielding was called for, but the best information he had did not indicate that. This is Reed, however, and he believes that if he was wrong in predicting some future event, he should have thought harder, done more research, or anticipated more possible outcomes. It doesn't help that Ben tried to warn him before taking off that "you *know* we haven't done enough research into the effect of cosmic rays! They might kill us all out in space?"[26] Reed obviously disagreed, feeling he was prepared for what his research led him to expect, but Ben's words contributed to his specific guilt over the effect of the accident on his best friend (as we discuss below).

Another explanation of Reed's sense of moral responsibility, absent any identifiable failing in terms of his duty or obligation toward the others, is that he is holding himself responsible for outcomes in general rather than any particular actions he took that contributed to them. In other words, he feels guilty for the accident based on having been involved with it at all. However, he needs to acknowledge that he was only in control of limited aspects of the situation and he only had access to limited information, and that he did the best he could with both—even if it turned out badly. It is normal to feel bad when a choice we make and act on backfires, but if we did the best we could, and did not do anything wrong, there is no reason to feel morally responsible (although regret for bad outcomes is perfectly appropriate).

Not all of the team would agree their lives were ruined by the accident, but if any of them would, it would be Ben Grimm, who was forever transformed into the massive rock-covered Thing, seen as a monster by many despite his warm and compassionate nature and his long history of bravery and resolve. Reed tries to find a cure for Ben's condition almost immediately following the accident, with his first "potion" providing only a short change, and subsequent attempts only slightly lengthening the transformation.[27] Each failure triggers intense guilt in Reed, who repeatedly makes promises such as "I'll keep working on a formula to make you normal again—permanently! No matter how long it takes, I'll never give up!"[28] By the time he thinks he has a permanent cure, Ben rejects it, by that time believing that Alicia only loves him as the Thing, not Ben Grimm.[29] Reed doubts Alicia feels this way or that Ben truly believes it, but eventually he has to accept the latter (if not the former), and all but stops trying to cure Ben for this very reason.

In the meantime, however, Reed is tortured by what his carelessness did to his best friend. Once, when remembering the accident and the powers they each acquired, Reed says to himself that "it was poor Ben who got the short end of the stick—And, in a way, it was all my fault!" (The "in a way" is a rare qualification on his responsibility for the accident!) Although "the power he gained was matchless, almost indescribable strength," he says, "the awful price for his awesome, newfound power—was higher than anyone should ever have to pay!" He once again swears to find a permanent cure, thinking "I owe that to Ben."[30] But after yet another attempt fails and Reed falls in despair, Sue tells him that "he no longer blames you for his condition. We all took the same risks when we flew into the cosmic ray field. Any of us could have been transformed into a monster as Ben was, or something far worse."[31]

This is confirmed in another story, when Reed kicks Ben out of his lab and Ben assumes he's working on another cure. "But it's hopeless," Ben thinks. "I'm just a thing…and that's all I'll ever be. I wish Reed'd stop torturin' himself…and me!" In his lab, Reed reiterates his responsibility for Ben's "nightmare" life, and imagines "if I'd only listened to Ben that ill-fated night years ago," a night "that marked the birth of the Fantastic Four and the beginning of one man's torment." We see here that Reed's guilt is based not only on his decision to pursue that space flight into unknown conditions, but also the fact that Ben tried to warn him against it. This pushes him to exhaustion, thinking "I'm so tired…No! I won't think like that! I'll carry on…and I'll succeed…for Ben's sake!"[32]

Eventually Reed believes he has at last found a cure, using a crystal from the chaotic and dangerous dimension he discovered and named the Negative Zone, but he ends up having to use it to repel Annihilus, the ruler of that realm, from invading their own. Reed "can only pray Ben will forgive me" before he collapses, only to be found later by Ben, who hears his best friend mumbling, "failed you…old friend…so close so very close. Maybe…next time…but it's better that you never know."[33] Even though Ben has effectively released Reed from the obligation born from his own guilt, Reed still holds himself responsible for making good on what he "owes" Ben.

Responsibility for Everybody…Well, Almost

Reed's guilt doesn't stop with Ben or the accident, however. As the usual leader of the Fantastic Four and the person responsible for their scientific plans and devices, any decision that goes awry brings forth his deep feelings of responsibility. When Annihilus triggers the cosmic powers of Reed and Sue's son Franklin, which threaten to destroy the solar system, Reed is forced to fire an antimatter gun at him, plunging him into a coma. Reed pleads with the others that he had no choice, but they all leave him in disgust.[34] Later, he goes into a rage, beating himself up and asking "why couldn't I have found another way? Why did I have to hurt him? Why?" Medusa, a member of the Inhumans who joined the team when Sue became pregnant with Franklin, tells him he only did what he had to do—the same argument he tried to make to the others, but by this point he no longer believes it either.[35]

To make matters worse, Namor the Sub-Mariner—whose regal arrogance and potent attraction to Sue often sets him at odds with her husband—attacks Reed on behalf of Sue and Franklin, arguing that he deserves neither, and Reed takes it to heart. When Ben catches him after one of Namor's blows, Reed says, "Maybe it would have been better if you hadn't caught me, Ben. Namor's right, after all—for what I did to Franklin and Sue—perhaps I deserve to die!"[36] In the end, Sue forgives

Reed and Namor admits his attack was just a ruse to bring the two back together, but it did reveal the depth of Reed's guilt over Franklin. This is just one example of the guilt that Sue and Reed feel about the constant dangers their adventures and fame put both of their kids in, guilt that is compounded when child protection authorities intervene.[37]

Let's not forget Johnny! Unlike Ben, the Human Torch is generally happy with his transformation, but his powers do go haywire from time to time, with his flame either going out completely, permanently on, or even supercharged. When this happens, it naturally falls to Reed to fix it, which he feels a strong obligation to do for his teammate, friend, and brother-in-law (even though his goal here is to return Johnny to his post-accident, enhanced state, not his pre-accident state as with Ben). One time when Johnny is stuck in "flame on" mode, rendering him incapable of human contact, Reed desperately tries to fix him, but when yet another attempt fails, Johnny lashes out, shouting, "Whatever's going with me, Reed, you caused. Fix it, now." When Reed develops a suit to control Johnny's flame while he continues to search for a cure, Johnny sees how drained he is and realizes Reed has been working as hard to fix him as he always has to fix Ben. "Look," he says to Reed, "I know I said some things about this all being your fault—and since it's no secret how you've blamed yourself for Ben's...condition for all these years—I just want to say...I was out of line."[38]

When Johnny later loses his powers completely, Reed quickly figures out why and tells his brother-in-law he's working on a way to restore him, but Johnny says dismissively, "I won't hold my breath." After Sue calls him on it, he apologizes, apparently sincerely, but continues to drive the knife in: "Look at Ben. How long have you been working on a cure for him to no avail...and you're the smartest man alive."[39] He explains that he's not being critical but realistic, preparing to adjust to a life as just Johnny Storm (which does not go well), but this is little con-solation to a man whose responsibility knows no bounds.

More recently, when Doctor Doom learns—on his wedding day—that Johnny slept with his fiancée, he not only makes Johnny flame on permanently but also makes him burn hotter and brighter than ever.[40] Again, Reed promises to fix him, but when other crises take precedence, Johnny grows impatient, saying, "Reed, you promised you'd make it stop! So stretch that big head of yours back into your damn lab and fix this!" After unsuccessful trips to the ocean and space, Johnny cools down, emotionally if not physically, and apologizes to Reed, who says Johnny is now his priority, "at the very top of my list."[41] At the risk of minimizing Johnny's condition, Reed does seem less guilt-ridden by now, balancing his obligation to his teammate and brother-in-law with those to other people in his life, and appearing to have some implicit understanding of even his limits.[42]

There are plenty of other questionable decisions Reed feels guilty about afterwards, including his role in exiling the Hulk into space after he is judged by the Illuminati to be too much of a danger to human-kind.[43] The Hulk lands on a savage planet that he eventually rules until it is destroyed, for which he blames his "friends" who banished him. Af-ter he returns to Earth and attacks them, Reed feels responsible, for the Hulk's exile if not the destruction of his world. When Sue tries to calm down the rampaging Hulk by telling him he isn't a monster, the Hulk replies, while punching Reed: "I know. He is."[44] During the Civil War among the hero community over the issue of superhero registration, Reed helps to design the cloned version of Thor, who ends up killing Bill Foster (Goliath), as well as the prison in the Negative Zone to hold cap-tured anti-registration heroes, both of which he felt remorse over later (especially when Sue left him).[45] With regard to these questionable ac-tions, a future version of Doctor Doom visits the team in the present day, presumably to prevent Reed from going even farther, and accuses him of possessing "a personal arrogance that places him beyond both man's and God's law."[46] As we discussed in chapter 1, Reed's enthusiasm to "solve everything" does sometimes lead him to forget that some methods cross moral lines. This is not arrogance regarding the irrelevance of ethics, as Doom implies, but rather a single-minded focus on his goal—a problem all the same, of course, but not a failing of moral character.

One thing Reed does not feel guilt or responsibility for is Galactus, the Devourer of Worlds whose life Reed saves, after which he is put on trial by survivors of the worlds Galactus destroyed afterwards, including the Skrulls.[47] Reed argues that he played a role, however indirectly, in the death of most of the Skrulls—even though they are "the most relentlessly evil race in the galaxy"—but that he could not let Galactus die when it was in his power to save him.[48] As he listens to testimony from those who lost families, races, and entire worlds, he thinks to himself that the scale of the destruction is "almost impossible to comprehend" but "I did not act without thinking. I believed what I did was right! And I still believe it!"[49]

In the end Reed pleads guilty to the act of saving Galactus but argues this act should not be considered a crime because Galactus is a natural and necessary aspect of the universe and must be assumed to serve the greater good—and when Odin, the All-Father of Asgard, appears and backs him up, the trial is declared over and Reed is acquitted. Even though Reed mourns the deaths Galactus caused, he believes he was right to save his life, while at the same time he realizes he is not morally responsible for what Galactus did afterwards, given that it was Galactus's choice, not his.[50] Nonetheless, this is impressively reasonable on his part, presumably driven by the fact that he could justify his act of saving a life as morally right, regardless of the subsequent consequences (recalling our discussion of deontology in chapter 1), as opposed to events like the original accident, in which he can identify possible failures of negligence that, if accurate, would leave him responsible.

Finally, and perhaps most surprisingly, at times Reed feels responsible for what Victor von Doom became after his own accident during their college days (as we discuss at length in chapter 8). Reminiscing to Sue about this time, Reed admits he was brash and arrogant then, provoking Doom unnecessarily and looking into his work without permission. Even though he tried to tell Doom about the mistake he found in his calculations that led to an explosion, Reed thinks Doom might have listened if Reed tried harder to acknowledge the brilliance of what he was doing. "I made so many mistakes back then," he says. "I have to wonder how much of this is my fault." When Sue tries to assure him he's not responsible for Doom's accident, he says it's not about the accident: "I feel guilty over the secret little thrill I got from proving myself smarter than him." As Reed prepares to visit Doom on his invitation, Sue tells him it's a trap and that "Doom's playing on guilt you shouldn't have. You're not responsible for what happened to him," to which Reed responds (as noted before), "We're all responsible for what happens to everybody."[51]

Later, after he traps himself with Doom in a "Mobius dimension" he invented that replays their past conflicts on an infinite loop, Reed reiterates that he was impressed with Doom's college plans to visit the afterlife (and locate his mother's soul in hell), but he cannot deny the fact that "I knew your science was flawed." Then he asks, "If I'd tried harder to make you listen to me, could I have saved the world from the path you took?" He admits that he probably could not have, but in light of the monstrous harm Doom did afterwards, including to Reed and his family, "'probably' isn't much consolation." In the end, he acknowledges that "I can't take the blame for all you've done, Victor. But someone has to take the responsibility." However, by trapping both of them in the

46

pocket dimension forever, Reed implies both of them should bear responsibility, even though only one of them is morally responsible for Doom's heinous actions.[52]

A Responsible Conclusion

Of course, Reed's statement about absolute and universal responsibility is idealistic but naive. Certainly, we are causally responsible for things when we were involved in the "chain of events" that led to them. Galactus would not have destroyed the Skrull homeworld had Reed not saved his life earlier. In that sense, Reed helped cause the Skrulls' destruction, but so was everyone else who was involved in that chain of events, including everyone involved in Reed's life that helped him to get the point when he saved Galactus's life. The same holds for Doom, whose life would have been very different had he never met the future Mr. Fantastic. Reed played an important role in Doom's life, but that doesn't mean he is responsible in a moral sense for everything that happened to him after they met, or who Doom became. Likewise, he is not morally responsible for what Galactus did after Reed saved his life. In both cases, Reed is only responsible for what he did—saving Galactus or intervening in Doom's experiment—but Galactus and Doom are morally responsible for their own actions afterwards. To hold himself responsible for any more than that, which he notably does not do in the case of Galactus, is excessive to the extreme.

Surveying all the examples presented above, we see that Reed's sense of responsibility is generally kept to things he actually did or failed to do, as well as things he feels capable of doing if he only pushed himself harder. The last one in particular drives him to the greatest depths of guilt and remorse because of the incredibly high expectations he places on himself as one of the most intelligent beings in the universe. And when he fails to live up to these expectations, he experiences just as incredible doubts, which not only impair his ability to do his best (which only reinforces the doubt), but also open him up to manipulation. In one relevant case, Doctor Doom plants a fake journal among Reed's college things that "reveals" that Reed intended for the four to be bombarded by cosmic rays on that eventful flight, as a pre-emptive defense against super-powered criminals.[53] This reinforces Reed's existing doubts and makes him hesitant to help Kitty Pryde (of the X-Men), leaving Doom to step in and prove he's the smarter man. In the end, Reed must overcome his doubts, based on the love and confidence of those who know him best, and (again) point out an error in Doom's work, saving Pryde and dealing the Latverian dictator yet another blow to his fragile ego.

In his best moments, Reed realizes that, although natural, guilt and doubt are counterproductive, especially to Mr. Fantastic's proclaimed goals of achieving the impossible and "fixing everything." After the Civil War and World War Hulk, the Skrulls launch a Secret Invasion that ends, due not to the valiant efforts of the gathered heroes, but rather to Norman Osborne, the Green Goblin, who then takes over S.H.I.E.L.D. in the period known as the "Dark Reign."[54] As Reed prepares to explore alternate timelines to see how it could have been prevented (as described above), he acknowledges to himself that

> guilt has a way of obscuring the obvious—it limits your vision. The only thing that matters when assessing a situation are the facts. You have to put everything else aside. If you can do that, you leave room for inspiration to strike.

He says this even while acknowledging to his family that "I made some choices that directly led to the deaths of some of our friends and almost tore this world to pieces…and for the life of me, I don't know where it all went wrong."[55]

Reed accepts responsibility, both causal and moral, for all that happened, thinking to himself that "all of humanity, my family…my children, they suffer for it. They live in the world I created…and I will find a way to make it right."[56] But he knows that he can't figure it out if he lets his guilt cloud his mind; instead, he has to find a way to accommodate the guilt for what he did and the responsibility for making it better. And the fact that he never gives up the drive to improve the world is what, in the end, truly makes him Mr. Fantastic.

[1] *Fantastic Four*, vol. 1, #1 (November 1961).

[2] *Fantastic Four*, vol. 3, #24 (December 1999).

[3] No less an authority than Spider-Man once told Reed, "The wisest man I ever knew told me with great power comes great responsibility. The smartest man I know lives that. Every day" (*Spider-Man/Fantastic Four* #2, October 2010).

[4] *Fantastic Four*, vol. 3, #585 (January 2011). In a great example of a "humble brag," Reed has "often wondered if the cosmic rays which changed us into the F.F.—did not affect my mind, making possible those intuitive leaps of imagination which are the core of all scientific achievement!" (*Fantastic Four*, vol. 1, #225, December 1980).

[5] *Fantastic Four*, vol. 3, #24 (December 1999).

[6] *Fantastic Four Special* #1 (2005). We see a more limited version of this early on, when Reed feels bad for Ben and Sue tries to tell him he can't blame himself. "Of course I can!" he tells her. "As leader of the F.F. I'm responsible for everything!" (*Fantastic Four*, vol. 1, #41, August 1965).

[7] *Dark Reign: Fantastic Four* #4 (August 2009).

[8] *Fantastic Four*, vol. 1, #3 (March 1962). Sue shares this feeling of gratitude, although not to "fate": As she tells a television interview for an anniversary special on the team, "It's an extraordinary life, and an extraordinary opportunity to give back to a world that has been so good to us" (*Fantastic Four*, vol. 3, #543, May 2007, "C'mon, Suzie, Don't Leave Us Hangin'").

[9] Immanuel Kant, *Groundwork for the Metaphysics of Morals*, trans. James W. Ellington (Indianapolis, IN: Hackett Publishing, 1785/1993), p. 423. He has more to say about this in *The Metaphysics of Morals*, trans. Mary Gregor (Cambridge: Cambridge University Press, 1797/1996), pp. 444-446.

[10] *Fantastic Four*, vol. 3, #570 (October 2009).

[11] *Fantastic Four*, vol. 1, #139 (October 1973).

[12] *Fantastic Four*, vol. 1, #358 (November 1991), "Whatever Happened to Alicia?" At other times, he acknowledged this might be an obsession, a type of "intellectual paranoia" that endangers those he wants most to protect (*Fantastic Four*, vol. 1, #366, July 1992).

[13] *Fantastic Four*, vol. 7, #6 (June 2023).

[14] *Fantastic Four*, vol. 1, #378 (July 1993).

[15] *Secret Wars*, vol. 1, #2 (June 1984).

[16] To be sure, Reed's not the only one who feels guilt about things they feel responsible for. For example, Ben feels responsible for endangering his girlfriend Alicia Masters, as we'll see in chapter 5, and even for "creating" Doctor Doom (*Fantastic*

Four, vol. 4, #9, August 2013); Johnny feels responsible for fans who get hurt imitating him (as well as people generally put at risk by his powers), as we'll see in chapter 4; and Sue feels bad for shaming Ben into the space flight that transformed them all, which loops her in on Reed's guilt over Ben as well as the danger their activities put their children in.

[17] *Fantastic Four*, vol. 1, #2 (January 1962).

[18] *Fantastic Four*, vol. 3, #543, "C'mon, Suzie, Don't Leave Us Hangin.'"

[19] *Fantastic Four*, vol. 3, #60 (October 2002). "'Mr. Fantastic,'" he says to her. "Does that sound like something anyone would really want to call themselves?"

[20] *Fantastic Four*, vol. 6, #35, "Stars" (November 2021). This explains the photo shoot for *LIFE* magazine as early as *Fantastic Four*, vol. 1, #24 (March 1964).

[21] They learned of this in *Fantastic Four*, vol. 6, #17 (February 2020), and Reed expressed his continued guilt despite this revelation in issues #20 (May 2020) and #46 (October 2022).

[22] For a good introduction to moral responsibility, including how it interacts with the debates over free will and why we consider it important in the first place, see Matthew Taibert, *Moral Responsibility* (Cambridge: Polity, 2016).

[23] Even though he didn't cause the cosmic rays themselves, one story claims that they originally passed through Reed while he was observing the origin of the universe and were modified by his thoughts of the four of them before hitting them, explaining why the powers the rays gave them just happened to emphasize their existing personality traits (*Fantastic Four*, vol. 3, #532, December 2005). It was actually Johnny who first suggested a purpose or design behind the rays' effects when he asked Reed if his idolization of the original Human Torch played any role in how the rays affected him, to which Reed responded, "It's all too deep for me, son" (*Fantastic Four*, vol. 1, #132, March 1973).

[24] *Fantastic Four*, vol. 6, #18 (March 2020).

[25] And he did, given the Overseer's actions: After Reed discovers what the Overseer did, he proclaims "my shields were strong enough. They *always* were" (*Fantastic Four*, vol. 6, #17, February 2020).

[26] *Fantastic Four*, vol. 1, #1 (and reiterated countless times since). In fact, Ben refused to join them until Sue called him a coward, so maybe Sue bears at least some causal responsibility for the accident as well! (She apologizes for this, and for calling him a "thing," before his wedding to Alicia Masters in *Fantastic Four*, vol. 6, #5, February 2019, "4-Minute Warning.")

[27] The first was in *Fantastic Four*, vol. 1, #8 (November 1962).

[28] *Fantastic Four*, vol. 1, #11 (February 1963), "A Visit with the Fantastic Four." (He says this *so many* times.)

[29] *Fantastic Four*, vol. 1, #25 (April 1964). We will discuss this more in chapter 5.

[30] *Fantastic Four*, vol. 1, #105 (December 1970).

[31] *Fantastic Four*, vol. 1, #239 (February 1982). Remember that it was Sue who called Ben a "thing" out of fright after the accident, a name that he took to heart.

[32] *Marvel Fanfare* #2 (May 1982), "Annihilation."

[33] Ibid.

[34] *Fantastic Four*, vol. 1, #141 (December 1973). Much later, Franklin will start losing his powers and resent his father for not trying harder to restore them (*X-Men/Fantastic Four* #1, April 2020).

[35] *Fantastic Four*, vol. 1, #142 (January 1974).

[36] *Fantastic Four*, vol. 1, #149 (August 1974).

[37] This happens in *Fantastic Four*, vol. 3, #528 (August 2005) and *Fantastic Four*, vol. 5, #8 (October 2014).

[38] *Fantastic Four*, vol. 3, #45 (September 2001).

[39] *Fantastic Four*, vol. 5, #3 (June 2014). Sue should talk: earlier, when Reed promised to fix her after she was infected by an alien parasite, she asked, "just like you promised Ben?" (*Fantastic Four*, vol. 3, #17, May 1999).

[40] *Fantastic Four*, vol. 6, #34 (September 2021).

[41] *Fantastic Four*, vol. 6, #39 (March 2022).

[42] By the next issue, Reed absorbs all the Watcher's knowledge and those limits are no longer an issue. However, his mind is warped by this, and he tells Johnny he knows how to fix him but won't, because his power is too useful to his new plans (*Fantastic Four*, vol. 6, #40, April 2022).

[43] *New Avengers: Illuminati*, vol. 1, #1 (May 2006). This is the same Illuminati (with slightly different membership) who would later confront the problem of incursions of Earths from other dimensions, as discussed in the last chapter.

[44] *World War Hulk* #2 (September 2007).

[45] We discuss the events of Civil War more in chapter 6. Amazingly, this is not Doom's most egregious display of projection. Once, he held Valeria in his arms while telling a captive Reed that "your problem, Richards, is your unquenchable vanity" and "in your unmitigated arrogance, you carry around an eternal sense of entitlement that is wholly undeserved...and yet, so fundamental to your sense of self that you're constantly willing to put everyone around you at risk to attain whatever goals strike your fancy," concluding that his "arrogance is a mask" to cover his "fundamental—and profoundly well-deserved—insecurity regarding your allegedly superior intelligence" (*Fantastic Four*, vol. 3, #70, August 2003). We will discuss Doom's own insecurity masked by arrogance in chapter 8.

[46] *Fantastic Four*, vol. 3, #552 (February 2008).

[47] Reed saved Galactus's life in *Fantastic Four*, vol. 1, #244 (July 1982), and Galactus consumed the Skrull homeworld in issue #257 (August 1983).

[48] *Fantastic Four*, vol. 1, #261 (December 1983); in issue #244, he agreed with Captain America when he declares Galactus to be "a living, sentient being," and Reed says "we are bound" to help him.

[49] *Fantastic Four*, vol. 1, #262 (January 1984).

[50] We discuss Galactus's status in the universe and whether he actually has a choice in his devouring in chapter 7.

[51] *Fantastic Four Special* #1 (2005).

[52] *Fantastic Four*, vol. 3, #507 (January 2004).

[53] *Fantastic Four vs. the X-Men* #2 (March 1987).

[54] *Secret Invasion*, vol. 1, #8 (January 2009).

[55] *Dark Reign: Fantastic Four* #1 (May 2009).

[56] Ibid.

Chapter 3
Susan Storm-Richards (The Invisible Woman)

Susan Storm-Richards, known as Sue to her friends and family and as the Invisible Woman to her foes, is widely acknowledged as the strongest member of the Fantastic Four. On the surface, this is due to her incredible forcefields, which she has used to shield entire cities and repel even the Hulk, which are a physical manifestation of her formidable willpower and resolve. This is just one aspect of Sue's strength, which is not only mental and physical, but moral as well. By surveying the various ways that Sue expresses strength through the history of the Fantastic Four—even early on, when "strong" would be the last word you might think of to describe her—we'll come to understand the many ways the term is understood, not only in philosophy but in ordinary life as well.

"Strength"? Really?

In the early years of the Marvel Universe, starting with the publication of *Fantastic Four* #1 in late 1961, female characters—regardless of whether they were superheroes themselves—were often written as simpering, submissive, and weak, especially in comparison to their male companions, who were usually their love interests, saviors, or both.

The first woman superhero of the modern Marvel age was no different in much of her behavior and dialogue, even down to her original name: the Invisible *Girl.* We need only mention a few examples, such as when Ben turns a firehose on Johnny in the Baxter Building and soaks Sue's designer clothes, at which she starts to sob, cursing "Men! You're all beasts!" before asking for forgiveness and proclaiming, "it isn't like me to get so emotional!"[1] When Sue feels neglected by Reed—not an uncommon feeling, even much later in their life together—she wonders if "a new hairdo would make him realize I'm not one of the boys!" Reed still fails to take notice, so she turns invisible, making the rest of the team think she is missing and start a search for her. When she reveals herself, she says, "I wanted you all to notice my new hairdo…and this seemed to be the only way to get your attention!"[2] In the same issue, Sue admits she's frightened as they approach the Great Refuge, home of the Inhumans, but thinks, "No matter how frightened I may be, I must never show it to Reed!"[3]

Of course, a weak portrayal of Sue needs a domineering and condescending Reed to complete the picture. For example, when Doctor Doom attacks Sue and Reed with a raygun, Reed suggests Sue use her forcefield to push him out a window, which she does, saving both their lives. But when she complains afterwards that "I don't understand any of this," Reed says, "I tried to explain, darling," and after he does, she appeals to "Reed…dearest" that "I've been such a fool!" Reed doesn't miss a chance to "correct" her, saying "not a fool, Sue…merely a female! You couldn't have reacted differently!"[4] He also gets impatient when she questions his orders or urges him to be careful, replying "I'll explain later, woman! Just do as I say!" or "stop sounding like a wife."[5] When Sue says she's "sick of living in a ridiculous costume! I'm a woman! I want feminine dresses—foolish hairdos," Reed promises to by her "a whole new wardrobe" and take her out on the town. When she's so happy that "I don't know what to say," Reed speaks for her: "Fine! Wives should be kissed—and not heard!"[6] And when she doubts her value when the team is chasing the Hulk, General "Thunderbolt" Ross says that her beauty will raise morale, and Reed agrees: "That's just the way we feel about Sue, General!"[7]

When Reed does acknowledge Sue's early accomplishments in the field—and they are frequent, as she often saves the team with her invisibility, forcefields, or sheer cleverness—it comes off as patronizing when set alongside his more sexist comments. Earlier in the issue in which she tries to get his attention with a new hairdo, Sue held the aquatic Inhuman named Triton in a force bubble filled with water until they could find a tank for him. When Reed tells her she can finally let the bubble go, she is relieved, saying she couldn't have held it much longer, to which Reed replies, "You held it long enough to save a life, my darling!"[8] After the team defeats the monstrous Blastaar on their first encounter with him, Sue falls into Reed, asking him "is it over? Is it really over…at last?" He assures her it is, after which she asks him to forgive her for "suddenly turning—feminine," but he refutes it, saying, "nonsense, dearest! You did your share…when it counted!"[9]

Reed often tries to shield Sue from danger, especially after they're married, usually by insisting she refrain from coming on missions. She resents this, of course, and eventually pushes back. In one story, Sue wants to lure Doom to the team, arguing that she's the only one who can do it. When Reed says he can't "permit" her to go alone, she says, "Please, Reed! Must we go through this every time a dangerous task falls to me? I've proven again and again that I can handle myself in an emergency situation."[10] In another case, Reed says the team needs stealth, and Sue knows she's the one; when he recommends caution (instead of objecting outright), she replies, "Please don't fuss so, Reed. I'm perfectly capable of taking care of myself," and thinks to herself later that "I've proven my value and resilience a hundred times over. I'm not about to go back to the sidelines now."[11]

To be fair to Reed, this event did occur shortly after Sue suffered a miscarriage, and other times he attempts to hold Sue back for valid reasons other than spousal concern.[12] For example, once he asked her to stay back for strategic reasons, because "you, more than any other, may be able to form a one-woman reserve unit—coming to the rescue with your force fields at some opportune moment," an explanation she accepts with understandable reservations.[13] Sometimes he does it for the sake of their children, such as when their son Franklin wants to join the team on a mission and Reed tells him he has to stay with his mother—which Sue knows means she has to stay behind too. When she says they might need her and he can't "cut me out of the danger," Reed said he isn't, and he wants Sue to stay with Franklin in case the danger comes to them, an argument Sue readily accepts.[14]

The ironic part about Reed repeatedly holding Sue back from danger is that she all too often ends up saving the team, not only in the later stories when her strength was widely recognized, but even in her earlier days of reserve, hesitance, and doubt—including before her forcefield powers even emerged. In their first meeting with Doctor Doom, Sue volunteers to be taken hostage to learn more about him. After Doom captures the other three, she destroys his control panel and frees her teammates—all with her hands tied behind her back (literally).[15] Soon afterwards, in an issue dominated by the team's introduction to the Incredible Hulk, Sue disarms the real threat, a spy named the Wrecker.[16] After Sue learns of her forcefield powers, this becomes an even more frequent occurrence, such as when the Frightful Four abduct her and attack the team: not only does Sue insert and expand forcefields in her restraints to break them, but she also shields the entire team from an explosion. "Protected by the power of one girl," the (outdated) exposition reads, "a girl whose will to survive is so strong that her force field remains even though she is unconscious."[17]

Eventually, these heroic feats would become more commonplace, as would Reed's acknowledgement of her tremendous ability and resolve. In another adventure in which Sue used a force bubble to save them all from an explosion—in space, no less—Reed asks her afterwards if she is all right, saying "your power drain must have been enormous!" She minimizes it, saying, "It knocked the wind out of me, Reed...but I'll make it."[18] In another story, Sue protects the four (and Ben's girlfriend Alicia) in a bubble flexible enough that they can roll it like a hamster ball to escape. When she tells Reed "the strain is too great" and she "can't hold out much longer," he tells her, "You can do it, lady! You're a lot tougher than you think!" and later tells her, "we owe you our lives."[19] Even the other Marvel heroes take notice: When an evil Reed imposter detonates a gamma bomb inside the Fantastic Four's headquarters where dozens of heroes have gathered for an intergalactic crisis, Sue contains all the bomb's force and radiation until an impressed Thor creates a wind funnel to carry it into space.[20]

The Indomitable Woman

As mentioned above, Sue is now widely acknowledged as the most powerful member of the team: for example, after she recently blocked out the sun to kill alien algae overtaking the planet, former S.H.I.E.L.D. director Maria Hill called her a "walking, talking mass-extinction event."[21] Although this was not a common opinion in the very early years, despite her impressive and heroic acts from the start, it is not an entirely new one either. At one of her lowest periods, after her miscarriage, Sue knows that it wasn't her fault, but cannot reconcile her helplessness in that situation with her abilities, particularly her force fields, which "some people have said" make her "the most powerful member of the FF."[22] Later, Reed's father, Nathaniel, a time-traveler who usually knows far more than he lets on, thinks that "my daughter-in-law possesses far greater power than even she suspects!"[23] When he tells Sue her power derives from another dimension and teaches her how to use it more effectively and forcefully, Reed is frightened, thinking to himself, "My God—! She doesn't realize the dangers of trying to harness such incomprehensible power!"[24]

This moment of doubt aside, Reed knows full well how powerful his wife is. After Sue uses a force bubble to protect bystanders from the falling rubble of a damaged building, Reed tells her that "once again, you prove that your power is really the most remarkable of all."[25] He goes even farther later when Sue renders their spacecraft invisible, to the naked eye as well as radar, to infiltrate a war fleet of the united Skrull and Kree alien races, inspiring the thought: "Susan makes it seems effortless. She really is the strongest of us all. In so many ways."[26] And this admiration is shown by the rest of the team as well: when their aircraft crashes into a lake, Johnny watches proudly from the shore as his sister manages "to put a force field full of air around the ship…and it's bobbing right to the surface!" Afterwards, Ben tells Reed "yer blonde better half is givin' me a kingsize inferiority complex."[27]

It is to these "many ways" of possessing and exhibiting strength that we now turn, using Sue as an example. These go beyond the amazing feats she performs in almost every story, ranging from using forcefields to repel foes (including the Hulk), keep a massive dam from breaking, covering New York City in a force bubble projected through Iron Man's armor, maintaining a forcefield bridge between two airplanes in flight to transfer passengers from one to another, and even giving the Thing somewhere to sit.[28] Although these are all feats of physical force, whether pushing something (such as a Hulk or a Thing) or repelling something (such as a flood), they do not result from Sue's actual muscles. Rather, it is her willpower, her mental strength, that allows her to do these amazing things.

Mind you, this does not mean Sue does not have physical skills as well. Although she may not have the strength of the Thing (or She-Hulk), Sue is fully capable of handling herself in one-on-one combat. In the very early years, we see her fighting Doctor Doom using judo, taught to her "by one of the world's greatest experts: Reed Richards!"[29] Just to be safe, she later gets lessons in martial arts from Danny Rand, the Immortal Iron Fist, whom she fights to a draw in a sparring session.[30] She later uses what she learned to defeat aliens trying to abduct Franklin, extending a force field around her limbs to extend their reach, her will giving them "a force beyond her purely physical strength" (and she does all this in a gown and heels).[31] She also puts these combat skills to good use in covert missions for S.H.I.E.L.D., where she says to herself, upon facing a thug with a knife, that she knows "seven ways I can take him down."[32]

These admirable (and frightening) skills aside, Sue's true strength remains more mental than physical. During her session with Iron Fist, she reflects on how both of their abilities, her force fields and his *qi*-powered blows,

> function as extensions of our will. The key to survival is our ability to focus those energies, and sustain them. The supremacy of our minds. It isn't raw strength that'll prove our undoing, but a fatal, unexpected distraction.[33]

It is this strength of will that enables her to hold her own against the Mighty Avengers, easily dispatching Iron Man, the Hulk, and her former teammate Luke Cage.[34] She even takes control of Thor's hammer Mjolnir (while he's holding it) and later turns Captain America's shield back on him with a perfectly shaped force field.[35]

This characterization of Sue's powers corresponds with a way of thinking about willpower supported by many philosophers and psychologists. For example, psychologist Roy Baumeister wrote that willpower acts like a muscle, requiring effort proportionate to any particular task, becoming stronger over time with practice and growing fatigued the longer the task lasts (or the more difficult it is).[36] When Sue "focuses all her energy, her indomitable will" to break several heroes out of a prison, the narration reads that "it cracks wide open before her mental assault," evoking a physical effort using muscles rather than her mind.[37] This doesn't apply just to her manipulation of force shields, which literally transforms mental exertion into physical force. When a building explodes over the team, burying them in rubble, she renders the debris over their heads invisible to find a way out, thinking to herself, "I'm going to have to push myself like never before—straining far beyond my uppermost limit! This will take all the inner strength—all the power—that I possess! The strain is excruciating! My head...feels like it's about to burst..."[38]

All of this is reflected in Sue's experience with her powers, limited only by her willpower and resolve, as they grow in power and precision over the years, but also coming at significant cost in terms of pain and exhaustion. Many are the examples of how difficult it is for her to maintain forcefields, especially against resistance, usually visible in terms of headaches, nosebleeds, and dizziness (or passing out altogether). This happens both when she uses her powers of invisibility, as in the case of the collapsed building above, as well as force fields to hold back powerful opponents: "I can feel it in my head. Each blow is like thunder."[39] When she has to hold a demonically possessed Franklin, glowing with otherworldly power, in a force bubble while the team sought help, she says, "The strain's beginning to wear on me—but I must maintain my forcebubble...Franklin's life depends on it!"[40] While she uses her force fields to protect her beloved teammates against the Hulk's rage, she thinks to herself, "Can't keep—this force wall—up much longer," and later, "Force field—Reed's only chance—! But—so tired now— How long— can I hold it—against the Hulk?" After she uses the last of her resolve to catch Reed in a force cushion, she collapses, muttering that she is "so weak," clearly indicating exhaustion rather than a general self-assessment![41]

Furthermore, even when she doesn't push herself to the limit, Sue nonetheless feels tired and weak after sustained use of her powers, which need time and rest to recuperate, just like muscles. This was revealed as soon as the issue after her expanded powers were discovered, when the team was escaping from one of Doctor Doom's plots. After freeing Ben from his restraints, she says, "if only I didn't always feel so weak after using my invisible force field."[42] When she doesn't give herself enough time to recover, Sue feels the strain of her powers even more. In one adventure, after she had nearly exhausted herself using her powers and needed to conserve them from an upcoming battle, she nonetheless uses them to keep a massive dam from breaking. But she soon realizes that

> I wasn't ready…wasn't quite prepared…to erect another force field! M-my strength is beginning to fail! M-my head feels like it's about to burst! Th-the pain is incredible! B-but I can't give up! N-not while the others are depending on me![43]

Sue's powers also require constant attention, again proportionate to the task at hand. This was mentioned in the issue where her force powers (as well the ability to render other things invisible) were discovered, and when Sue later encloses the team in a force bubble, she says "I hope I can maintain it."[44] When the team needed to get to the top of a tower that stretched ten miles from the ground, she propelled them straight up with a growing column of force. She began to shake near the top and then started to lose her focus: "My concentration—only slipped a fraction—but my force field's destabilizing!"[45]

Even though Sue has limits, she refuses to accept them, typical of the hero she is. After the team discovers invisible asteroids threatening Earth, she constructs two force shields overhead, a porous one on the outside to detect the asteroid and a harder one on the inside to protect them and the nearby civilians. When the first asteroid arrives, she holds the explosive blast of the asteroid between the two force shields, which Franklin says "takes strength she didn't know she had," while she has Johnny dispel the heat into space. When they see more asteroids coming, Reed tells Sue, "It took everything you had just to hold back one. We can't—", to which Sue responds, simply, "We have to, honey. We do what we can."[46] Sometimes, doing what we can means finding a way to ignore our limits. In one interstellar adventure teaming the Fantastic Four with the Avengers, after Sue realizes she is reaching her limits but needs to fight on, she asks her psychic colleague Mantis to "use your telepathy on me. Block my pain and fatigue—the body's warning systems. Then let's see how hard I can push," akin to an epidural often used during childbirth to enable mothers to endure the intense pain of delivery.[47]

Moral Strength

It should come as no surprise that Sue's most tremendous exertions are made to protect others or save lives, the heroic ideal that all in the Fantastic Four exemplify. This reflects not only her mental strength but also moral strength, or what is more commonly called *strength of character*. This can refer to one's possession of virtues in general, as we discussed in chapter 1, as well as a person's resolve or determination to do the right thing (in a deontological sense) even in the face of difficulty or temptation.

Immanual Kant, the deontologist we met in chapter 1, wrote about strength of character in very similar terms that Baumeister uses to describe willpower. To Kant, one's resolve to do the right thing "can never settle down in peace…if it is not rising, [it] is unavoidably sinking."[48] He also wrote that "the way to acquire it is to enhance the moral *incentive* (the thought of the law), both by contemplating the dignity of the pure rational law in us and by *practicing* virtue."[49] In essence, Kant meant that we must always keep the thought of what is moral and right in our minds and act in accordance with it, and with repeated use of this "muscle," we will get better at behaving ethically—or, in the terms of Sue and the rest of the Fantastic Four, being a hero.

We see this strength of character most often in Sue's resolve not to give in to the agony or exhaustion from using her powers, visible in many of the quotations through this chapter.[50] This heroic determination to survive and prevail is not just observed when using her abilities, but also in inspiring proclamations such as "the FF will fight to save our universe with our dying breaths!"[51] During the cataclysmic battle with Onslaught (which resulted in the Fantastic Four and most of the Avengers being "killed"), the narration hails "her stoic professionalism" in tending to injured colleagues, continuing that "her strength is an inspiration to all," even though she is inwardly worried about Franklin (who ends up saving them all at the last moment and shunting them to a pocket universe of his own creation).[52]

Another time, when the team was captured and Sue was trying to keep their spirits up with inspiring words, Lyja—a Skrull ally who was once married to Johnny—thinks that "she speaks with such confidence—such courage!"[53] Although she always shows courage, Sue was not always known for confidence, although there were early signs, such as when she stood up to Namor's insistence that she be his bride, and then stopped the rest of the team, who threatened to "gang up" on him afterwards.[54] Nonetheless, her confidence developed even more over the years as her experience and powers grew, to the point where she tells Spider-Man, when he asks whether she is concerned about a secret meeting of many of their foes, "Through the years, I've beaten every one of them. Over and over. Badly. So you tell me…Do you think I should be afraid of them…or should they be afraid of me?"[55]

This strength of character is all the more admirable given the ordeals Sue has suffered over the years since the fateful accident that gave them their powers. Soon after suffering her miscarriage, she is emotionally manipulated by the villain Psycho-Man into becoming a dark version of herself named Malice, an event she describes as emotional rape.[56] When the team next confronts him and is captured, he makes it worse, making Sue see visions of her teammates dying and blaming her for it, followed by her long-deceased parents asking her to join them.[57] After they escape, Sue finds Psycho-Man, relieves him of his emotion-control device and explains what he did to her, telling him that "you defiled me, Psycho-Man. And now you are going to be punished." Rather than kill him (as he fears), she promises to "pay him back in kind," and upon hearing a scream that She-Hulk describes as "somebody having their soul ripped out," the team finds Sue alone. She tells them merely that "the Psycho-Man is no longer any threat to us. He won't bother anyone. Ever again."[58]

Afterwards, Sue announces to the team that Psycho-Man forced her to look deep within herself and see how she had changed since the accident that altered all their lives, gaining amazing powers but also losing "an innocence. A child-like naivety." She acknowledges that she is not the same, especially after what Psycho-Man did, and tells her husband, "There is no Invisible Girl anymore, Reed. She died when the Psycho-Man twisted her soul. From now on, I am the Invisible Woman."[59] With this announcement, she embraces a long-overdue change of name she had long dismissed, having told Luke Cage years earlier that, while "anachronistic," the more mature title was too "long and unwieldy," and arguing to a television interviewer who accuses her of failing to be a "modern, liberated woman" that she is "not a prisoner of words or labels."[60]

Another expression of Sue's strength of character is her heroic sense of sacrifice, which we have seen in her commitment to using her powers to save others even at the risk of pushing herself farther than she can endure. In an early adventure, the villain Klaw tortures Sue with sonic vibrations to coerce her into helping in his ongoing battle with the Black Panther, but she refuses, saying "even my life is more dear to me than loyalty to those who trust me!"[61] Years later, a group of alien survivors of Galactus's hunger develop a way to shield worlds from his view, which Sue has the potential to counteract. Afraid that Galactus will find to way to use her power, the aliens threaten to destroy Manhattan unless she surrenders her life to them—and she agrees.[62] As the aliens prepare to execute her, while a captive Ben and Johnny look on, her brother begs her to fight back and "do something." The alien leader responds, "She is. She is demonstrating the characteristic for which your race is most widely known. She is being noble."[63]

At the same time that she willingly risks and offers her life for others, Sue is resolutely opposed to killing (as are the rest of the Fantastic Four, as we discussed in chapter 1). We already saw that she refused to kill Psycho-Man, despite his inhumane treatment of her; she realized much earlier, after the Skrull who killed her father died in a battle with other Skrulls, that "revenge isn't so sweet, after all."[64] She similarly passes on the opportunity to kill the mass-murderer Thanos—he of the infamous "snap"—despite thinking that "the world would be a lot safer" without him. She admits to herself that "I haven't sunk low enough to commit cold-blooded murder. At least not yet."[65]

This stance against killing extends to her espionage work for S.H.I.E.L.D. as well, despite the "looser" rules against the practice in that particular line of work. But it isn't simply a matter of abstinence, as Sue reveals when her former S.H.I.E.L.D. partner breaks bad and dares her to kill him, taunting her that "it must be awful to finally have to consider killing." Her exasperated response is very telling:

> Think about what I can do! Give you an instant embolism from a hundred yards out. Crush your windpipe. Fill your lungs. Drive a force-field spike through your heart without blinking. I'm a living weapon. I'm "finally" thinking about killing?! I have to think about it all the time. I never worry about being strong enough to take a life, Aidan. I worry about being strong enough *not* to.[66]

Given the awesome powers at her disposal, it is a testament to her strength of character that she never takes the easy way out and eliminates threats permanently. This also shows that she poses just as significant a threat with her powers as Ben and Johnny do with theirs, and requires just as much self-restraint to not let it loose.[67]

Finally, Sue's strength of character also shines in the many leadership roles she has adopted, whether leading the collected Marvel heroes in the "Infinity War" crisis, negotiating peace between warring peoples, or serving as the queen of Old Atlantis (after Namor kills their king).[68] But her most impressive and meaningful role as leader is taking charge of the Fantastic Four. Reed is normally the leader of the team (as discussed in the last chapter), but when he is missing or incapacitated, Sue easily steps up and takes his place, such as when Reed is shot on an exploratory mission in the Negative Zone.[69] Later, after Reed is apparently killed by Doctor Doom, Sue leads the team again, instinctively and without hesitation, despite being deep in shock and refusing to believe he is truly gone.[70] During this time, Lyja admires her courage and confidence (as seen above) and temporary team member Scott Lang (Ant-Man) admits he's "constantly amazed at how she maintains such a cool head in times of extreme crisis."[71] At the reading of Reed's will, Sue is obviously distraught, but thinks to herself, "can't break down...must remain calm...strong. I'm the leader of the team, now. I can't allow the others to see me break down." She also reflects on how others have long seen her: "When we started the team, I was always regarded as the weak link in the chain. Now I've got to be the strong one—for all our sakes."[72]

After Reed returns after being held captive by Hyperstorm (an all-powerful future version of their son Franklin), he finds Sue less compassionate and "soft" than he remembers, perhaps reflecting how leadership forced her to confront hard decisions and make tough calls (in addition to her distress over losing him and slowly coming to terms with it).[73] At the same time, Reed is depleted and defeated, telling Sue when she gives orders to the team before remembering he's back, "you're doing a fine job leading the team...without me."[74] Later, Sue struggles to accept Reed's new state, thinking, "he should be leading the team, but his experiences with Hyperstorm have really shaken his confidence." When she sends him to a lab with Nathaniel to work on a way to fight back, he refuses and reminds her he used to be the team leader and "maybe it's a responsibility I should reclaim!" She simply replies, "Maybe...but not now!"[75] Even after Reed recovers and resumes leadership, the team notices the difference. When Johnny is critical of his directions, Sue urges him to "be gentle" and reminds him that Reed "didn't necessarily get used to the fact that the rest of us had come up with a way of working that is maybe a little more instinctual than intellectual" under her leadership.[76]

This is not to say, of course, that Sue is not intellectual herself. Although it may not compare to Reed's, her intelligence complements her mental strength, especially when it comes to clever and inventive uses of her powers.[77] Ironically, even though she was often captured or taken hostage in the early years, she usually managed to free herself, such as when she escaped from the Red Ghost by finding the control panel for the force field she was held in and cutting the correct wire.[78] A few issues later, Doctor Doom captures the team, but it is Sue who thinks of a way out and disarms the Latverian tyrant.[79] She gradually comes to appreciate her own intelligence over the years: When fighting an Atlantean warrior underwater, whom Sue acknowledges is stronger and faster than her, she thinks to herself, "my best weapon is my brain," taking advantage of the other fighter's temper until she can find an opening for attack.[80] Much more recently, it was revealed that she earned a Ph.D. before that pivotal space flight—not in marine biology, as she jokes, but archaeology.[81]

Sue's intelligence has long been on display in how she uses her powers of invisibility against foes, but more recently has figured out how to manipulate light in new ways, such as affecting color, helping to disguise her on S.H.I.E.L.D. missions as well as faking being burnt to a crisp during a team adventure.[82] She uses her force fields in precise and intricate ways also, such as manipulating the internal steering mechanism of the Fantasticar after the control panel is destroyed; using a force "key-probe" to unlock the team's restraints after they are captured; and even threading force particles through the particles of Doom's personal force field to destroy his armor.[83] She also forms much larger and inventive force constructs, including ramps to slide around the city, the missing parts to an airplane while in flight, and horses for the team to ride.[84] No less an expert than Reed calls Sue's use of her force powers "brilliant"—'nuff said![85]

More Than Meets the Eye

If this chapter seemed like a Susan Storm-Richards gushfest…fair enough! But you can hardly blame me for wanting to dispel the common perception, both in the Marvel Universe as well as the real world, of Sue as the team's "weakest link." As Reed reflected on his wife recently, he thought that,

> To the public, her contributions are often overlooked…But to those who know and love her…Sue is the most powerful of us all. Because she has always pushed the boundaries of what is possible…precisely because she doesn't know the meaning of the word defeat.[86]

Through providing copious examples of Sue's amazing abilities, this chapter tried to show that her strength is not just shown by how big a force-field battering ram she can make or how hard she can push it through a brick wall. Strength is a much broader concept than mere physical force—as even Ben Grimm knows—and Sue exemplifies mental strength as well as strength of character as well. She's often thought of as the heart of the team, given her compassion and protective impulses, which are all strengths as well. It would seem that saying that Sue is the strongest member of the Fantastic Four means more than what's evident at first sight—almost like the other types of strength were…invisible!

[1] *Fantastic Four Annual*, vol. 1, #1 (1963), "Sub-Mariner Versus the Human Race!"

[2] *Fantastic Four*, vol. 1, #47 (February 1966).

[3] Ibid.

[4] *Fantastic Four Annual*, vol. 1, #2 (1964), "The Final Victory of Dr. Doom!"

[5] *Fantastic Four*, vol. 1, #45 (December 1965); *Fantastic Four*, vol. 1, #47.

[6] *Fantastic Four*, vol. 1, #65 (August 1967).

[7] *Fantastic Four*, vol. 1, #12 (March 1963).

[8] *Fantastic Four*, vol. 1, #47.

[9] *Fantastic Four*, vol. 1, #63 (June 1967). Nonetheless, he snaps at her for "going feminine" (*Fantastic Four*, vol. 1, #107, February 1971).

[10] *Fantastic Four*, vol. 1, #236 (November 1981), "Terror in a Tiny Town."

[11] *Fantastic Four*, vol. 1, #272 (November 1984).

[12] On the other hand, when Sue was abducted by the Frightful Four in an early story, Reed told the others that "this is the reason I shied away from romance all these years! Once an enemy knows that one of us is in love, he can strike at us…through our loved one!" (*Fantastic Four*, vol. 1, #38, May 1965). Here, Reed isn't even thinking of Sue as a fellow hero, but merely a love interest his enemies can exploit.

[13] *Fantastic Four*, vol. 1, #173 (August 1976).

[14] *Fantastic Four*, vol. 1, #216 (March 1980).

[15] *Fantastic Four*, vol. 1, #5 (July 1962).

[16] *Fantastic Four*, vol. 1, #12 (March 1963).

[17] *Fantastic Four*, vol. 1, #38. This contradicts later evidence, reviewed below, that her powers require mental focus and exertion—although I suppose her unconscious mind may be able to trigger her powers in the pursuit of survival (such as when her forcefield "activated itself automatically" to protect her from an electric shock burst in *Fantastic Four*, vol. 1, #50, May 1966).

[18] *Fantastic Four*, vol.1, #208 (July 1979).

[19] *Fantastic Four*, vol.1, #359 (December 1991).

[20] *Fantastic Four*, vol.1, #368 (September 1992); see also *Infinity War*, vol. 1, #3 (August 1992). Mind you, this was not the Thor we know but rather Eric Masterson, a fairly new Thor at this point (and later to be known as Thunderstrike)—but I am confident the Odinson himself would have been similarly impressed, verily!

[21] *Fantastic Four*, vol. 7, #6 (June 2023). In the next issue Hill tells her colleague Nick Fury that "I didn't know she and her brother could end all life on this planet," which she calls "an escalation. A new use of their powers to do something they couldn't do before" (vol. 7, #7, July 2023).

[22] *Fantastic Four*, vol. 1, #270 (September 1984).

[23] *Fantastic Four*, vol. 1, #376 (May 1993).

[24] *Fantastic Four*, vol. 1, #408 (January 1996). In the next issue, the mysterious Hyperstorm (actually a grown version of Franklin from the future) tells her she has "barely scratched the surface of your true potential!" (*Fantastic Four*, vol. 1, #409, February 1996).

[25] *Fantastic Four*, vol. 3, #1/2 (March 1998).

[26] *Empyre* #1 (September 2020).

[27] *Fantastic Four*, vol. 1, #176 (November 1976).

[28] Respectively, *Fantastic Four*, vol. 1, #369 (October 1992); *Fantastic Four*, vol. 1, #411 (April 1996); *Fantastic Four*, vol. 3, #600 (January 2012), "Forever"; *Invisible Woman* #5 (January 2020); and *Fantastic Four vs. the X-Men* #4 (June 1987).

[29] *Fantastic Four*, vol. 1, #17 (August 1963). It's not only her: After the Sandman tricks him into triggering the water sprinklers in the room where they're fighting, Johnny thinks that "I've still got one thing in my favor—the long hours the Thing spent teaching me every rough and tumble trick in the book…and the lessons I've had in judo and karate from Mr. Fantastic!" (*Strange Tales*, vol. 1, #115, December 1963, "The Sandman Strikes!").

[30] *Fantastic Four*, vol. 3, #6 (June 1998).

[31] *Fantastic Four*, vol. 3, #7 (July 1998).

[32] *Invisible Woman* #1 (September 2019).

[33] *Fantastic Four*, vol. 3, #6.

[34] *Fantastic Four*, vol. 5, #8 (October 2014). Luke replaced the Thing in *Fantastic Four*, vol. 1, #168 (March 1976) when Ben temporarily lost his powers.

[35] *Fantastic Four*, vol. 5, #642 (March 2015).

[36] For an approachable treatment of his academic work on the subject, see Roy F. Baumeister and John Tierney, *Willpower: Rediscovering the Greatest Human Strength* (New York: Penguin, 2011).

[37] *Fantastic Four*, vol. 1, #370 (November 1992).

[38] *Fantastic Four*, vol. 1, #383 (December 1993).

[39] *Doomwar* #4 (July 2010).

[40] *Fantastic Four*, vol. 1, #223 (October 1980). Earlier, Sue fears blacking out from the strain when using her forcefields to free Reed from a metal jar, but succeeds nonetheless (*Fantastic Four*, vol. 1, #42, September 1965).

[41] *Fantastic Four*, vol. 1, #167 (February 1976). In fact, the first time strain is mentioned is when she uses a force bubble to protect Johnny from the Hulk, losing control of it only after Hulk leaps away with him (*Fantastic Four*, vol. 1, #25, April 1964).

[42] *Fantastic Four*, vol. 1, #23 (February 1964).

[43] *Fantastic Four*, vol. 1, #411 (April 1996).

[44] *Fantastic Four*, vol. 1, #22 (January 1964). However, a later story suggests that Sue instinctively triggered her forcefield powers after the fateful accident to shield her and Reed from Johnny's first flaming outburst (*Fantastic Four*, vol. 3, #12, December 1998).

[45] *Fantastic Four*, vol. 3, #19 (July 1999). You no doubt remember the early episode when Sue maintained a force bubble around the team even after she lost consciousness, but this is "temporary": soon afterwards, she encases herself in a force bubble underwater to keep from drowning, but as her air starts to run out, she worries about losing consciousness and losing control over the bubble, which is already weakening (*Fantastic Four*, vol. 1, #125, August 1972).

[46] *Fantastic Four*, vol. 7, #18 (May 2024).

[47] *Empyre* #6 (November 2020).

[48] Immanuel Kant, *The Metaphysics of Morals*, edited by Mary Gregor, Cambridge: Cambridge University Press, 1797/1996, p. 409.

[49] Ibid., p. 397.

[50] I'm sure she would make them invisible if she could!

[51] *Fantastic Four*, vol. 3, #44 (August 2001).

[52] *Fantastic Four*, vol. 1, #416 (September 1996). In the way the word is used her, "stoic" means unemotional, which is a tragic oversimplification of what the actual Stoic philosophers recommended, which was not to eliminate emotion altogether but simply to not let emotions control you. For a readable introduction, see Massimo Pigliucci, *How to Be a Stoic: Using Ancient Philosophy to Live a Modern Life* (New York: Basic Books, 2017).

[53] *Fantastic Four*, vol. 1, #383 (December 1993).

[54] *Fantastic Four*, vol. 1, #9 (December 1962).

[55] *FF*, vol. 1, #4 (July 2011).

[56] *Fantastic Four*, vol. 1, #280 (July 1985). (The miscarriage occurred in *Fantastic Four*, vol. 1, #267, June 1984.)

[57] *Fantastic Four*, vol. 1, #283 (October 1985).

[58] *Fantastic Four*, vol. 1, #284 (November 1985).

[59] Ibid. Incidentally, many years later Sue captures Psycho-Man—who clearly they *do* see again—in a force bubble and he says, much like Doctor Doom has said to Reed countless times, "Curse you, Richards!" Sue calmly tells him she goes by her maiden name now. When he says, "Curse you, Storm!", she says, "that's better" (*Fantastic Four*, vol. 6, #46, October 2022).

[60] *Fantastic Four*, vol. 1, #169 (April 1976) and #245 (August 1982), respectively. The interviewer—named Barbara Walker and clearly drawn to resemble the legendary Barbara Walters—also accuses Sue of having ineffectual powers and being the perpetual hostage of the group, both of which she counters effectively and with grace.

[61] *Fantastic Four*, vol. 1, #56 (November 1966).

[62] *Fantastic Four*, vol. 3, #518 (November 2004).

[63] *Fantastic Four*, vol. 3, #519 (December 2004). In the end, she is not killed: Reed shows up and fires a ray at Sue that takes her powers away and orders the aliens to leave, which they do. He then reveals that his device merely switched Sue and Johnny's powers—after which Galactus arrives and claims Johnny as his new herald. (Comics!)

[64] *Fantastic Four*, vol. 1, #37 (April 1965).

[65] *Fantastic Four*, vol. 1, #370.

[66] *Invisible Woman* #5.

[67] This is not to say she doesn't make threats on occasion, such as when she warns Doctor Doom, whose damaged brain Reed has agreed to examine, that "I could always do a little more damage up there. A couple of strategically placed air bubbles in your brain and you'll be reduced to a drooling house pet. If you're good maybe I'll feed you from the table" (*FF*, vol. 1, #2, June 2001).

[68] Sue takes charge in the Infinity War in *Fantastic Four*, vol. 1, #369 (October 1992); she negotiates peace between Mole Man and the Skrulls in *Spider-Man/Fantastic Four* #3 (November 2010) and between the various undersea communities

starting in *Fantastic Four*, vol. 3, #584 (December 2010). She becomes queen of Old Atlantis in issue #587 (March 2011), telling Namor when he challenges her that "in case you missed it, these are my people now. I rule here. And I am a queen that bows to no king." (His reply? "God, you are magnificent," at which she just rolls her eyes.)

[69] *Fantastic Four*, vol. 1, #252 (March 1983). Johnny makes it official when he tells her, "with Reed out of action, I guess you're team leader"—thanks for the show of confidence, little brother!

[70] *Fantastic Four*, vol. 1, #381 (October 1993)

[71] *Fantastic Four: Atlantis Rising* #1 (June 1995).

[72] *Fantastic Four Unplugged* #2 (October 1995).

[73] *Fantastic Four*, vol. 1, #407 (December 1995). Also, she has had another period of possession by Malice: in #376 (May 1993), she acknowledges she welcomed her "dark side" back, before rejecting it in issue #384 (January 1994).

[74] *Fantastic Four*, vol. 1, #408 (January 1996).

[75] *Fantastic Four*, vol. 1, #409 (February 1996).

[76] *Fantastic Four*, vol. 3, #1 (January 1998).

[77] She does pick up some things from Reed, though: After she exhibits some scientific expertise, Ben says "if I didn't know any better, Suzie-Q, I'd swear I was listenin' to Reed his own self talkin' just now," to which she replies, "Marriage will do that, Ben" (*Fantastic Four*, vol. 3, #11, November 1998). Later, she tells a villain that tried and failed to trap her in a pocket universe, "please—theoretical physics is my pillow talk" (*Fantastic Four*, vol. 6, #48, December 2022).

[78] *Fantastic Four*, vol. 1, #13 (April 1963).

[79] *Fantastic Four*, vol. 1, #16 (July 1983).

[80] *Fantastic Four*, vol. 3, #32 (August 2000).

[81] *Fantastic Four*, vol. 7, #12 (December 2023). Interestingly, Reed also minored in archaeology in college (4 #16, May 2005).

[82] *Invisible Woman* #3 (November 2019); *Fantastic Four* #7, #9 (September 2023).

[83] Respectively, *Fantastic Four*, vol. 1, #124 (July 1972); *Fantastic Four*, vol. 1, #225 (December 1980); and *Fantastic Four Annual*, vol. 5, #1 (2015).

[84] Respectively, *Fantastic Four*, vol. 3, #7; *Fantastic Four*, vol. 3, #11; and *Fantastic Four*, vol. 7, #18.

[85] *Fantastic Four Unplugged* #5 (May 1996).

[86] *Fantastic Four*, vol. 6, #47 (November 2022).

Chapter 4
Johnny Storm (The Human Torch)

Johnny Storm is a surprisingly complex character. Often regarded as an immature, impetuous "hothead" who cares more about women and cars than being a superhero, Johnny is actually a dedicated hero who regularly and readily risks his life to save others. He is the only member of the Fantastic Four who sincerely relishes his new life and the fame it has brought him, but at the same time he doubts and diminishes his value to the team. Most interesting, perhaps, is that he is the most dangerous one of the four, not only to civilians but to the women he loves, making it difficult to be with anyone while the other members enjoy meaningful long-term relationships.

In this chapter we'll look at several of these contrasts in Johnny Storm, acknowledging the sources of his less illustrious reputation—including his own efforts to perpetuate a certain image—while highlighting the many ways in which his behavior contradicts them. In particular, we'll focus on the danger posed by Johnny's powers and how difficult it actually is to control them, and how all of this leads him to be too fast to sacrifice himself for others—a noble and heroic trait to be sure, but only when exercised for the right reasons.

The Johnny We Think We Know

Let's start with the typical picture of Johnny Storm before we plumb his not-so-hidden depths. From his first days as the Human Torch, he has been characterized as an impetuous hothead, acting before he thinks. In an early issue, after Doctor Doom drags the Baxter Building into space, Johnny leaps out of a window after him, forgetting that the lack of oxygen in space makes him unable to flame on.[1] His sister Sue often calls him out on it, referring to him as "my impetuous kid brother" and telling Reed that "sometimes that hotheaded brother of mine makes me want to scream. I've never known anyone to be so impetuous...and one of these days it's going to land him in trouble."[2] During a fancy dinner for the launch of a scientific grant in the Fantastic Four's honor, Ben says that Johnny "loved the adventure of it. Runnin' without thinkin'."[3] No one is more aware of this trait than the young man himself: When Reed starts acting suspicious after wearing Doom's armor, Johnny wonders, "If a guy like Reed can fall apart, what hope is there for a hothead like me?"[4]

Impetuousness is obviously not a virtuous trait, but rather a vice, one that Aristotle wrote about as one example of *incontinence*, or lack of self-control. Specifically, he wrote that

> It is keen and excitable people that suffer especially from the impetuous form of incontinence; for the former by reason of their quickness and the latter by reason of the violence of their passions do not await the argument, because they are apt to follow their imagination.[5]

Reed sees this when he tells Ben, after he tries to stop Johnny from rushing into danger, that "it's no use, Ben! He won't listen to reason!"[6] It is easier to think of Johnny as being "excitable" (or rash) rather than being "keen" (or intelligent), but we'll see later that Johnny is not the lunkhead he is often thought of (including by himself).

Although impetuousness is a vice, missing the ideal in terms of patience and thoughtfulness, we should note also that when Johnny is too quick to act, it is usually in the service of heroism, seeing someone in trouble and acting on the impulse to help. During a brief spell with the Avengers, Johnny considers how Reed would react to a crisis, thinking that "he'd have a plan of attack immediately," as well as Sam Wilson, the Falcon (between spells as Captain America), about whom he thinks, "I can practically feel him strategizing on the fly." As for Johnny himself? "Without standing around for orders, I just do what I do best. Lead with my face," rushing into battle by himself while his teammates watch in alarm.[7] Johnny's impetuousness impairs his ability to do the most good with his powers, but on the bright side it is also a reflection of his heroic spirit, to which we'll return soon.

A darker aspect of Johnny's reputation as a "hothead" is his temper, which often expresses itself more in terms of youthful petulance than true anger. We see this often when Johnny is impatient for Reed to solve a problem, whether it's searching for his missing sister, curing Ben's condition, or fixing the occasional problems with Johnny's powers, such as not being able to flame on or off (as we saw in chapter 2). When Sue and Franklin go missing, Johnny yells at Reed for indulging his intellectual curiosity instead of finding them. When Reed argues that he's trying to gather facts, and that "going after them half-cocked…and getting ourselves killed…won't do them any good," Johnny apologizes, admitting he was "thinking with my heart…not my head," letting his passions overwhelm his reason.[8]

To his credit, when Johnny blows his top at Reed like this, he invariably apologizes. Once, after blowing up at Reed for not working hard enough to save Ben's life—just before he does in fact save Ben's life—

Johnny admits that "I lost my temper—blew my cool." Reed tells him he's being too hard on himself, that "you wouldn't be human if you hadn't" gotten upset and "you wouldn't be the Torch if you hadn't apologized—like the man you are."[9] Reed is generous in acknowledging Johnny's human imperfection, but at the same time, Johnny's quick apologies suggest that, with just a little thought and reflection ahead of time, he could possibly avoid needing to make them altogether. However, the fact that they continue to the modern day shows he has not learned that lesson. After Doctor Doom turns on his flame permanently, Johnny lashes out at Reed, saying he "promised you'd make it stop! So stretch that big head of yours back into your damn lab and fix this!" After he argues that nothing takes precedence over his problem, including a court case involving Reed and Sue's kids, Sue slaps him and he flies away.[10]

Other times, however, Johnny's anger is sincere and understandable. Usually it comes out when someone he loves is hurt or killed, such as when Alicia Masters, to whom he was married at the time (after she had split from Ben), was nearly hit by a brick during a hate rally, or when Doctor Doom appears to kill Reed before they both vanish.[11] In the latter case, as Johnny destroys a squadron of Latverian fighter jets, the team's Skrull ally Lyja—to whom he was *actually* married, because she was impersonating Alicia at the time—thinks that "Johnny is lashing out in grief...directed more by his heart than his head! A fatal flaw in a warrior!"[12]

In thinking this, Lyja touches on a philosophical argument about anger that goes back centuries. On the one hand, Aristotle approvingly described "righteous indignation" or properly motivated anger, writing that "the person who is angry at the right things and towards the right people, and also in the right way, at the right time and for the right length

80

of time, is praised."[13] In this view, anger is a natural and appropriate reaction to injustice, and a person who does not feel rage at seeing others mistreated does not have the necessary moral sensitivity to others' suffering. Johnny does not suffer from a lack of righteous indignation, as we see not only from his reactions to threats to his loved ones, but also to societal injustices in general, such as racism and hatred.[14]

On the other hand, though, even the most appropriate anger can be difficult to control—especially if you're already a hothead to begin with! In his book *On Anger*, the Stoic philosopher Seneca wrote that "it is easier to exclude the forces of ruin than to govern them…once they have established possession, they prove to be more powerful than their governor, refusing to be cut back or reduced."[15] Johnny's impetuousness does him no favors when it comes to maintaining control when he is angry, but his heroic nature serves to hold him back from going too far. As Lyja watched him take on the Latverian jets, she also noted that "even in his righteous anger…he is careful to spare the pilots!"[16] In a more recent adventure in which he flew off in a rage to save a friend, Johnny remains aware that he is being rash, and once he collects himself he pursues his mission while being careful not to hurt innocent people.[17]

Johnny Storm may be a jumble of emotions, but much of the time he manages to balance them—even if it does not happen immediately—to make the best decision. This refutes another common portrayal of him that combines the ones we've discussed so far: his immaturity, such as when Sue says he acted like "a spoiled kid" when he attacked the Inhumans in pursuit of Crystal, his true love (at the time).[18] We see this in a lighthearted way in his constant bickering and prank wars with Ben, which exasperate the others but rarely do any serious harm. During one episode, Reed chides both of them, asking "when are the two of you going to grow up?", but this sentiment is more often directed toward Johnny (especially given Reed's guilt over Ben's condition, as described in chapter 2).[19] Even a grizzled future version of Johnny tells his younger self, after the latter teases Ben in a moment of crisis, that "at some point, you're going to have a get a little serious."[20]

To be sure, (young) Johnny is aware of this too, telling Alicia that "they all still consider me the callous, uncaring, smart-alec kid," and for the most part he shares this impression of himself.[21] Ironically, it is his marriage to Alicia (before her true identity is discovered) that makes him feel he's growing up; before their wedding, he tells Reed that "I've never really felt like a grown-up before...I was always the kid in the group," but he believes marriage will force him into maturity.[22] Soon afterwards, he tells his former love Crystal, in a moment of mutual temptation, that "I'm not a kid anymore! I've taken on adult responsibilities—and I won't break the vows I made to my wife!"[23]

Johnny seeks the feeling of adulthood in other responsibilities as well, such as when he joins the New York Fire Department to prove to his family that he's reliable (by showing that others can rely on him).[24] Reed later tells him that, while he expected him to bail after a couple weeks, he stuck with it, and "I'm proud of you."[25] Even though Reed generally sees Johnny as mature (and more capable than most), Sue treats him more like her oldest child rather than her brother, much less a grown man. When Reed reminds her that she's "his sister, not his mother," she explains that she had to be both after their mother died, and even when Reed argues Johnny has matured a lot, she says "he still has the attention span of a toaster."[26] The validity of his sister's opinion aside, Johnny shows through his heroism that he is mature when it matters—especially when it regards the serious risk his powers pose to those around him.

Warning: Very Flammable

In his earliest appearances, Johnny was shown to be happy-go-lucky, reveling in his newfound powers and the fame they brought. His powers were also portrayed, for the most part, as easily controllable and not at all dangerous to others. When he speaks directly to the readers to answer "some questions about myself" at the end of the eighth issue, Johnny explains that "I control my flame through reflex action, just as you control your breathing without conscious thought! When touching another human being, I automatically turn off the flame of the part of my body which establishes contact!"[27] However, even then he would occasionally lose control, such as when he confronted an angry newscaster criticizing him for being a showboat and his temper made him flame on unintentionally, which only reinforced the man's impression that Johnny's "a menace to society."[28]

To be sure, Johnny has caused significant damage over the years. Inspired by Daredevil, whom he is helping look for, Johnny tries to threaten guys in a bar for information. Not being much of a tough guy, however, he soon loses his patience, flames on, and ends up burning the bar down.[29] Even worse, during a fight at Empire State University with a trio of violent aliens—including his ex-wife Lyja, whom he believed to be dead—he uses his powerful nova blast in self-defense, destroying much of the campus (after he previously urged everyone to evacuate). When Sue arrives, he tells her that "it was an accident! I…I was desperate! I panicked! I lost control!"[30] Johnny surrenders to the police, telling his sister, "I'm guilty! I've made a mistake…and I've got to pay for it!"[31] But the damage is done, and Johnny is once again regarded as a menace, both by J. Jonah Jameson (who hurls that accusation at Spider-Man on occasion) and the public at large, which lasts long after his legal case is

83

over (thanks to Matt Murdock, the lawyer without fear, who had returned by then).[32]

It isn't just the damage he causes, whether through carelessness or just as a blameless accident, that is a concern with the Human Torch. In later years, we learn that his power is not automatically or subconsciously controlled, as the early issues stated, although it took a different Human Torch to make it clear. When Reed switches Sue and Johnny's powers (for reasons explained in the last chapter), Sue is initially elated to have such power and the freedom of lighter-than-air flight. But when she tries to catch a falling Ben, her hand *doesn't* automatically flame off, and Reed tells her she's "radiating an uncomfortable amount of heat" even when flamed off. Reflecting on her brother, Sue thinks to herself, "I never gave you credit. You always seemed to have so much fun with this power. I never realized how impossible it is to keep it in check."[33] Later she apologizes to him in person—while making him sweat, which he hasn't done "in, like, forever"—and he remembers "how long it took me just to learn to sneeze without fireballing the room."[34] Later, after their powers are switched back, Sue empathizes with her stressed brother, reiterating that "I know how dangerous your torch-power is. … You have to be so aware of everything—what's flammable, what's not, is it too close, the winds, your moods…You act so carefree, I never suspected you had to be so careful."[35]

In this way, Johnny is much more dangerous to those around him than even Ben, who is harmless when not angry (or clumsy).[36] When Reed recounts the team's history during an interview, he compares the two, saying that "while Ben lived in despair…poor Johnny lived in perpetual terror. He was the only one of us whose powers were a clear and present danger to anyone near him—and it haunted him day and night."[37] Immediately after the accident, according to a recent retelling of their origin, Johnny tells Reed he flames on "every time I get worked up," that "I catch fire in my sleep," and that he worries that he can never be around gasoline, cars, or people ever again.[38]

As well as being volatile, Johnny is also passionate, especially about women that he becomes romantically involved with. I would need another book to detail the ups and downs of Johnny's stormy love life, but suffice it to say he is generally unsuccessful at sustaining a long-term relationship and is very aware of this fact. Although it may be easy to chalk this up to immaturity, a more generous explanation is rooted in his powers themselves.[39] Soon after Sue had Johnny's powers, the team sees each other's dreams, with Sue experiencing one of Johnny's in which many of his former loves approached him, saying they want to be with him and asking why things didn't work out. After they gang up on him, he flames on, setting them on fire while shouting, "You don't understand what I can do to you!" Later, she tells him she always assumed he simply didn't want to settle down with anyone, but never thought that "you were afraid you might seriously hurt someone you loved. That in the heat of the moment you might...forget." She's surprised he still feels this way, given the control he's gotten over his powers in the years since the accident, and tells him that "you can't live your life afraid to let anyone get close." Johnny responds, "you keep a loaded gun around, no matter how careful you are, sooner or later it'll go off...and someone'll get hurt. Just a matter of time."[40]

The danger that the crimefighting life poses to romantic interests is a pervasive aspect of nearly all superhero stories, but the main danger is usually understood to come from their enemies, either retaliating against their loved ones or using them to strike back at the heroes. Although Reed and Sue focus more about the risk of their enemies getting to their kids, Ben has always worried about the threat of his lifestyle to Alicia, at one point leaving her—and later breaking an engagement to another woman—because he didn't want to put either of them in danger.[41] Johnny is different, however, in that his powers themselves pose a significant threat to his romantic interests. During a pregnancy scare with a one-night stand, Johnny is confronted by Sue about why he never called the woman back, and he explains that "it's incredibly dangerous to make a commitment. It's to protect her." Johnny is vague—and perhaps a little evasive and self-serving as well—about which danger he means in this instance, but the woman clearly recognizes the threat from enemies when she asks Reed, "if I decide to go through with this pregnancy, every super villain in town's going to want a piece of this baby, right?" When Reed is evasive himself, she understands his answer is yes, and she jumps into the timestream, never to be seen again.[42]

Trauma and Tragedy

Aside from the danger his powers pose for others, Johnny's experiences with them are more complex than his easygoing demeanor would suggest, as Sue realizes when she has his powers for a short time. As Reed explains Johnny's initial transformation after the accident, "imagine flames engulfing you from head to toe, except...you don't burn. Your skin, your hair, and your organs are unaffected, but panic keeps your brain from processing that...for hours."[43] Johnny himself explains:

> There is a moment, between my self and the flame—a burning, eternal, sickening moment—when, no matter how many times I've done this before...I feel like this is it. This is the time when my head will truly be consumed by burning searing excruciating flame. It's in that split-second just after I call up my power, just before I am engulfed...it's a split-second of panic, of fear. Even when doused, I burn. I always feel as if on fire.[44]

Much later, when a villain named Ayesha manipulates the team's powers, she asks how Johnny can burn without a fuel source and then makes his flames consume him. "My flames—it hurts—I can't shut down my power—I'm starting to burn!" he screams to Sue, and the narration confirms that "this has always been the Torch's greatest nightmare."[45]

Perhaps even a greater fear is that someone will be hurt or die as a result of his powers: as he tells Alicia when she says everyone makes mistakes, "mine cripple...mine can kill!"[46] We've already seen this fear play out in terms of his romantic life and his loved ones being in danger of his flames, but there have also been notable cases of less direct but no less meaningful accidents. After the fight with Ayesha referenced above, she swaps the Fantastic Four's minds with her underlings, who are inexperienced with their powers and use them recklessly. Johnny feels responsible for the harm the new Torch causes right off the bat and fears what he will do once he actually learns to use his powers. "Too many have suffered already. It's my power and my responsibility. Even if it costs my life, I won't allow one more person, innocent or guilty, to be harmed by my flames."[47] Although he had nothing to do with the other person gaining his powers, nor any control over what he does with them, Johnny feels responsibility for the harm his powers "cause," which is excessive but not unexpected from a superhero (as we saw from Reed in chapter 2).

More tragic is the case of Tommy Hanson, the 13-year-old fan who idolizes the Human Torch and dies from third-degree burns after lighting himself on fire with rocket fuel, telling Johnny with his final breath, "I only did it to be like you." After Tommy's parents accuse him of murdering their son, Johnny is racked with guilt, telling Sue that kids like Tommy treat superheroes like movie stars and want to emulate them. "That's why...why I can't be me anymore," he says before announcing his decision to quit. "I can't risk it happening again, Sue. From now on there is no Human Torch…The Human Torch is dead!" It takes the intervention of the all-powerful Beyonder to show him Tommy's life before he died, a life with no friends and absentee parents, whose only joy was reveling in the exploits of his favorite superhero. "The death of this boy is not a burden for you to bear," he tells Johnny. "He did not die because of you. It was through you that Tommy Hanson lived!"[48] This seems to put Johnny's mind at ease, and later, the doctors handling Tommy's case identify the man who showed Tommy his model airplane and recklessly left him alone with the rocket fuel as the person morally responsible for what happened.

Not long after, another admirer, a 16-year-old boy named Teddy Bannion from New Jersey, takes his own life, writing in a suicide note that "I know I can never achieve the greatness that the Torch has attained, and knowing that, I see no point in going on. So I've gone out in a fitting way—as a real human torch." Upon hearing this, Johnny loses control, nearly burning the garage in which he was working on his car alongside Alicia, who later tells him that "you can't blame yourself for what that kid in Jersey did. You act responsibly as the Torch," and that it's not his fault people "twist the good things you do" to justify their own bad decisions.[49] In saying this, Alicia is invoking the idea that adequate precaution—what lawyers call "the due standard of care"—can indemnify a person from responsibility for harm they might cause. But even this assumes that Johnny can be responsible at all for what people do in his name (such as the man who gained his powers after Ayesha's mindswap), which ignores those people's responsibility for their own choices.[50]

Johnny then decides to visit New Jersey, and after Teddy's sister blames him for her brother's death, he meets Teddy's friends, who have formed a suicide pact to go out the same way Teddy did, seeing it as the only path to glory given the meager circumstances of their lives. Johnny is obviously alarmed and distraught, but when he tries to talk them out of it, one of them asks, "can't you just dig that we're so inspired by you?" He says he can't, and then swears to never flame on again so "you've got nothing to imitate." When he informs the rest of the team of this, Ben tells him that quitting won't solve those kids' problems and they'll only find some other person to emulate. Johnny sees his point, "but if there's even a small chance you're wrong—that what I'm doing will save even one kid—then I've got to do it. I won't have any more deaths on my head."[51]

What Johnny forgets is the innumerable lives he has saved as the Human Torch. He is reminded of this by yet another admirer, Rusty Collins, a mutant who also has flame powers. Despite accidentally burning someone when his powers first manifested, Rusty is training with X-Factor (a team of the original X-Men), who "helped me realize the good I could do with that power is worth doing in spite of any potential bad. The good I do—the lives I've saved—that's a reason to go on, to not give in to the doubts, the fears." After they team up to face and defeat Teddy's father (dressed in super-powered armor), Johnny tells Rusty, "I know the good I can do outweighs the bad. But it's going to be a constant struggle to remember that." To help with this, Johnny's friendly neighborhood Spider-Man stops by to remind him how, when he was ready to give up his webs long ago, Johnny gave an inspirational lecture at his high school about never giving up, even when things seem tough, that helped Peter find his way back to heroism. He suggests that Johnny do the same thing again, which he does, starting with giving an anti-suicide talk at Teddy's school, using his fame to inspire others, which further offsets its occasional negative effects.[52]

Can a Hero Be…Too Heroic?

One reason Johnny saves so many lives as the Human Torch is that he repeatedly risks his life for others, but often does so impetuously and excessively, even for a hero. As far back as their second issue, Johnny volunteered to set a trap for the Skrulls, and then drew active gunfire to draw them out.[53] Later, as he rushes off to destroy an asteroid in the Negative Zone, Reed urges him to hold back, but Ben says, "save yer breath, pal. He's too busy bein' a hero again!"[54]

Speaking of Ben, Johnny often risks his own life to save his best friend. In one story, he uses his powers in reverse for the first time to draw all the heat from Reed's lab to save Ben during an experiment, then flies into space to expel it so he doesn't burn the entire city down, only to black out and fall back to Earth, awakening and flaming on at the very last minute.[55] When Doctor Doom banishes Franklin to hell, Johnny flies through a mystical portal without a thought, until the hellfire makes him experience burning for the first time since their fateful accident.[56] Recently, during a battle against evil symbiotes (like Venom), Johnny helps Spider-Man and Eddie Brock (Venom's original host) to escape by using his nova blast, even though Spidey warns him he'll pass out and become possessed by the symbiotes himself. "I know," Johnny says. "So hey, Pete. Do me a favor and tell everyone I said something and heroic before I fell, yeah?"[57]

Johnny may sacrifice himself with style and panache, but that doesn't take away from the sheer heroism of his actions. He makes what is perhaps his greatest sacrifice during a climactic battle in the Negative Zone. This tale begins when Johnny allowed an alien, disguised as a beautiful woman in a nightclub, access to the Negative Zone portal in the Baxter Building. After crossing over to fix his mistake, Reed chided him for going to the dangerous realm by himself, risking not only his life but count-less others by leaving the portal open in the meantime. He warns Johnny of ominous things coming, and when Johnny asks what he should do at that point, Reed says, "you ask yourself a question…what is it you stand for? When you answer that, then you'll know."[58]

Later, Johnny, Ben (in human form at the time), and several of the children of the Future Foundation stand in the Negative Zone guarding the portal from an invasion wave threatening their own dimension. Their plan requires one of them to remain in the Zone to repel the in-vaders, which Ben immediately commits to doing. After sending the children back through the portal, Ben says goodbye to Johnny, thanking him for the amazing week they spent together while Ben was human, but Johnny pushes him through the portal just before it closes. He asks Ben, "when you see Reed…you tell him…tell him this is where I made my stand," and turns to face the horde, shouting "flame on!" before being overwhelmed and presumably killed.[59]

Johnny soon returns alive but worse for wear, having endured years in the Negative Zone (where time moves more slowly), repeatedly being killed and brought back to life, until he eventually becomes the ruler of the dimension.[60] Reflecting on this incident shortly after Johnny returns, Ben apologizes for having taken the new potion that turned him human for a week just before Johnny needed him the most. Johnny embraces his friend and says, "Ben Grimm, you are an idiot. Don't you know I'd go through it all again, twice…if it meant you could feel human again?"[61] Years later, a depowered Johnny repeats his heroic sacrifice, pushing his longtime friend Wyatt Wingfoot away from an interdimensional portal so Johnny can face the danger alone, saying "I died once, and if I have to, I guess I can do it again."[62]

I could fill this book with examples of Johnny risking his life and sometimes sacrificing it for others, whether a teammate, close friend, or random civilian. All of the Fantastic Four do this on a regular basis, of course, as do most superheroes—almost on a monthly basis, as it happens! But Johnny seems to do it more often and more willingly, with even less thought to his own safety.

There are many reasons this might be the case, including some we've discussed already in this chapter. He feels responsible for the danger posed to others by his powers, and regards himself as more disposable due to the danger his injury or death would save those around him. Related to this, he may feel that his difficulty maintaining a stable romantic relationship, partially based on the danger he poses to his partners, makes him the most eligible sacrifice when heroism calls, because he wouldn't leave a love interest (or child) behind. He may also think he is compensating for being the member of the Fantastic Four who is happiest about the accident and most grateful for his powers and the fame it has granted him, so he deserves to take a greatest share of pain and suffering—especially from Ben, whom (as we saw) he pushed out of the Negative Zone to face the invading horde himself.

At the core of all these explanations is self-deprecation, Johnny's feeling that he is not as worthy of life, love, and happiness as the other members of the team. We see this in cases like Ben and the Negative Zone as well as Wyatt Wingfoot years later, when Johnny is quick to spare others the risk of death and easily take it on himself. This is not a recent development: In an early adventure, Doctor Doom steals the power cosmic from the Silver Surfer and threatens Reed and Sue. When Johnny appears and confronts Doom in their defense, Reed and Sue try to tell him how powerful Doom has become, but Johnny argues that "I'm more expendable! You and Sue need time to escape—and to cook up a plan to beat him! And you're gonna get that time—compliments of the Human Torch!"[63]

Later, when Reed and Sue are relieved to find Johnny alive after an-other battle with Doom, Johnny says, "I failed you! When you needed me—the most—I let you down—!"[64] Whatever the reason he feels like his life is worth less than others', thinking himself a failure only rein-forces it. In another adventure, when the other three lay aged and dying, Johnny thinks to himself, "If anyone should be dying, it's me! I'm the useless member of our quartet—I'm the one who never pulls his weight. And now it looks like I'm gonna fail for the very last time!"[65] Johnny makes a last-ditch effort to save them, and when it doesn't seem to work, he flies into a rage of self-hatred, shouting that he failed like he had al-ways done when people rely on him. "What's wrong with me, anyway? Why can't I ever do anything right?" he asks. "My life's a total sham-bles…I've had every opportunity offered to me in the world—and I've blown them all!" He continues to tear himself down, diminishing his powers as "surface glitter and flash" that make him "nothing more than a glorified matchstick," and in reference to romance he says that "no one's ever stuck with me—because I've never had anything real to give them!" He concludes two pages of this by saying, "I'm always at my worst—that's why the only three people who have meant anything to me are gone! There's no one else to shift the blame to now, Storm, face it—you're a born loser!" A voice from off-panel tells him he's wrong, and when he turns he sees Reed, Sue, and Ben, back to normal, telling him his solution worked and that he's not a failure after all.[66]

As much as the others try to convince him he's a valuable member of the team, it is obvious Johnny's self-doubts go much deeper than one episode.[67] Much of this can likely be traced to his reputation as being dumb, another mischaracterization that pervades his entire history in the comics, so much that he often believes it himself. His buddy Spider-Man jokes about Johnny's low intelligence the most, such as when he accuses Johnny of thinking Captain America's last name is "America."[68]

Even heroes that don't interact much with the Fantastic Four regard him as stupid: After the assassin-turned-hero Elektra kisses him, she says "so that's what handsome idiot tastes like."[69] Consistent with his tendency toward self-deprecation, Johnny embraces this misapprehension himself to make jokes at his own expense. During his time with the Uncanny Avengers, he told the others, when they need to solve a time travel problem, that in the Fantastic Four he was "the Ringo. Time travel wasn't my forte."[70] When Sue tells him why she blasted part of the Baxter Building into space to protect them from a Skrull invasion, he asks for more details, adding "feel free to explain it to me like I'm a second-grader."[71]

But the idea that Johnny is not smart is simply wrong, and there is ample evidence of this from the comics, almost from the very beginning. In the twelfth issue, Reed defends Johnny's "mechanical skill" to General "Thunderbolt" Ross when working together to capture the Hulk.[72] When Kosmos and Kobik analyze the team's character traits, as explained in chapter 1, they discover that Johnny has "high-order problem-solving ability" and demonstrates "a powerful intellect, which his usually aggressive nature typically leaves him without the patience to use."[73] Later, he explains an advanced car engine he built to Sue, including an unstable molecule turbine and a quantum turbine, which recalls the time Reed praised him after their original space crash for designing and building "an eight-barrel, air-cooled engine from scratch."[74] Recently, when Reed wants to rebuild their original spacecraft to "complete our original mission" and "travel to those distant stars," he invites Johnny to help.[75]

In fact, Reed is his most frequent booster, praising his intellectual abilities on many occasions, such as when he devises a plan to defeat Galactus after becoming his herald, asks Doom for help with Sue's third pregnancy, and figures out how to deal with alien algae by blocking the sun, which Johnny writes off as a stupid idea until Reed says, "Jonathan.

My god. I think that could actually work."[76] During a particularly reflective period, Reed thinks to himself that "for all his fire and bravado, Johnny is often underestimated—even by himself."[77] When Tony Stark makes a crack about Johnny, Reed thinks that "Johnny's much more intelligent than he admits," which combines Reed's own high opinion of "the best brother-in-law I could have" with Johnny's opposite regard for himself.[78]

When Reed is critical of Johnny, it tends to be his negligence of his own intelligence: at one point, he regards Johnny as the least "intellectually motivated" of the four, and he urges him to take more interest in science (besides what he needs to build advanced engines, presumably).[79] To be fair, though, Johnny occasionally shows he might be smarter than Reed, such as when "the smartest man in the world" tries to communicate telepathically with Galactus and says "if I think hard enough—thought waves have an infinite range," to which Johnny replies, incredulously, "*Thought waves?!*"[80]

As I hope to have shown in this chapter, Johnny Storm is hardly the simplistic young hothead that he is often known as (and just as often regards himself). Furthermore, this reputation, and the degree to which he has accepted it as part of his self-image, may explain his excessive willingness to sacrifice his life for others—a characteristic that seems noble but is hardly virtuous. Johnny needs to have a keener appreciation of how valuable he is as a friend and family member, a teammate, and a person—which would not necessarily make him risk his life in heroic efforts less, but it would make such self-sacrifice all the more meaningful, because it wouldn't represent the loss of someone he deems worthless anyway.

[1] *Fantastic Four*, vol. 1, #6 (September 1962).

[2] *Amazing Spider-Man*, vol. 1, #18 (November 1964); *Fantastic Four*, vol. 1, #224 (November 1980).

[3] *Marvel 2-in-One* #1 (February 2018).

[4] *Fantastic Four*, vol. 3, #33 (September 2000).

[5] Aristotle, *Nicomachean Ethics*, ca 350 BCE, translated by W.D. Ross, Book 7, Ch. 7, at https://classics.mit.edu/Aristotle/nicomachaen.html.

[6] *Fantastic Four*, vol. 1, #364 (May 1992).

[7] *Avengers*, vol. 7, #678 (March 2018).

[8] *Fantastic Four*, vol. 1, #364. Another common example of Johnny's petulance is his repeated insistence that he's quitting the team, usually after some romantic frustration (such as when Frankie Raye dumps him after discovering his powers in *Fantastic Four*, vol. 1, #166, January 1976).

[9] *Fantastic Four*, vol. 1, #113 (August 1971).

[10] *Fantastic Four*, vol. 6, #39 (March 2022).

[11] *Fantastic Four*, vol. 1, #280 (July 1985); *Fantastic Four*, vol. 1, #382 (November 1993).

[12] *Fantastic Four*, vol. 1, #382. Lyja's deception was revealed in *Fantastic Four*, vol. 1, #357 (October 1991), and the entire Ben-Alicia-Johnny episode is discussed more in the next chapter.

[13] Aristotle, *Nicomachean Ethics*, Book 4, Chapter 5.

[14] For instance, see his reaction to the hate rally in *Fantastic Four*, vol. 1, #280-281 (July-August 1985), the latter inspiring him to call himself "Captain Philosophy." (For a recent take on righteous anger in response to injustice in the real world, see Myisha Cherry, *The Case for Rage: Why Anger Is Essential to Anti-Racist Struggle*, Oxford: Oxford University Press, 2021.)

[15] Seneca, *On Anger*, Book I, 7(2), collected in *Seneca: Moral and Political Essays*, ed. John M. Cooper and J.F. Procopé (Cambridge: Cambridge University Press, 1995).

[16] *Fantastic Four*, vol. 1, #382.

[17] *Fantastic Four*, vol. 3, #20 (August 1999).

[18] *Fantastic Four*, vol. 1, #99 (June 1970).

[19] *Fantastic Four Annual* (vol. 1) #1 (1963), "Sub-Mariner Versus the Human Race!" Later, however, Medusa would tell Sue that she and her husband Black Bolt "often consider all four of them your children," referring to Ben and Johnny as well as Franklin and Valeria (*Fantastic Four: The Wedding Special* #1, 2005, "The Life Fantastic").

[20] *Fantastic Four*, vol. 4, #12 (November 2013).

[21] *Fantastic Four vs. the X-Men* #3 (April 1987).

[22] *Fantastic Four*, vol. 1, #300 (March 1987).

[23] *Fantastic Four*, vol. 1, #317 (August 1988).

[24] 4 #7 (September 2004).

[25] 4 #9 (October 2004).

[26] *Fantastic Four*, vol. 3, #61 (November 2002). In a later issue, after returning from an extended trip with Reed and the children of their Future Foundation, she begs Johnny to focus and then tells him, "for five years I've worked with children who have greater attention spans than you" (*Fantastic Four*, vol. 6, #3, January 2019).

[27] *Fantastic Four*, vol. 1, #8 (November 1962).

[28] *Strange Tales*, vol. 1, #112 (September 1963), "The Human Torch Faces the Threat of 'The Living Bomb!'"

[29] *Daredevil*, vol. 1, #261 (December 1988).

[30] *Fantastic Four*, vol. 1, #371 (December 1992).

[31] *Fantastic Four*, vol. 1, #372 (January 1993).

[32] Johnny goes so far as to compare himself to mutants: "The scorn! The fear! The ridicule! This must be what it's like to be a mutant!" (*Fantastic Four*, vol. 1, #379, August 1993).

[33] *Fantastic Four*, vol. 3, #520 (January 2005).

[34] *Fantastic Four*, vol. 3, #523 (April 2005).

[35] *Fantastic Four*, vol. 3, #525 (June 2005).

[36] Ben does not share this opinion: in one issue, he tells Johnny that only they know "how easy it'd be for us to take out a city block without half tryin'," and "maybe that's why I always give you a hard time, Johnny—to keep you... keep *us* on our toes. 'Cause you and me, we always gotta be alert, always gotta remember" (*Fantastic Four*, vol. 3, #55, July 2002).

[37] *Fantastic Four*, vol. 6, #35 (November 2021), "Stars."

[38] Ibid.

[39] It may even be one of his powers: When Johnny flirts with a princess from the microverse immediately after losing the latest "love of his life," someone remarks that he bounces back fast, and Ben responds, "Yeah. That's Johnny's real super-power!" (*Fantastic Four*, vol. 6, #46, October 2022).

[40] *Fantastic Four*, vol. 3, #526 (June 2005).

[41] *Thing*, vol. 1, #23 (May 1985) and *Fantastic Four*, vol. 3, #569 (September 2009); in the former, after Johnny starts seeing Alicia, Ben wonders if Johnny realizes "it's just too plain dangerous ta be datin' a member of the Fantastic Four." (We'll discuss this more in the next chapter.)

[42] *Fantastic Four Annual*, vol. 3, #32 (2010).

[43] *Fantastic Four*, vol. 6, #35, "Stars."

[44] *Daredevil*, vol. 1, #261.

[45] *Fantastic Four*, vol. 3, #11 (November 1998).

[46] *Fantastic Four vs. the X-Men* #3.

[47] *Fantastic Four*, vol. 3, #12 (December 1998).

[48] *Fantastic Four*, vol. 1, #285 (December 1985). For any fellow fans of the 2009 film *(500) Days of Summer*, this Tom's last name is spelled with an 'o', not an 'e,' so no multiversal variant here, I'm afraid.

[49] *Fantastic Four*, vol. 1, #342 (July 1990). (Hmm, Tom Hansen was from New Jersey too…)

[50] Again, see chapter 2 for more on moral responsibility.

[51] Ibid.

[52] *Fantastic Four*, vol. 1, #342 (July 1990). Johnny's speech in Peter's high school can be seen in *Amazing Spider-Man*, vol. 1, #3 (July 1963), and is referenced often, usually when Spidey has to return the favor and help Johnny out of a funk in *Marvel Team-Up*, vol. 1, #147 (November 1984).

[53] *Fantastic Four*, vol. 1, #2 (January 1962).

[54] *Fantastic Four*, vol. 1, #256 (July 1983).

[55] *Fantastic Four*, vol. 1, #106 (January 1971).

[56] *Fantastic Four*, vol. 3, #69 (July 2003).

[57] *King in Black* #2 (February 2021).

[58] *Fantastic Four*, vol. 3, #578 (June 2010).

[59] *Fantastic Four*, vol. 3, #587 (March 2011).

[60] *Fantastic Four*, vol. 3, #600 (January 2012), "Whatever Happened to Johnny Storm?"

[61] *Fantastic Four*, vol. 6, #35 (November 2021), "Death in Four Dimensions."

[62] *Fantastic Four*, vol. 5, #645 (June 2015). Once again, he returns, this time in the same issue (and with his powers restored).

[63] *Fantastic Four*, vol. 1, #58 (January 1967).

[64] *Fantastic Four*, vol. 1, #60 (March 1967).

[65] *Fantastic Four*, vol. 1, #214 (January 1980). Related to this, he has also long regarded himself as the weakest member of the group, as recognized and exploited by the villainous Monocle in *Fantastic Four*, vol. 1, #205 (April 1979).

[66] *Fantastic Four*, vol. 1, #214.

[67] They also extend to other teams: When he was fighting alongside Captain Marvel (Carol Danvers) in a recent intergalactic adventure (*Empyre* #6, November 2020), with billions of lives at stake, he's worried about failing and wishes his family were there. Captain Marvel rests a hand on his shoulder and says, "We *are* here. Once an Avenger, always an Avenger, Johnny. We're all family," referencing his brief period in the Uncanny Avengers, starting from *Uncanny Avengers*, vol. 3, #1 (December 2015).

[68] *Marvel 2-in-One* #4 (May 2018).

[69] *Uncanny Avengers*, vol. 3, #17 (February 2017).

[70] *Uncanny Avengers*, vol. 3, #22 (June 2017).

[71] *Secret Invasion: Fantastic Four* #1 (July 2008). It turns out that "Sue" is actually a Skrull herself—Johnny's ex-wife Lyja, no less—who starts to give herself away when she mocks Johnny's intelligence.

[72] *Fantastic Four*, vol. 1, #12 (March 1963).

[73] *Fantastic Four*, vol. 1, #351 (April 1991).

[74] *S.H.I.E.L.D.*, vol. 3, #4 (June 2015); *Fantastic Four*, vol. 6, #35, "Stars."

[75] *Fantastic Four*, vol. 6, #14 (November 2019). What's more, they do it without using their powers: Reed says "original tools and specs," to which Johnny adds, "or it doesn't count."

[76] *Fantastic Four*, vol. 3, #522 (March 2005); *Fantastic Four*, vol. 7, #6 (June 2023).

[77] *Fantastic Four*, vol. 6, #48 (December 2022).

[78] *Empyre* #3 (September 2020).

[79] *Fantastic Four*, vol. 1, #274 (January 1985); *Fantastic Four*, vol. 3, #54 (June 2002), "A Choice of Dooms!"; *Uncanny Avengers*, vol. 3, #2 (January 2016). Johnny should read about Immanuel Kant's duty to cultivate one's talents, discussed in chapter 2!
[80] *Fantastic Four*, vol. 1, #75 (June 1968). (Indeed.)

Chapter 5
Ben Grimm (The Thing)

We all know Ben Grimm, the ever-lovin' blue-eyed Thing, idol o' millions, and many fans' favorite member of the Fantastic Four. Transformed by the group's accident into a powerful rock-covered behemoth that many call a monster—while his friends and family know he's just a big softie—Ben never lets his tragic fate stop him from using his power for the good of others. When an interviewer tells Sue that she's "the heart of the soul of the Fantastic Four," she corrects her, saying, "that's Ben."[1]

Despite his unflinching heroism and flippant humor, Ben is a deeply tortured soul, condemned to a body of stone that threatens to deny him the simple pleasures most people can enjoy, including the rest of his teammates whose transformations were less catastrophic. He displays a level of self-loathing that is as strong as his positive traits or virtues, and despite assurances from his loved ones that he is a good and worthy person, he is usually the first to agree with gawking onlookers that he is indeed a monster. Even the devoted love of Alicia Masters, the blind sculptress who has always "seen" the gentle, noble man underneath the rocky exterior, all too often fails to convince him of his true worth and value as a person as well as a hero.

Why Everyone Loves Ben

There are many reasons why Ben's self-loathing is harmful, but before we get to that, let's make clear that it's simply incorrect as an assessment of his character. As we laid out in chapter 1 along with the rest of the team, Ben exhibits many of the core virtues of heroism, and this is confirmed repeatedly by those who know him well. His best friend Reed considers Ben his "bedrock of friendship and loyalty," citing his "indomitable will" and "limitless strength" and trusting that "he'd carry the weight of the world on his shoulders" to protect the people he loves.[2] In addition to what Sue told the interviewer above, she tells Ben during one battle that "you're the bravest and honorable man I've ever known."[3] Speaking of honor, when Ben asks the living embodiment of that virtue, Captain America, to make "a leap of faith" and trust him when Sue appears to be marrying Doctor Doom—actually Reed trapped in Doom's armor—Cap agrees without question.[4] Even Johnny, who never passes up a chance to bust Ben's pebbles, tells him that "of all of us, you always were the best man."[5]

For all the love he receives from his family and friends, Ben's biggest fan has to be Alicia, whom he finally marries in 2018 after being a couple on and off since meeting in 1962's *Fantastic Four* #8. Before taking their vows, they tell each other (and everyone in attendance) what they mean to each other, and Alicia uses this opportunity to explain her unique perspective and list many of his best qualities:

> I've heard the stories about "the blind girl and the monster." And they make me laugh. Don't they understand? I can sculpt you from memory. More than anyone, I can *see* you. Every part of you. Inside and out. The fearless pilot. The noble warrior. The truest friend. The gentlest soul I'll ever know. My dear, sweet Ben.[6]

His sweet, gentle nature stands in stark contrast to his rocky exterior: he often breaks down in tears at moments such as Reed and Sue's wedding rehearsal, their actual wedding, and Franklin's birth—Franklin *Benjamin* Richards, as he is named by his appreciative parents.[7] He is also very well read, often seen absorbed in great literature such as *War and Peace* or quoting Charles Dickens.[8]

There are interesting comparisons and contrasts to be made between his early life and his current status as the "idol o' millions."[9] He grew up poor on Yancy Street on Manhattan's Lower East Side and joined the local Yancy Street Gang after his brother Danny died. "Of all the bad cards I got dealt," he reflects later, "none of 'em compared to losing you, Daniel."[10] Eventually he followed his brother as gang leader, but after his parents died and he moved in with his aunt and uncle—cleaning up his act and earning a college football scholarship—he also earned the resentment of his old gang, which famously lasts to this day in the form of regular if harmless harassment. He became a football star at State University, where he roomed with Reed Richards (and aggravated Victor von Doom), eventually earning "a college degree or two" (also known as "many advance degrees in engineering").[11] After graduating, he served in the Marines as an ace fighter pilot before helming the infamous space flight that changed his life forever.

Despite his intellectual and professional accomplishments, Ben normally plays the fool, which could be hailed as a virtuous display of humility if it were not for his self-loathing streak, which makes his understatements of his own achievements more serious. When Ben is introduced at the inauguration of the Fantastic Award, a grant for space exploration in honor of the team, the emcee calls him "the infamous astronaut who plotted the four through their discoveries," but after Ben hails the accomplishments and virtues of other three, he says of himself, "I just drove the bus."[12] He's honestly surprised when Nick Fury asks him to be the test pilot for a new supersonic aircraft, and Nick has to "remind" him of his military record when Ben pretends to get sick on a flight.[13] He serves the same role for Tony Stark, who could surely afford the best, and who credits Ben with "a rare mix of street smarts and test-pilot cool."[14] Even Captain America, himself no stranger to downplaying his abilities, acknowledges the training Ben underwent to become a pilot and calls him on his "hick routine," telling him that "as an ex-test pilot, your science know-how is better than mine!"[15]

Naturally, Ben's teammates are always there to remind him of his know-how. Reed is all too familiar with how much his best friend knows, having watched while he earned "a college degree or two." During a time-travel adventure, Reed offers to explain the mathematics and physics to Ben, but admits that he would only pretend not to understand.[16] When they encounter a powerful alien force that communicates with Ben telepathically, Reed asks why it chose Ben's mind, and Ben tells him "you're just jealous 'cause until now ya weren't sure I had one."[17] He takes advantage of ways to use Ben's brains in the field, assigning him to not only fly their many aircraft and spaceships but navigate them as well.[18] Even Johnny compliments Ben's piloting skills, although Ben has a hard time believing him—which Johnny appreciates, saying "it makes you even more crazy."[19] Leave it to Doctor Doom, then, to be the lone soul who agrees with Ben's impression of himself, telling Reed and Sue's daughter Valeria that her Uncle Benjamin is "sentient only by the basest of definitions."[20]

The Ever Self-Loathin' Thing

We can't blame Doctor Doom for Ben's negative evaluation of himself, however. Self-loathing has many different aspects and reveals itself in various ways, many of which are exemplified by the ever-lovin' Thing, even if that love rarely comes from himself.

At its most basic, self-loathing is a lack of positive regard for oneself or a denial of one's basic worth as a person. For example, when Ben thinks that "I'm a nobody…just a crummy pimple in the acne of life," he is implicitly comparing his worth to others, and feels he does not live up to what other people have to offer the world, despite his many acts of heroism and bravery.[21] Another way self-loathing is often expressed is in terms of self-hatred, such as when Ben says to himself:

> I hate being an orange-skinned freak! I can't even walk down the street without scaring someone half ta death. Sometimes I think I've hated myself from the first moment I was exposed to those cosmic rays which turned me into…a Thing.

He finishes this particular diatribe with a reference to his worth (or lack thereof): "I ain't worth spit."[22] This attitude is not only harmful for his own emotional well-being, but sometimes results in negative behavior towards others. When Ben asks why Alicia left him for Johnny, she explains that "I gave you all the love I had, but it wasn't enough! You were so bitter, so self-absorbed! I tried, Ben, but…" He suggests she could have tried harder, but she replies that she needed someone more supportive of her—and he normally is, but not when he focuses too much on his own shortcomings.[23]

Self-loathing can have many roots, including negative experiences in early childhood and adolescence—of which Ben definitely had his share. But in his case, we can reasonably assume its primary cause is the accident that transformed him into "a monster" who frightens people based on both his appearance and the damage he can do if he loses his temper (or is attacked by a supervillain).

Once, while Alicia was with Johnny (before she was revealed to be a Skrull), we see Ben sitting in a Yancy Street bar, feeling sorry for himself and thinking about the "beautiful people. Havin' a beautiful time. ... Everybody's tryin' not to look my way. Don't wanna eye the freak. Don't much blame 'em."[24] Ben's characterization of himself as "ugly" or a "monster" is relentless, especially in his earlier years, and is unfortunately reinforced by other insensitive and frightened onlookers. In the second issue of the comic, after the shapeshifting Skrulls impersonate the Fantastic Four to turn the public against them, Ben says they're being hunted like monsters, which makes sense to him: "Maybe I am a monster! I look like one—and sometimes I feel like one!"[25] This continues to this day: in a recent issue, a kid points at him and calls him a monster, and when Alicia, by then his wife, tells him she's sorry, he says, "Like I care. Trust me, by now I'm used to it."[26] Even more recently, another kid runs from him, yelling "it's a monster," to which Ben replies, "I'm not a monster, kid!" before hanging his head and repeating, quietly, "I'm not a monster."[27] Even with his marriage to Alicia and the greater level of acceptance over the years of how he looks, we see that Ben's feelings of self-loathing have never disappeared completely.

Even though others try to assure Ben he's not ugly, he hardly accepts it. Sometimes he challenges them, such as when Sue tries to tell him he's a not a monster but "one of the most wonderful people in the world," to which he responds sure, "and maybe some day you'll be able to look at me when ya say it—without flinchin' at the sight!"[28] Other times he dismisses the praise, such as when the Inhuman named Crystal leaves the team after her first spell as a member and tells Ben, "you'll always be the kindest—and the gentlest—and the most beautiful person I've ever known." Through sniffles, he jokes that "yeah, that's my problem! I always been just another pretty face!"[29]

If there's a bright side to Ben thinking of himself as a monster, it's that he has become more sensitive to others who are subject to the same fear and ridicule. For example, Ben forms an uneasy connection with the Mole Man, who fled underground when rejected by others for being ugly; Ben even joins his subterranean society after Alicia rejects him for Johnny.[30] Later, he stands up for the Moloids, the Mole Man's minions whom Ben frees from enslavement, saying "nobody should have to be a monster that don't want to be."[31] More recently, the team visits a planet in which the population attempted to replicate the Fantastic Four's own transformation, with the attractive "successes" remaining in Hightown and the unattractive "failures" being shunted to Lowtown, out of sight from the others. When Ben finds himself in Lowtown, the residents blame him for their fate, and once he calms them down, he says "none of you are monsters. Not really. No more than yours truly." Later, he leads them in an uprising against Hightown, which he proclaims is "for everybody—even us freaks!"[32]

Perhaps the one Ben feels the most sympathy toward is the Hulk, whom he often fights but usually resents it, knowing that the green goliath is feared and hated even more than Ben. During one of the times the U.S. Army asks the team to help capture the Hulk, Reed hopes he can cure him and makes the colonel in charge promise to hand him over, with Ben adding, "I ain't got much love for the Hulk…but there's a man inside there somewhere. I'm in a position ta know." When the team finds the Hulk, Ben lands the blow that knocks him out, but when Reed says "good work," Ben just tells him to "shaddup." After Reed manages to change the Hulk to his human form of Bruce Banner, the colonel reneges on his deal and holds him captive. Furious, Ben breaks Banner free, watches him change back to the Hulk, and stands beside him as two monsters against the world.[33]

Although his meetings with the Hulk are more frequent, even more poignant are Ben's interactions with the *golem* of Jewish tradition, a creature of clay that rabbis summon to protect those who need him.[34] This also ties in with Ben's own Jewish faith, which was hinted at throughout his history but explicitly referenced only in recent years. When Hank Pym (Giant-Man) asks him to teach at Avengers Academy, Ben alludes to a tenuous tenure at Hebrew school, which may explain why he did not have his bar mitzvah until thirteen years after becoming the Thing.[35] At least Rabbi Lowenthal, the rabbi who presided over the ceremony, did the same at Ben and Alicia's wedding.[36]

On one of his visits to the old neighborhood, Ben runs into Mr. Sheckerberg, a local pawnbroker with whom Ben had numerous run-ins in his younger days. When Sheckerberg asks him why the press never mentions his faith, Ben says "anyone on the internet can find out, if they want," but he figures "there's enough trouble in this world without people thinkin' Jews are all monsters like me." This leads Sheckerberg to compare Ben to the golem, "a being made of clay—but he wasn't a monster. He was a protector."[37] When Ben meets a troublesome golem on Yancy Street later, he suggests they talk, "monster to monster." He calls the golem by the name Joseph, which he remembers is the traditional name of all golems, "after a half-human, half-demon creature that useta help the Jews out in ancient times." He guesses that Joseph is just duplicating behavior he saw on Yancy Street, like the gang that protected it from outsiders, and convinces him he is no longer needed here. As Joseph walks into the East River to dissolve, Ben says that "someday, someone'll be doing the same thing ta me that I'm doing ta you...that's just how it always ends for us monsters, sooner or later."[38]

As much as he despairs over people's reactions to his appearance, Ben's deeper resentment is due to the effect his appearance has on his personal life, especially romance, love, and family. As his inner mono-logue at the bar mentioned above goes on, he remembers that he "loved Alicia Masters—but she dumped me for the Torch. An' why not? His skin's smooth. An' soft to the touch. Mine's like concrete. He can kiss her. He can...be a man." Then he thinks about how Reed and Sue have kids, and Johnny and Alicia can have them someday, "but not me. Never be a dad, never be a gran'pa—the Grimm family ends right here."[39] We'll discuss his relationship with Alicia more soon, but this is a familiar feeling to Ben throughout his life as the Thing with reference to various women, not just his eventual wife.

Sometimes Ben even feels like a lesser member of the Fantastic Four family. When comforting Kristoff Vernard, Doom's protégé, who feels rejected by both his mentor and his occasional allies the Fantastic Four, Ben references himself and Spider-Man in saying, "Reed, Sue, Johnny...they're blood. They don't question it. But me an' Spidey, we get where yer comin' from. The feelin' like yer only bein' included outta pity. 'Cuz everyone feels like they hafta," to which Spidey adds, "That any moment they'll finally get sick of you and tell you to get out." Johnny assures him that's not true, and Ben admits that "even I figgered it out by now," but even if he knows it in his head, it may not have completely penetrated his heart.[40] When Reed takes responsibility for talking Ben into their space flight, Ben explains that it was his own decision, and Reed's repeated apologies only contribute to his suspicion that Reed keeps him around out of guilt. When Sue says that too is not true, Ben says he knows, but "sometimes ya get too far gone."[41]

Much like people who think too highly of themselves (especially those whose names rhyme with "broom"), self-loathers such as Ben fail to assess their own qualities accurately. We touched on Ben's humility before, a normally admirable virtue that keeps one from getting a big head and also saves others the discomfort of having their relative inadequacies emphasized.[42] But it clearly becomes excessive—and stops being virtuous—when it leads to denial of one's good qualities in light of an overwhelming focus on the bad ones. After his self-pity party in the bar, Ben walks outside to see a burning tanker trailer rolled on top of a car with a baby trapped inside. Without thinking, he rushes into danger, throws the tanker into the East River, and tears the car roof open to rescue the baby. Does this make Ben feel worthy? When a police officer says to him, "Real nice piece o' work, fella. You ought'a be proud," Ben dismisses it, saying it was "nothin' special" and telling another officer that "you guys would'a done the same."[43] The baby touches his face and the mother kisses him on the lips, neither of them horrified in the least by his appearance, but there is no visible reaction from the self-described monster.

Ben's heroism is easy to reconcile with his self-loathing once we recognize that his low feelings of self-worth make him more likely to risk his life to save others who he feels are more worthy in comparison. Sue captures Ben's attitude well when she wonders, "Why is it you can fight for anyone else besides yourself?"[44] By its very nature, heroism involves putting other people's well-being above one's own, but once again, self-loathing takes it too far. We saw this to some extent in the last chapter with Johnny, who considers himself expendable for his own reasons, but Ben takes it to another level entirely. On the bright side, though, he does turn his own tragic fate into a positive, using his tremendous strength and rocky hide to help others, doing what others cannot—even if he minimizes the incredible contribution he makes to so many people's lives.

Although he feels he is less worthy than other people, Ben has enough self-awareness to realize that there are many others in (even) worse situations than his. In another issue in which he is feeling sorry for himself after Alicia takes up with Johnny, he meets an elderly unhoused woman whom he helps out, thinking to himself afterwards that he "may be a monster but at least I always had a home."[45] While working a case with Johnny Blaze, the Ghost Rider—to whom he says "us monsters have to stick together"—Ben thinks how lucky Blaze is that he can become human and that he shouldn't feel so sorry for himself, before realizing that this applies to himself too once he thinks about his teammates and Alicia (whom he was with at the time).[46] When a reporter tells him he's "considered one of the best of your generation of astronauts" and asks him if he misses his old life, Ben actually acknowledges "there's worse fates" than his, and that "I think o' the places I've been, the things I've done. The guys I trained with may never reach the moon. Me, I've been ta the stars."[47]

Ben explores the bright side of his situation after an adventure with the Black Widow, in which he pulls a massive bomb up from over three miles under the surface of the ocean. Showing a level of appreciation for his life that is far too rare (especially in his early years), he muses to himself:

> 'S funny. I been the Thing now for a lotta years. And most o' the time I hated it. All I wanted wuz ta be plain ol' Ben Grimm again. But…today, I did sum'pin' no one else could'a done by pullin' that bomb up. I saved a hunnert million people. I maybe saved the whole blamed world. Me, the Thing. If I'd been Ben Grimm, Reed, Suzie, Franklin, Alicia—they all woulda died. Kinda makes the pain worth it.[48]

After Johnny and Alicia get married, Ben has an epiphany. While watching little Franklin sleep, Ben thinks about Alicia and the romantic opportunity he had with the villain Thundra—don't get me started—plus his experiences on other worlds and in other dimensions. He realizes that he needs to (as they say) work on himself first: "Long as I ain't any good for myself, I wouldn't have done [Thundra] no good, either. I gotta solve my problems in this world—not on Battleworld, or in Thundra's dimension, or on another Earth." But all is not settled, for the next thought on his mind is "what if I *don't* solve 'em?", followed by the admission that he'll always love Alicia, no matter who else she ends up with (even Johnny).[49]

The Romance of Alicia and Ben

Ben's romance with Alicia Masters represents the most heartbreaking expression of his self-loathing as well as his salvation from it. From the first time they meet as manipulated tools of her adoptive father, the Puppet-Master, Alicia knows who Ben is: "This man—his face feels strong and powerful! And yet, I can sense a gentleness to him—there is something tragic—something sensitive!"[50] She reiterates this opinion many times throughout their relationship, such as when she tells baby Franklin, after Ben goes missing, that he's the "strongest...yet tenderest...most wonderful man in the world."[51]

Just as much as his specific virtues, Alicia also appreciates Ben's heart, a poetic way of describing his goodness in general, especially his kindness and resolve. During Alicia's bachelorette's party, Jen Walters (She-Hulk) asks her "what makes an artsy Soho sculptor fall for a guy like Ben Grimm?" Alicia explains in terms of her art:

> Marble, stone, clay. It speaks to me. It's my rainbow. And Ben *is* that rainbow, come to life. He walks with me in the park, and never forgets my birthday and shows more heart in a day than most people do in a year. You ask how I could fall for a man like that. I ask, how could I not?[52]

Soon afterwards, on their honeymoon, Ben ends up once again fighting the Hulk, now under the control of Ben's angry father-in-law, who speaks through the jade giant as well. At a low point, Ben tells his new wife that "the Hulk's got me beat every way. He's bigger than me! Stronger than me! Smarter than me!" Alicia assures him that "none of that matters. Because this fight isn't about brains or brawn. It's about heart. And no one has more heart than my Ben."[53]

Ben often acknowledges the irony of a blind woman "seeing" him better than anyone else, starting with their second issue together, when she tells him he is just like the white knight she sculpted: "You are good, and kind, and you will never desert your friends when they need you most!" Ben replies, "It's a funny thing, kid! Despite your blindness, you see things much better than I do! You—you make me feel ashamed of myself!"[54] Later she tells him that "I may not be able to see you, dear, but I know you, maybe better than you do."[55] Here, she recognizes that, because self-loathing people often have a negatively skewed opinion of themselves, they can often benefit from trusting in the way others see them (however they do it).

Despite all the praise she regularly lavishes on him, especially in response to his expressions of self-hatred, Ben still feels he's not good enough for her. It doesn't take long after they first get together for Ben to tell the rest of the team, "I'm fixin' to bust up with Alicia! It ain't fair for a slob like me to waste that doll's time!"[56] He often tells her that "you deserve better" and thinks that "she's got too much going for her—beauty, brains, and talent—to waste her time with an ugly meathead—a thing…like me!"[57] This last statement reflects two important aspects of a self-loather's thinking about romantic relationships: That their partner is too good for them (or that they're not good enough for their partner) and that they would be better off with someone else, hence the guilt about "wasting their time."

Through their long and—forgive me—rocky courtship, Ben has seen Alicia tempted by, attracted to, and sometimes even leave him for other men, to whom he cannot help but compare himself. Due to his self-loathing, these other men always seem better for Alicia than Ben is, and their mere existence in her life only confirms his low opinion of himself as her partner. It also arouses suspicions in him that Alicia only pities him because of his condition. In an early adventure, when Sue says that Dragon Man, a child-like android who attacks them, really needs kindness and protection, Ben thinks to himself,

> Yeah! That's the way Alicia must feel about me, too! It can't be love! It's just pity! The pity of beauty—for a beast! I ain't heard from Alicia for days! Mebbe she found someone better! Better! Wotta laugh! How could he be worse!?[58]

Naturally, Ben feels the same way when he actually sees Alicia with another man, thinking to himself that "I gotta face facts. She wuz never really in love with me. She wuz just pityin' the poor monster all along."[59] This is another aspect of self-loathing that links it with its frequent underlying condition of depression: the tendency toward negative and binary thinking. Not only does the sight of another man confirm Ben's belief that he was never good enough for Alicia, but it also leads him to jump to the conclusion that she never loved him at all, instead of acknowledging that, even if she doesn't love him anymore, she did at one time.

Although that incident was a false alarm—the other man was just Alicia's art dealer—Ben had been confronted with a more significant "threat" much earlier in the form of a shiny man on a gleaming surfboard. In the now-classic "Galactus Saga," the Silver Surfer comes to Earth to warn humanity of the impending arrival of Galactus, who intends to consume the planet to stave off his unquenchable hunger.[60] After Ben knocks him across the city, the Surfer falls through the skylight of a certain blind sculptress's studio, and she senses "unimaginable loneliness" in him. When he tells her of Galactus's plans, she argues for the value of humanity, asking him, "Can't you see that? Are you as blind as I?" Through Alicia's passion and courage, the Surfer for the first time understands beauty, and he starts to consider rebelling against his master.[61]

At the conclusion of the tale, after Galactus leaves in defeat, Alicia runs past Ben to the Silver Surfer, telling him she knew he would do the right thing based on the "certain proud nobility" she sensed in him. As they continue to talk, Ben sinks into self-loathing, thinking to himself as he slumps away:

> He talks like...a poet! And she's listenin'...like it's the first time she ever heard a guy speak to her! I can't even git mad! He didn't try ta beat my time! It just happened! Anyhow, if I wuz Alicia...who would I pick? A gleamin' gladiator like him...or an ape like...me? Face it, ugly! It ain't no contest!

After he slumps away, Alicia wants to introduce the Surfer to Ben, saying he's "the most wonderful man who ever lived," but it is too late (for now).[62]

Years later, during a time she was not with Ben, Alicia went into space with the Surfer and the two grew close. When they return to Earth briefly and meet Ben, she says, "You've always been my Rock of Gibraltar, Ben. My anchor. My...touchstone. But when I ride that board with him, I'm no longer blind. I feel alive in ways I can barely imagine, much less describe." She tells Ben she's unsure about the nature of their relationship, but when he watches her run into danger for the Surfer, he accepts they are "meant for each other," and gives them his blessing as they return to space.[63]

This seems mature of Ben, but it also serves to confirm his belief that he was never good enough for her, which replays itself through Alicia's relationships with other men. After being apart for a while, Ben is tempted to reach out to Alicia, but decides that "she deserves better than that. Gettin' jerked around by a yoyo like me." He calls architect Arlo North instead about designing a youth center on Yancy Street and is surprised the voice on the other end of the line is Arlo's girlfriend, Alicia.[64] He tells Sue later that he checked Arlo out and "there's nuthin' sinister or hinky about 'im. Basically, Alicia found herself a great guy. An' how am I supposed to compete with that?"[65] Even when Alicia was with Johnny, which disturbed Ben on an entirely different level, he acknowledged that at least they make a better-looking couple.[66]

Separate from his low opinion of himself, Ben has also more practical concerns about being with Alicia. For example, he worries about what kind of life he can offer her. While vacationing with her in London, Ben wonders again what she sees in him and when "she'll finally get tired a' waitin' fer me ta pop the question an' she'll marry someone else!" He contemplates the idea of them getting married and questions "what kinda marriage would that be for her? 'Meet my husband, the orange monster! An' our kids—Rock-Head and Stone-Face—an' don't they take after their dear ol' dad?'"[67] Later, as their relationship starts to crumble, he asks her directly, "what kinda life can I offer you?" before returning to his familiar theme of "you deserve a whole lot more than bein' the girlfriend of a freak!"[68]

Like his best pal Johnny and his love interests, Ben also worries about Alicia's safety, being in such close proximity to the Fantastic Four and all the danger they encounter (or invite). Early on, he was quite naïve about this, telling her that "you'll always be safe, baby—as long as I'm around!"[69] But it doesn't take long for Ben to appreciate how much danger his lifestyle puts Alicia in. During their London trip, she is transformed by the criminal organization Hydra into a murderous spider-creature, after which he realizes that "because a' me, Alicia almost died. Because a' me! I just ain't right fer her. For her sake, she can't keep seein' me. She just can't," which coincides with his general self-loathing: "An' she's much better off without me. I know it."[70]

Later, Ben asks Reed how he deals with the danger their lifestyle puts Sue in—apparently without thinking about the powers and abilities she has herself, even before she was widely acknowledged as the most powerful member of the team. Reed replies, "I think I've accepted that Sue has the same right to choose her lifestyle that you or I do."[71] Although it is easy to see that romantic partners deserve to have their choices respected, as well as their reasons for them, it is difficult for self-loathers such as Ben. They feel they know better than their partners how bad they are for them, and they have to use that superior insight to protect them—not just from the dangers of vengeful supervillains or intergalactic tyrants, but from the disappointment that "inevitably" follows from being with someone so horrible. This also explains why Ben often feels he is exploiting the fact that Alicia cannot see him in the same way that sighted people can, telling her early on that "it ain't right for me to take advantage of ya—just 'cause you can't see!"[72] Later, he asks himself how he could "let her" marry him, "with her bein' blind and all—not really being able to see what I look like," completely ignoring her agency or choice in the matter.[73]

There are encouraging signs that Ben can get past this, however. As he ponders their relationship after Alicia is abducted and tortured by Annihilus, the ruler of the Negative Zone, he wonders "if I really got any right ta expose Alicia ta the kind of constant danger that goes with bein' my gal" before his thoughts turn back to his looks and being "a freakshow." But he also realizes that "she reckons she knows what I look like, knows from what her fingertips tell her," and seems to accept Reed's advice: to trust her to know what she wants and what she's getting with him and to make her own decision whether to remain with him or not.[74] The fact that they are (as I write this) happily married gives one hope that he has finally accepted her decision—even if he will never stop worrying about her safety, as we see in a recent adventure in a nightmare realm when he imagines Alicia turning to a Thing while thinking to himself that "my biggest fear is destroyin' what I love."[75]

Another wrinkle (or crack) is added to Ben's self-loathing about his appearance when we learn that he believes that Alicia prefers him as the Thing. This makes him ambivalent about the possibility of becoming human again, despite Reed's repeated attempts to correct what he regards as his greatest failing (as we saw in chapter 2). This impression dates to their very first meeting, recounted above: After Alicia touches his face and feels his strength, gentleness, and sensitivity, Ben uses Reed's serum to change back to human form. When she hears him speak and reaches for his face again, she says, "Your voice! You are the strong, kindly one! But—you seem different now!" When the serum wears off and he begins to revert back to the Thing, she corrects herself: "No—wait! I—I was mistaken! It *is* you—it *is* the same wonderful man!" Holding her in his arms, Ben is sad that the serum didn't last longer, "but the clinker is," he thinks, "she likes me better as the Thing!"[76]

Soon after, Ben takes another of Reed's cures while holding a piano up with one hand, and when he becomes human he falls and hurts himself. Reed apologizes to Ben for not reminding him to use common sense and put the piano down first, but more important is Alicia's alarmed reaction, asking him if he's hurt and why he feels so different (again). "I—I love you so that I don't want you to change!" she pleads. "I don't ever want anything to change you!" Ben turns to Reed and says, "I appreciate what you're tryin' to do for me, but nothin' makes sense! I love Alicia, and she loves me best as—the Thing! So why don't you forget about tryin' to change me back" and try to cure her blindness instead (which would, of course, only trigger his parallel anxiety about her seeing him as others do).[77] Later, Ben rejects a cure which Reed promises will be permanent, saying, "Alicia loves me this way…How do I know how she'll feel about me if I become just plain Ben Grimm?" Reed argues that Alicia loves him for who he is, not how he looks, but Ben is adamant that he needs to be able to change at will, because "I don't wanna give up bein' the Thing."[78]

Reed's assurances aside, Ben does have good reason for his suspicion. When he finally agrees to try a permanent cure—which, if ever reversed, cannot be repeated—Johnny asks him how it feels to be Ben Grimm again, to which he answers, "I can live with it, kid. But Alicia's the one who counts! I gotta see how she feels about me not being the Thing any more!" On the way to their first date as two "normal" folks, he worries she might find him "too different—too dull," and she confirms his concern, telling him "everything seems different now." She feels his face, finding "a rugged handsomeness" to his features, but Ben feels a difference in her touch. Their date is interrupted by the Android Man—seriously, that's his name—and Ben is forced to trigger a permanent reversion to the Thing in order to protect Alicia from him. When Johnny reiterates later that he can never change back, Ben mopes and walks away, saying "why be boring old nobody Ben Grimm, when I can be the Thing…forever," once again emphasizing his tragic choice between being human and (possibly) losing the woman he loves.[79]

After keeping this concern a secret for years, Ben confronts Alicia on the issue after Doctor Doom traps them in a miniature world in which they live as a married, dual-human couple.[80] While considering Reed's latest offer of a cure, Ben tells Alicia, "All the years I've known you an' loved you I ain't never been able ta shake one feelin'. The feelin' that it's really the Thing you love, not Ben Grimm." She replies, "What? Th-that's absurd, Ben. It's you I love. I don't care what form you wear." But Ben thinks that "she hesitated! Only fer a second, but she hesitated. Was it because I never asked that before, or...," while Sue has the same impression later.[81]

Ben's concern becomes serious enough that, as revealed by a mysterious adult version of Franklin, he subconsciously rejects any attempt to revert him to human form. As Reed tells Sue, "Ben has said many times he fears Alicia loves him only as the Thing, and although she has denied that in both word and deed it is a deep rooted fear." He goes on to identify "the tragedy...the beautiful, blind Alicia is the one spark of joy in Ben's life. Yet so long as he loves her his mind will reject all cures. So long as there is Alicia he will always be...the Thing!"[82] For his part, Reed feels he must continue to "try" to cure Ben, so neither he nor Alicia ever suspects the truth.[83] When, after splitting from Alicia, Ben discovers that he can change at will on the Beyonder's Battleworld during the first Secret Wars, Reed lets him believe it has to do with the world itself and not the fact that he's no longer worried about Alicia's reaction—a deception that, once revealed, provides a new reason for Ben to resent his best friend (and for Reed to feel guilty about his).[84]

A Happy Ending?

Is Ben doomed to suffer from self-loathing the rest of his days? There is good reason to be optimistic on this front. Although he will likely never be free of feeling like a monster or a freak, the one thing he has come to accept is the love of Alicia. After a significant period of separation and other relationships—Alicia with Arlo, Ben with a teacher named Debbie

whom he almost marries—Ben and Alicia reconnect, leading to his proposal of marriage and their wedding soon thereafter.[85] They later adopt
two children, Nikki and Jo, a Skrull and Kree (respectively) whom they
rescued from an intergalactic fight arena, and later a dog named Princess.[86] Does this mean, however, that all of his issues regarding Alicia are
behind him (or them)?

On their honeymoon, Ben tells his new bride he's nervous and she
thinks she knows why, telling him that "it wasn't that long ago you used
to worry that I only loved you as the Thing." He replies, "Yeah. But we're
well past that, right?" After a pause, he asks again, "Right? Say sumthin'."
She asks about his wedding band, which he explains is made out of vibranium to withstand lots of clobberin', but it will fall off when he re-
verts to human form for his one week each year (which they timed for
their honeymoon, of course). She says, "good," to his puzzlement, then
gets down on one knee to offer him a human-sized ring, explaining that
"whoever you are...inside and out...I want to be with you. Have family
with you. For as long as we both shall live."[87]

That should settle the issue of whether Alicia loves Ben more as the
Thing, but there is still the problem of Ben's thinking he's an ugly monster. More recently, Ben reads Alicia some *Fantastic Four* comics (as
published in the Marvel Universe), reading the words and describing the
pictures for her. She makes sure he tells her when "anyone shows up
who's big and handsome and rocky and orange," and asks him, "just how
handsome *is* this guy?" He starts to answer that he's not handsome at all,
but she stops him with a "Ben." He reconsiders, saying, "Well...I suppose—I mean...I guess in th' right light...there's mebbe a chance he ain't
half-bad, sweet pea." She gives him a kiss and says, "right answer,
babe."[88] She's learned that it's not enough to tell him how handsome *she*
thinks he is—she has to make *him* say it if she wants him to start believing it.

It is hard to believe that Ben Grimm will ever completely get over being the Thing, but his development over the years gives us cause to hope that, at least, he won't dwell on it as much going forward. The fact that he now chooses to remain the Thing—at least for 51 weeks out of the year—also sends an important message that it is okay to be different, even if some people find that difference to be alarming, disturbing, or frightening. After his son Jo disguises himself as human to fit in better at school, Ben tells him, "I get it, kid. There've been a lotta times I wished I didn't look like this. And that I still looked like everybody else." When Jo asks why Ben would want to be anyone else, given that he's "a legend throughout the galaxy," Ben answers, "I don't. Not anymore. And that should go double for you."[89] Later, when Ben is offered a permanent cure, Jo asks if he will take it, and Ben asks, "what do you think, son?" Jo hails his legendary status again, adding "as you once told me, we should be proud of who we are," and Ben declines the cure, saying "with all I got goin' for me—I wouldn't ever change an ever-lovin' Thing."[90]

[1] *Fantastic Four*, vol. 3, #543 (May 2007).

[2] *Fantastic Four*, vol. 6, #47 (November 2022) and #48 (December 2022).

[3] *Fantastic Four*, vol. 3, #12 (December 1998).

[4] *Fantastic Four*, vol. 3, #27 (March 2000). For more on Captain America's honor, see chapter 4 in my book, *The Virtues of Captain America: Modern-Day Lessons in Character from a World War II Superhero*, 2nd ed. (Hoboken, NJ: Wiley & Sons, 2024).

[5] *Fantastic Four*, vol. 1, #299 (February 1987). To be clear, Ben was agreeing to be the best man at Johnny's wedding—to Alicia, no less, although she was actually a Skrull—but the context makes clear that Johnny meant it more generally. Compare this to when Ben asks Reed to be *his* best man, and Reed says back: "Aw. You're my best man, too, Ben" (*Fantastic Four*, vol. 6, #3, January 2019).

[6] *Fantastic Four*, vol. 6, #5 (February 2019), "4-Minute Warning." For his part, after mistaking Ben for a monster, Shang-Chi (the Master of Kung Fu) reflects that "I have sensed nobility in this man… a dedication to cause," concerned more with helping others than himself (*Marvel Two-in-One* #29, July 1977).

[7] *Fantastic Four*, vol. 1, 37 (April 1965); *Fantastic Four Annual*, vol. 1, #3 (1965), "Bedlam at the Baxter Building!"; *Fantastic Four*, vol. 1, #94 (January 1970).

[8] *Thing*, vol. 1, #23 (May 1985); *Fantastic Four*, vol. 3, #16 (April 1999).

[9] This history is based on a number of sources in the comics, such as *Fantastic Four*, vol. 3, #56 (August 2002) and *Fantastic Four*, vol. 1, #11 (February 1963), "A Visit with the Fantastic Four."

[10] *Fantastic Four: 4 Yancy Street* #1 (October 2019).

[11] *Fantastic Four*, vol. 1, #28 (July 1964) and #367 (August 1992).

[12] *Marvel 2-in-One* #1 (February 2018).

[13] *Marvel Two-in-One* #77 (July 1981) and #26 (April 1977).

[14] *Marvel Two-in-One* #12 (November 1975); *Iron Man*, vol. 3, #14 (March 1999).

[15] *Marvel Two-in-One* #42 (August 1978).

[16] *Marvel Two-in-One* #100 (June 1983).

[17] *Fantastic Four*, vol. 3, #530 (October 2005).

[18] For instance, in *Fantastic Four*, vol. 1 #240 (March 1982).

[19] *Fantastic Four*, vol. 3, #16.

[20] *Fantastic Four*, vol. 3, #70 (August 2003).

[21] *Fantastic Four*, vol. 1, #97 (April 1970).

[22] *Marvel Two-in-One* #80 (October 1981).

[23] *Fantastic Four*, vol. 1, #296 (November 1986).

[24] *Fantastic Four vs. the X-Men* #3 (April 1987).

[25] *Fantastic Four*, vol. 1, #2 (January 1962).

[26] *Fantastic Four*, vol. 6, #14 (November 2019).

[27] *Fantastic Four*, vol. 7, #1 (January 2023).

[28] *Fantastic Four*, vol. 1, #11, "A Visit with the Fantastic Four." Recall that Sue is the one who called him "a thing" when he first transformed, which he then took as his codename (*Fantastic Four*, vol. 1, #1, November 1961).

[29] *Fantastic Four*, vol. 1, #105 (December 1970).

[30] *Fantastic Four*, vol. 1, #296.

[31] *Fantastic Four*, vol. 3, #575 (March 2010); later in the same issue, he rescues three of the most intelligent young Moloids, who later join Reed's Future Foundation and regard "the Ben" as their hero (*Fantastic Four*, vol. 3, #579, July 2010).

[32] *Fantastic Four*, vol. 6, #16 (January 2020).

[33] *Fantastic Four*, vol. 1, #166 (January 1976).

[34] This was not Ben's first experience with a golem: He met "the" Golem in *Marvel Two-in-One* #11 (September 1975), an animated statue who debuted in *The Incredible Hulk*, vol. 1, #134 (September 1970) and had his own short-lived feature in *Strange Tales* around the same time. Ben does not suggest any faith-based connection with this Golem, though he does regard him as a fellow monster.

[35] *Amazing Spider-Man*, vol. 2, #661 (July 2011), "The Substitute, Part One"; *Thing*, vol. 2, #8 (August 2006).

[36] *Fantastic Four*, vol. 6, #5, "4-Minute Warning."

[37] *Fantastic Four*, vol. 3, #56 (August 2002), the canonical confirmation of Ben's faith (aside from Jack Kirby's famous Hanukkah card featuring the Thing), with reporter Ben Urich later writing that "it's well-documented that Ben Grimm is Jewish" (4 #22, November 2005). Curiously, in a earlier holiday tale, a young Jewish kid who is sick of hearing about Christmas has to explain the meaning of Hanukkah to Ben (*Marvel Holiday Special 1994*, "Losin' the Blues"). Maybe he did miss a lot of Hebrew school after all!

[38] 4 #22.

[39] *Fantastic Four vs. the X-Men* #3.

[40] It's the rocks, you know—even Reed was surprised early on when he couldn't hear Ben's heartbeat or feel a pulse (*Fantastic Four*, vol. 1, #113, August 1971).

[41] *Spider-Man/Fantastic Four* #4 (December 2010).

[42] For more on this approach to humility or modesty, see Irene McMullin, "A Modest Proposal: Accounting for the Virtuousness of Modesty," *The Philosophical Quarterly* 60(2010): 784–807; Mark D. White, "A Modest Comment on McMullin: A Kantian Account of Modesty," *Journal of Philosophical Research* 40(2015): 1-5; and McMullin, "A Response to Mark D. White's 'A Modest Comment on McMullin: A Kantian Account of Modesty'," *Journal of Philosophical Research* 40(2015): 7-11.

[43] *Fantastic Four vs. the X-Men* #3.

[44] *Thing*, vol. 2, #6 (June 2006).

[45] *Marvel Fanfare*, vol. 1, #20 (May 1985).

[46] *Marvel Two-in-One* #80.

[47] *Fantastic Four*, vol. 3, #9 (September 1998).

[48] *Marvel Two-in-One* #10 (July 1975). He follows up by saying, "Sheesh! I'm a philosopher a'ready." Yes you are, Ben—yes, you are.

[49] *Fantastic Four*, vol. 1, #303 (June 1987).

[50] *Fantastic Four*, vol. 1, #8 (November 1962).

[51] *Fantastic Four*, vol. 1, #90 (September 1969). (She's referring to Ben, not Franklin, just in case you weren't sure.)

[52] *Fantastic Four: Wedding Special* #1 (February 2019), "(Invisible) Girls Gone Wild."

[53] *Fantastic Four*, vol. 6, #13 (October 2019). I would be remiss if I didn't mention Alicia's heart as well: While Ben is fighting the Hulk, she's trapped under a rockslide with other vacationers. She urges them to stay calm and starts feeling the rock to find a way out. When someone asks her how she can do this, she replies, "I work with stone and chip away large chunks of it for a living," adding that "I've also had to get my husband out of bed in the morning." (It should not be surprising that the members of the Fantastic Four consider her a member of the team, going back to *Marvel Two-in-One* #70, December 1980, when Reed tells her "you may not be a member of team officially…but you've always been one of us. Welcome to the Fantastic Four!")

[54] *Fantastic Four*, vol. 1, #9 (December 1962).

55 *Marvel Two-in-One* #29.

56 *Fantastic Four*, vol. 1, #29 (August 1964). As it happens, she feels very similarly about herself. In the same issue, she tries to break it off with him, prompting him to say, "Hah! I knew it! I was right all the time! You finally realized I ain't good enough for you! And it's true, honey! I don't blame ya!" But Alicia turns the tables on him: "No, Ben! No, my darling! It is I who am not good enough for you! You're so wonderful...any girl would be proud to have your love! I can't let you waste your time with me...just out of...pity!" She repeats this later: In *Fantastic Four*, vol. 1, #107 (February 1971), Reed makes Ben able to change at will, and Alicia worries that only the Thing "could love a blind girl." Unlike Ben's obsessive self-loathing, however, Alicia's statements of self-doubt are only occasional and fairly normal.

57 *Fantastic Four*, vol. 1, #226 (January 1981); *Marvel Two-in-One* #81 (November 1981).

58 *Fantastic Four*, vol. 1, #45 (December 1965). Years later, Reed and Valeria would increase Dragon Man's intelligence significantly and would become an ally of the Fantastic Four, helping supervise and teach the children of the Future Foundation (*Fantastic Four*, vol. 3, #579).

59 *Marvel Two-in-One* #67 (September 1980).

60 *Fantastic Four*, vol. 1, #48 (March 1966). We discuss Galactus's hunger and the Silver Surfer's complicity in it in chapter 7.

61 *Fantastic Four*, vol. 1, #49 (April 1966).

62 *Fantastic Four*, vol. 1, #50 (May 1966).

63 *Fantastic Four*, vol. 3, #4 (April 1998).

64 *Thing*, vol. 2, #5 (May 2006).

65 *Thing*, vol. 2, #7 (July 2006).

66 *Fantastic Four*, vol. 1, #298 (January 1987).

67 *Marvel Two-in-One* #30 (August 1977).

68 *Thing*, vol. 1, #10 (April 1984).

69 *Fantastic Four*, vol. 1, #14 (May 1963).

70 *Marvel Two-in-One* #32 (October 1977).

71 *Marvel Two-in-One* #67—after which Ben thinks "that guy's got smarts where it really counts...dealin' with people," which is hardly a common impression of Reed Richards. Ben even thought earlier that "Reed'd have made a good shrink!" (*Marvel Two-in-One* #60, February 1980), although when Reed tries to analyze his brother-

in-law's relationship problems, Johnny reminds him that "psychology is one diploma you don't have on your wall" (*Fantastic Four*, vol. 3, #13, January 1999).

[72] *Fantastic Four*, vol. 1, #68 (November 1967).

[73] *Marvel Two-in-One* #60. One time he even adds the difference in their ages: As he tells She-Hulk, "lotsa times I felt like I was takin' advantage of Alicia. I was a lot older'n her...an' she couldn't see the ugly mug she was with!" (*Fantastic Four*, vol. 1, #299).

[74] *Thing*, vol. 1, #5 (November 1983); Alicia was attacked by Annihilus in *Fantastic Four*, vol. 1, #251 (February 1983) and discovered by Ben in #256 (July 1983).

[75] *Fantastic Four: Grimm Noir* #1 (April 2020).

[76] *Fantastic Four*, vol. 1, #8.

[77] *Fantastic Four*, vol. 1, #16 (July 1983).

[78] *Fantastic Four*, vol. 1, #25 (April 1984).

[79] *Fantastic Four*, vol. 1, #79 (October 1968). This isn't the place to discuss it—this book is long enough as it is!—but another reason Ben is ambivalent about becoming human again is the greater amount of good he can do as the Thing, as he found out with the Android Man as well as a battle the Wizard immediately after transforming the issue before (#78, September 1968). Even when he is able to become human for one week a year, it backfires, such as when he cannot prevent Johnny from sacrificing himself in the Negative Zone in *Fantastic Four*, vol. 3, #587 (March 2011), as discussed in the last chapter.

[80] *Fantastic Four*, vol. 1, #236 (November 1981).

[81] *Fantastic Four*, vol. 1, #238 (January 1982), "The More Things Change..."

[82] *Fantastic Four*, vol. 1, #245 (August 1982).

[83] Reed ponders this additional responsibility with regard to Ben in *Fantastic Four*, vol. 1, #246 (September 1982) and Alicia in *Marvel Two-in-One* #92 (October 1982).

[84] Reed tells Sue about his deception (which takes place in *Secret Wars*, vol. 1, #12, April 1985) in *Fantastic Four*, vol. 1, #271 (October 1984), and Ben and Reed have it out in *Thing*, vol. 1, #23 (May 1985).

[85] Ben meets Debbie in *Fantastic Four*, vol. 3, #554 (April 2008), proposes to her in issue #562 (February 2009), but breaks off the engagement on their wedding day in issue #569 (September 2009) for her own safety. Ben and Alicia reconnect in *Fantastic Four*, vol. 5, #1 (April 2014), get engaged in *Fantastic Four*, vol. 6, #1 (October

2018), and are married in *Fantastic Four*, vol. 6, #5, "4-Minute Warning." (There will be a quiz on Friday.)

[86] *Empyre: Fantastic Four* #0 (September 2020); *Fantastic Four*, vol. 7, #11 (November 2023).

[87] *Fantastic Four*, vol. 6, #12 (September 2019), "Honeymoon Crasher."

[88] *Fantastic Four*, vol. 7, #9 (September 2023).

[89] *Fantastic Four*, vol. 6, #39 (March 2022).

[90] *Fantastic Four*, vol. 6, #46 (October 2022).

Chapter 6
Civil War

One of the reasons the Fantastic Four were such a breath of fresh air upon their introduction in 1961 was that the members bickered and squabbled with each other. Instead of the bland, "let's get 'em, pals" tone of comics published by their Distinguished Competition at the time, we saw Reed growing impatient with Sue, Sue telling Ben to watch his temper, Ben losing his temper at Johnny's pranks, and all of them making fun of Reed's preoccupation with scientific minutiae.

When things get serious, though, the four usually come together as a team (or a family) and have each other's backs as they face a common threat (nearly every month, as it happens). As we saw in chapter 1, they all share the main heroic virtues, and any minor differences in ethical approaches normally get lost in the rush to save lives and stop whatever danger faces the planet, galaxy, or universe.

But not always! Occasionally a situation brings out key differences between members of the Fantastic Four and threatens to tear apart Marvel's first family. We discussed one such story briefly in chapter 1, in which Reed shot Franklin with an antimatter ray to stop his cosmic powers from overloading and possibly destroying the universe, shocking the rest of team and driving Sue away for some time.[1] In general, this is emblematic of a lot of the internal debates among the team: Reed takes an action, often in secret, that the others disagree with when they find out. To be fair to Reed, in the case of Franklin he had to make a split-second decision to disable his son and save the world, and he did beat himself up afterwards for not thinking of another option in the fraction of a second he had. In most cases, however, Reed makes a very deliberate, pragmatic or utilitarian decision, often without telling the others, who typically prefer a more principled or deontological way of thinking (as well as a greater degree of openness and communication).

Appropriately enough, the event that may have caused the most dissent and disagreement among the group was the first superhero Civil War, which tore all the Marvel heroes apart over the issue of government registration of superheroes and its implications regarding privacy, safety, and autonomy.[2] Although the main protagonists in the Civil War were Captain America and Iron Man, with Spider-Man in the middle, the members of the Fantastic Four also had strong reactions to the debate, with Reed taking controversial steps toward the registration effort, Sue opposing his actions (and registration itself), and Ben taking himself out of the debate altogether—by leaving for France. (What about Johnny? He was injured early on, but he allied with Sue once he got back on his feet…or off them, as the case may be.)[3]

Superhero Registration Before the Civil War

Years before Iron Man and Captain America led the forces supporting and opposing registration (respectively), the Fantastic Four faced the same issue, without it becoming a massive crossover event like the later episode. It begins simply enough, with Johnny reading a newspaper article headlined "Super-Hero Registration Act Eyed by Congress," which his wife at the time, Alicia, logged in a computer database.

The members' reactions to this news are relatively muted. Sue appreciates that the public is anxious about the disasters superheroes are often involved in (even if they don't cause them) while she is suspicious of

130

military plans for registered heroes and their powers. Johnny anticipates an eventual ban of superpowers altogether, like the government tried to do with mutants, and fears that, similar to common arguments against gun control, "if powers are outlawed, only outlaws will have powers." Sharon Ventura—Ben's girlfriend at the time, transformed into a Thing and going under the name Ms. Marvel—agrees that people can be frightened of people who are "different," but Ben dismisses this, saying "Baloney! I been the same and I been 'different.' Stuff don't hurt any less when yer orange." When Sue expresses concern about the security of heroes' private information, including secret identities, Ben says that the good guys will be mad, the bad guys won't comply, and the government can't be trusted to keep the information safe. Finally, Reed merely recommends hearing what the government has to say at their congressional hearing the next day.[4]

At the hearing, though, Reed takes a harder stance against registration, as previewed by his quotation from James Madison regarding the way individual rights are often phased out: "I believe there are more instances of the abridgement of the freedom of the people, by gradual and silent encroachments of those in power, than by violent and sudden usurpations."[5] The supporters of registration argue that the government needs to know what abilities are available for military conscription—validating Sue's earlier suspicion—as well as for their own protection. Henry Peter Gyrich, who once exercised a very forceful management over the Avengers as their government liaison, explicitly cites the utilitarian principle of "the greatest good for the greatest number" with respect to the need to be aware and on guard of renegade superpowers. He suggests that not only may registration be required but limitation as well, adding another popular wording of the utilitarian principle: "the needs of the many outweigh the needs of the few." Finally, he suggests that "cooperative" superhumans could, in the spirit of altruism, aid the government in rounding up any "who refused to cooperate"—and not once did he make any reference or distinction between heroes or villains.[6]

Ironically, Reed also relies on utilitarian arguments in opposition to registration—showing that such reasoning is very dependent on the aspects of a situation someone chooses to emphasize, not to mention how they estimate them. First, when the congressional delegates question the value of superheroes, Reed provides overwhelming evidence—in thousands of pages of reports, with appendices—of the lives saved over the years just by the Fantastic Four, not to mention the Avengers and other heroes. For their part, Johnny and Ben make more practical points about the difficulty of trying to extract personal information from super-powered criminals, whose activities will likely go unopposed while the government is checking superheroes' identification. Sue alone makes a principled point, telling one congressman that she's worried about their names being held in yet another computer in Washington, and that "I want my son to grow up knowing what freedom in the United States is supposed to mean, not what it would have meant if he hadn't been 'special.'"[7]

Later, when asked about the role of superheroes in society, Reed explains that superheroes not only do an immeasurable amount of good, but they are also uniquely able and qualified to do so:

> We live in a world where so-called super-villains are an everyday fact of life. So are beings of great power and even some of cosmic significance. And in this world, super heroes do a job nobody else can do. They're not paid, they suffer injuries, and aren't insured. Most do it out of the sense of altruism Mr. Gyrich referred to earlier. And out of a sense of holding society together against the forces of chaos that their foes represent. The very nature of these

activities often puts them beyond the experience of non-super humans...and makes it very difficult for a non-super human to exercise a considered judgment regarding their activities.[8]

This last part, we can assume, was in reference to Mr. Gyrich's failure to oversee and assess the Avengers' activities during his time supervising them—which incidentally led to a congressional inquiry into *their* value to society.[9]

Sue backs him up, responding to the point anticipated by Johnny and made by a representative of the National Rifle Association, who opposes superhero registration for the same reason he opposes gun control. He would hardly be happy with where Sue takes the argument, saying that while gun owners have no need for high-capacity weapons, the world does need superpowered individuals to combat extraordinary threats:

> Bearing arms is a constitutional right, but some people choose to interpret that right in its broadest sense...thereby including weapons like assault rifles, weapons designed for only one purpose, and it certainly isn't deer hunting. All this at a time when an invasion from hostile forces or nations seems remote. But the invasion by super-powered individuals and teams continues even as we speak. Literally. The existence and activities of such people determined to break the law are an ongoing menace to the forces of order everywhere. We're not talking about a theoretical or hypothetical threat; we're talking about the real thing, here and now.[10]

When Reed takes the rhetorical baton back, he builds on Sue's point that superhumans are necessary to confront such threats by emphasizing that conventional forces cannot do it, as evidenced by the U.S. Army's continued failure to subdue the Hulk. To make matters worse, he puts on the record Gyrich's time with the Avengers, during which the team was "hamstringed" and nearly "destroyed," which could have rendered them incapable of protecting the world and saving lives.[11]

After questioning the government's motives and expertise in collecting the information it claims to want—as well as the issue of who even counts as a "superhuman"—Reed turns to the principled concerns of privacy and individual rights, as Sue alluded to earlier. He concludes by saying, "Gentleman, I submit that the full ramifications of this bill have not been thoroughly understood and the further reflection is essential," and the matter is quickly tabled.

Hero Against Hero

During the episode recounted above, the government never cited any actual disasters that prompted the push for registration—only hypothetical ones (which, given their scale, cannot be dismissed as unreasonable concerns). But years later, a series of catastrophes involving superheroes culminated in a massive explosion in Stamford, Connecticut, during a fight between the teen hero team the Young Warriors—who were filming a reality series at the time—and the literally volatile villain Nitro. The explosion killed over 600 people, including sixty children playing at a school nearby.[12] These calamities prompt widespread public outcry about the danger posed by superheroes—especially young and untrained ones—and lead the United States government to pass the Superhuman Registration Act, which requires all heroes (even technologically-powered ones like Iron Man) to register with the government, provide their secret identity, and submit to training and accountability.

Speaking of Iron Man (Tony Stark), he warns the Illuminati—the secretive group of the smartest heroes in the Marvel Universe we met in chapter 1—of the coming legislation even before the Stamford incident, explaining that "an environment of fear has been created where this bill can not only exist but will pass." He predicts that it will take just one more disaster to push the bill forward, and the ensuing controversy will split the hero community—unless they get ahead of the legislation, supporting it and managing it for the safety and well-being of their own community as well as the public. Most of the Illuminati object and storm out of the meeting, with only Reed saying that "Tony's right. He's completely right."[13]

As he leaves, Reed says to Tony, "Well, I have to go home and fight with my wife about this for the rest of my life."[14] This may have been a slight exaggeration, but in spirit he was not wrong—and he gets off to a bad start when he refuses to tell her anything about the Illuminati meeting.[15] After the Stamford incident, Johnny gets attacked and injured by a crowd upset at superheroes, after which the heroes gather to discuss registration, with many of the same opinions and arguments made as before—although this time around Sue dismisses the concern about secret identities, because their names are public, but Spider-Man argues he has loved ones to protect.[16]

Once the bill is passed, Tony takes charge of implementation for the government, rounding up unregistered heroes and fighting normal supervillain threats, while Reed and Hank Pym work on other ideas regarding enforcement and detention. Reed tells Sue that "Tony's big plan for the superhuman community is the most exciting thing we've ever worked on," and that "I haven't been this excited since I saw my first black hole." When Sue brings up the fact that they're hunting down their friends, Reed simply says they can always register and asks her to "look at my projections if you need to see the social dangers they're creating." He hails Tony and Hank as "concept-machines," but when Sue asks about a file mysteriously labeled "42," he says it's classified. She leaves to see Johnny in the hospital, and Reed says, without looking up, "mm. Give Johnny all my love."[17]

We see the pattern between Reed and Sue emerging from just this exchange: Reed takes some action that he justifies in terms of the greater good, and when Sue learns about it, she points out that it crosses a moral line. This explains why she is called, in a television interview soon after the end of the Civil War, his "moral compass," without which "he flounders."[18]

This also reflects another distinction between them, with Reed focusing on the project at hand while Sue attends to the people around her—in this case, Johnny. When Reed travels to Wakanda to try to enlist the Black Panther to their cause, T'Challa asks about Johnny. Reed admits "I haven't checked in for a day or two," but he assumes Sue will let him know "if anything was wrong." T'Challa offers a "word of advice, Reed. Call Susan."[19] We see this contrast again when Spider-Man unmasks on live television (at Tony's urging), and Reed and Sue each phone him to follow up. Reed calls first, congratulating him on a job well done, commending his courage, and offering help if he needs it. Sue calls next while Reed is still on the line and asks how Peter is "holding up," and when Reed answers for him, saying "he's handling it very well," Sue interrupts: "Reed, I'm sure he's handling it, but that's not what I asked. I asked how he's feeling." Although they both reach out to Peter in his time of need, Sue shows more compassion and concern for his emotional well-being, whereas Reed seems more interested in acknowledging Peter's contribution to the larger mission.[20]

The Law Is the Law...Or Is It?

Yet another point on which Reed and Sue disagree reveals itself when the entire team gathers in Johnny's hospital room. When Reed implies that heroes cannot (or should not) fight the government or resist the law,

Sue tells him they're rounding up their fellow heroes and friends "because they won't betray their principles," then accuses him of "just following orders," invoking the defense given by Nazi leaders during the Nuremberg trials when they were held accountable for their actions in the Holocaust during World War II.[21] Later, when Reed accuses her of breaking the law to help unregistered heroes evade capture, Sue says the law is wrong. Reed says if she believes that she needs to act to change the law, but until then she has to obey it. She repeats her "just following orders" comment and explicitly mentions the Nazis rounding up entire populations into concentration camps, asking him, "isn't that a whole lot like what you're doing?"[22] After Reed, clearly frustrated, begins to make a fist, Sue leans in, saying: "Use it, put it away, or I'll take it off at the wrist."[23]

When Sue asks if she ever knew him, Reed shouts that "I'm doing this for the same reason I've ever done anything, Sue! Because it's the law! Because it's right!" She responds that it's not right, which gets to the crux of the matter: Is the law right just because it's the law, or can the law be wrong and still be the law—and if so, is there still an obligation to follow it?

These questions were at the core of a protracted debate between two prominent legal philosophers, H.L.A. Hart and Lon F. Fuller, during the Nuremberg trials. The issue at hand was the one Sue invokes above: whether the claim of accused Nazi war criminals that they were "just following orders" should excuse them from legal responsibility for their actions. Both philosophers agreed that Nazi law and the actions taken under it were heinous and inhumane, but they disagreed about the status of that law itself. Hart was an advocate of *legal positivism*, a philosophy of law that says the validity of a law—whether it has the status of official law—was separate from the morality of that law. In other words, a bad law, like Nazi law, could still be law if it was enacted in the appropriate way.[24] Fuller disagreed with legal positivism and maintained that moral aspects of a law could have an effect on its standing as official law, an example of an approach to legal philosophy known as *natural law*. Accordingly, he argued that Nazi law was so atrocious that it should not be considered law at all.[25]

Even though Hart was strongly opposed to what the Nazis stood for and did, his positivist approach to the law provides some support for the argument that accused Nazis were simply following orders under the recognized and valid law of the day. This aligns with Reed's view that people—especially heroes—should follow the law simply because it's the law, whether they agree with it or not, as long as it is the law. Later, when Peter Parker asks him why he chose to support registration, Reed tells him a story about his uncle Ted, who was called to testify before the House Un-American Activities Committee about his presumed communist beliefs. His uncle told them to "go to hell," after which he lost his friends, his job, and eventually his life. Peter calls Ted brave, but Reed says,

> You're missing the point, Peter. He was wrong. Whether HUAC was right or wrong wasn't the point. It was the law. Take away the law, and what are we? Savages. Up to our necks in blood. The law is the law, Peter. I support it because I honestly believe we have to support it, no matter what.[26]

Here, we see Reed's pragmatic argument for obeying the law: even if individual laws may be wrong, citizens are obligated to obey them because the institution of law in general is essential to maintaining order.[27]

Sue takes a more principled approach to the obligation to obey the law. Returning to where we left off in the Richards–Storm debates, Sue tells Reed that "sometimes the law is wrong. Sometimes the government is wrong. When that happens, you have to stand up and speak out. Even if you're alone. Especially if you're alone."[28] A person can believe in the value and importance of the law in general while opposing particular laws that seem wrong or unjust. This is the spirit of *civil disobedience*, about which Dr. Martin Luther King, Jr., wrote so eloquently in his 1963 "Letter from Birmingham Jail," citing another prominent figure in the natural law tradition:

> One may well ask: "How can you advocate breaking some laws and obeying others?" The answer lies in the fact that there are two types of laws: just and unjust. I would be the first to advocate obeying just laws. One has not only a legal but a moral responsibility to obey just laws. Conversely, one has a moral responsibility to disobey unjust laws. I would agree with St. Augustine that "an unjust law is no law at all."[29]

In this view, tolerating unjust laws does not respect the law overall, which is compromised by their existence and can only be improved by the people's resistance or refusal to follow them. Above, Reed recommended going through official channels to change laws Sue disagrees with, but protesting bad laws by refusing to comply with them is another way to effect change (especially by those with little contact with or access to the workings of governance).

At one point Reed becomes flustered and shouts, "Can't you understand, Sue? I'm doing this because I'm trying to protect you!" Sue reacts by forming a forcefield column around her that extends through the floors of the Baxter Building, above into the sky and below them into the ground, asking him, "Do I look like I need protecting, Reed? Do I?" Rather than wondering how to protect her, she tells Reed to ask himself, "What are the rights and freedoms we say we cherish worth? Because I think they're worth dying for if necessary."[30] With that statement, and their subsequent split, Sue draws a bold line between her principled, deontological position, and Reed's pragmatic, utilitarian one.

But these arguments have an effect on Reed. Just before the confrontation with Sue, Reed was busy designing containment fields customized for the abilities of each captured unregistered hero, during which he thinks to himself,

> I look at the numbers. I look *only* at the numbers. The figures. The readouts. I don't think about the result. About the person in the containment tube about to be interred in a Negative Zone prison. I think only about the numbers. And I realize—maybe that's what I've always done.

After Sue leaves, he starts computing the estimated costs of repairing the Baxter Building, thinking to himself again, "Just think about the numbers. Don't think about the rest. You can't."[31] Slowly, Reed seems to realize that, as important as utilitarian considerations are, they cannot be considered in isolation from other ethical aspects of a situation. To protect himself from the full implications of this realization—a goal that fails once he starts to argue with Sue—he tries to keep his focus on the numbers, which represent the additional good done or the increased probability of success, rather than what he is doing in their pursuit.

Do the Ends Justify Reed?

Speaking of what Reed is doing, there are several significant and questionable actions he takes during the Civil War as a means to the end of supporting registration. One is helping to create a cloned version of Thor (who at the time was presumed dead after the latest Ragnarok event), who subsequently went berserk and killed Bill Foster, the scientist and hero known at various times as (Black) Goliath and Giant-Man.[32] Another is using the Thunderbolts, a team of supervillains, to help track down and arrest unregistered heroes. Reed tells the Wasp (an Avenger on the pro-registration side) that, "after what just went down" with the cloned Thor, "it's the only course of action we've got left." He justifies this by explaining the measures they've taken to control the villains, including having them "chipped and tagged, their every movement monitored by microscopic nanobots," which only signal how far they'll go to prevail.[33]

But the act with which he is most directly involved is the creation of the Negative Zone prison mentioned above. It wasn't a new idea: some time earlier, Reed conceived of an escape-proof prison in the dangerous antimatter dimension to house superpowered convicts.[34] After registration is made law, the Negative Zone prison is the project labeled "42" that he keeps secret from Sue—apparently even he knew she would disagree with it. It only makes matters worse that Reed endorses the detention of unregistered heroes there, outside of United States law and without legal procedure.[35] No less a morally questionable figure than Doctor Doom himself criticizes Reed for having "built and maintained secret prisons" and "contributed to the dissolution of your country's *habeus corpus*," the right to appeal one's detention, which was denied to unregistered heroes held in the Negative Zone.[36]

As time goes on, Reed continues to question what he's doing. As they stand by while Daredevil, one of their oldest friends and allies, is handcuffed and loaded into a transport bound for the Negative Zone, Reed expresses his doubts to his former teammate She-Hulk. Even though crime is down and public sentiment is on their side, he reconsiders their choices regarding the cloned Thor and the Thunderbolts. Without explicitly endorsing those actions, She-Hulk reminds him of the good they've done over all, restoring faith in superheroes and preventing a stricter regulation if they had all resisted, concluding that "you guys gave us all a future."[37]

Reed is in a similarly reflective mood when he meets Johnny for coffee, admitting to a mistake with the cloned Thor but otherwise standing behind that they've done. When he makes the same "we have to follow the law even if we think it's wrong" argument that he previously made to Sue, Johnny dismisses it by asking, "Since when? You don't even obey the laws of physics." Then he gets serious and reminds Reed that they stole the spaceship to go on their fateful trip, and "the FF overthrows an extraterrestrial government three times a year. We've deposed evil warlords, defied gods. Now all of a sudden we turn on our friends because of a bad law?" Reed cites the power superheroes wield and the fear that inspires in the public and says the law is necessary, to which Johnny says the magic words (at least in philosophy): "and the ends justify the means?" Reed answers, "only 1.396% of the time. And this is one of those rare occasions."[38]

At least Reed acknowledges that there is a problem with pursuing utilitarian goals, no matter how valid and worthy, with no thought to deontological constraints based on principle. His laughable numerical estimate—to three decimal places, no less—would delight the person who finally drives home the Faustian bargain Reed has made. After his "Cup o' Joe with Johnny"—podcast coming soon—Reed invites the Mad Thinker, one of the Fantastic Four's frequent foes and a genius nearly on his own level, to check his math. Reed explains that he was inspired by science fiction author Issac Asimov's idea of *psychohistory*, a fictional mathematical theory of history that models mass human behavior, to create such a tool for real ("the first entirely new field I ever created").[39] He used it to confirm Tony Stark's predictions about registration and the conflict between the heroes, and found the only way to prevent even worse outcomes was to engage in the "many distasteful acts" they performed. The Mad Thinker echoes the language of moral dilemmas when he says, "so you chose the lesser of two evils," but Reed corrects him:

"the lesser of thirty-one evils, each more horrible than the next...It was the only possible choice. In the other scenarios, mankind does not survive."

Hearing all of this, the Mad Thinker confirms Reed's calculations, agreeing that every step of the plan was necessary and yet so much can go wrong if not managed perfectly. Then he turns to Reed himself and invokes the "dirty hands" aspect of such inescapable moral dilemmas: "So brilliant, yet so naïve. You thought you could make these moves without personal cost, without doing evil yourself?" He says Tony could never have understood Reed's math, "but he does have the gut instincts of a futurist and the political sense to know that his actions would make him reviled among his former friends in the super hero community." Tony accepted this, the Mad Thinker says, and "few outside of this room will ever understand the sacrifice he's made. Even if he wins." He describes Reed, on the other hand, as "understanding every intricacy of the big picture, while blindly walking further and further down the path of evil," then quotes from Mark 8:36 in the King James Bible: "for what shall it profit a man, if he shall gain the whole world, and lose his own soul?"

As if on cue, Sue suddenly fades into view next to Reed and the Mad Thinker, saying to her husband, "so it's not the law, or your poor, persecuted uncle," citing the rationales for his behavior he gave to her and others. He reiterates that it was all meant to protect her and their children, saying "I'm going to do whatever it takes it save their lives." (Compare this to what he says to Captain America later, during an Illuminati meeting about the incursions: "You seem surprised that I would be willing to sacrifice myself for my family."[40]) Sue walks away, saying "we've beaten the odds before. Just by doing the right thing. I'm with Captain America. We're going to beat the odds again," to which Reed simply responds: "No. Don't you see? You're not."

Reed was right: The Civil War comes to an end during the final climactic battle between the two sides when Captain America surveys the damage they're all doing to New York City and stands down, telling his fellow anti-registration heroes to do the same.[41] Afterwards, Reed writes Sue a letter, celebrating the successes of the registration movement—including public approval of the Negative Zone prison—while regretting what they had to do it to achieve it. He promises her, "no more traps. No more clones. None of those painful things we had to do on that path to respectability," and asks her to come home, which she does.[42]

But things are not the same going forward. As they talk in the Fantasticar high in the clouds, Sue remembers how she fell in love with him based on all his fine qualities, some of them virtues: "Tall. Handsome. Brilliant. Curious. Adventurous. And good. So good." She remembers how deontological he could also be: "you cared about what was right. You helped anyone who needed it. You'd go anywhere, risk anything to make things right." She explains that, before all of this, "I thought you could do no wrong. Now I know better. I still love you, Reed. But it won't ever be the same…"[43] They take some time off from the team, nominating Black Panther and Storm to replace them, and then vacation on Saturn's moon Titan. There, Sue asks when he's going to tell her the rest of his plan to save the world, now that the immediate crisis has passed. He says he sees a way to "guide things now, not simply to avert destruction, but to create good." When she accuses him of sounding like Doctor Doom, he assures her that when he figures everything out, "I'll present a course of action to you and the others. We'll decide what to do together, as a family. If any of us don't agree, none of us will go forward. That's a promise. No more secrets. No more deception."[44]

Reed sets a high bar for himself—one he fails to clear on several occasions after this—but at least Sue believes in him again, even more cautiously. Soon afterwards, a future version of Doom who was extremely

144

critical of Reed's actions during the Civil War calls her naïve for continuing to trust him. She denies any naïveté, explaining that she knows Reed as well as she knows herself, and even though "recent events have…forced me to confront weaknesses of his that I preferred not to dwell on," she is confident she knows "both how far he'll go and exactly where he draws the line."[45] If she does know these things, and if he does acknowledge a line he cannot cross, it is precisely because she does serve as his moral compass—one that has now been sorely tested.

What About Ben?

Although the focus of the Fantastic Four's ideological debate during the Civil War was between Sue and Reed—just like if Captain America and Iron Man were married—Ben struggled with the moral dilemma mostly by himself. (Johnny was in the hospital for much of the crisis, and when he was feeling better he joined Sue on the anti-registration side.)

Ben sets himself apart from most of his fellow heroes by refusing to take a side in the conflict. While the family visit Johnny in the hospital, Ben tries to keep Reed and Sue calm for Johnny's sake, and when Reed asks Ben to help him round up unregistered heroes, Sue says he's not interested. Reed says that, because Ben's identity is public, he has no reason to resist, but Ben disagrees, pointing out that "I'm still an American. I have as much at stake if this country tears itself apart as anybody else. So I think—I think you both better get outta here and cool off before somebody says somethin' that can't be unsaid."[46] Note that Ben's first statement regarding the conflict is about the disruptive nature of it rather than the right or wrong of either side, a point he raises throughout the crisis.

Sue and Reed eventually leave separately, and Ben spends an hour keeping Johnny company. When Sue returns by herself to talk to Ben, he asks her, "we're not gonna get in a fight, are we?" Sue asserts that they should not be rounding up unregistered heroes, and without disputing this point Ben asks, "Then what do you think we should do doing, Sue? You wanna take up arms against our own government?" She argues that "disagreement isn't disloyalty, Ben. Sometimes the most patriotic thing you can do in a democracy is disagree."[47] Here, Sue invokes historian Howard Zinn's famous statement that "dissent is the highest form of patriotism," in which patriotism is understood as supporting the principles your country stands for rather than its government, policies, or laws at any particular time—especially if they betray those very principles.[48] However, Ben is not disputing the right to dissent—his concern is with violating the law itself, an act of civil disobedience Sue and the rest of anti-registration heroes embrace, but about which he is less certain.

While leaving Johnny's room Ben sees a television news report about an incident on Yancy Street involving his old gang harassing reporters. When he arrives there, Carol Danvers (who was Ms. Marvel at the time) asks him to help her apprehend Silverclaw, a former Avenger who refuses to register, but he ignores her. Next, the police tell him that the Yancy Street Gang is interfering with their efforts to arrest unregistered heroes, and ask him to speak with them. "Right," he says. "Good thing they always listen to what I say." After Ben calls out the gang, he debates the current situation with Cee, their leader, who asks, "What's up? Thought you'd be happy we're taking on the fascists." Ben pokes fun at him for learning a new word, but Cee presses him on what the pro-registration forces are doing, saying "even you gotta see this is wrong, right?"[49]

Ben refuses to commit immediately to whether it's right or wrong, admitting only that "I'm thinkin' about it." This is admirable in its own way: he acknowledges that there are valid arguments to be made on both sides, regardless of the actions taken in support of them, and he doesn't want to settle on a position until he's deliberated on it sufficiently. While we often see heroes struggling with moral dilemmas, talking them through either with themselves, fellow heroes, or civilian friends, we rarely see one admit, in the meantime, that they haven't yet made up their mind.

However, it doesn't take Ben long to make a declarative statement, and it sums up the position he states later to several people:

> Look, as a concept, do I think it's wrong? Yeah. But it's the law. There's lots of laws I don't like. That's life. I'm not big on the idea of fighting my own government. On the other hand—'cause I do think the law's wrong even though I won't fight it doesn't mean I support it. Doesn't mean I'm gonna help round up the guys who do want to fight it.[50]

Aside from his antipathy about conflict itself, his answer captures most of the important aspects of Ben's thinking: He opposes registration on principle, as well as the law mandating it, and while he doesn't want to violate the law directly, he won't help anybody trying to enforce it either. In this way he stands between Reed's belief "the law is the law" and Sue's position of civil disobedience.

But Cee calls this uncomfortable middle ground out. "Look, Grimm—just 'cause you're as big as Switzerland doesn't mean you *are* Switzerland. You can't stick around and be neutral. You gotta take a stand here. Same as us." Ben points out they'll get arrested if they continue to interfere with the police, and probably even get hurt, both of which Cee acknowledges before saying, "We don't have powers, we're not gonna take down Galactus tomorrow, but we gotta stand up for what's right, y'know?"[51] In this they agree with Sue, going farther than mere dissent and actively resisting, engaging in civil disobedience in response to a law they consider unjust. Ben asserts on several occasions that he is a patriot and therefore cannot fight his government, but this again conflates his government and its actions in one particular case with the country in general and the principles it (generally) stands for. If he truly believes the registration act is wrong, it isn't enough to refuse to support it, which is passive resistance at best and plain acquiescence at worst.

Later, a battle breaks out between the two groups of heroes, with the Yancy Street Gang, manipulated by the Puppet-Master, in the middle, and Cee is killed. Before the sides can start fighting again, Ben throws a prison transport vehicle between them and steps forward, holding Cee's body in his arms. "Look," he tells his friends. "Look at what your freakin' war has done. He was just a kid! I barely knew him. But he had parents, he had a life, he had a future…and you took all of that away from him!" Growing angrier, he yells, "Don't you see what you're doing? Don't you see that you're tearing apart everything that makes this place worth fighting for? Look around! Take a long freaking look around!"[52] He is asking his friends and colleagues to put their ideological differences aside and consider the costs of their war, which is hurting the very people and communities they're dedicated to protecting.

Missing the point completely, Captain America and Iron Man both ask Ben to fight for their respective sides. Daredevil (on the anti-registration side) tells Ben he can make a difference and the whole world is watching, so "what're you going to do? What do you say?" Ben says, "ta hell with both of you." He gives them an explanation that builds on what he told Cee, more definitive this time around and ending with a final decision:

> I've been thinking about this fer a long time, but this has made up
> my mind for me. Registration's wrong, and I won't support a law
> I don't believe in. But I'm still a patriot, I'm not gonna fight my
> own government, or let the government say I'm a criminal. So the

way I see it, that leaves me only one choice. I'm checking outta the country. Don't bother leavin' a light on. I may not come back.[53]

He elaborates further on his decision to leave when he tells Reed about it, repeating much of what he said above (including the bit about being a patriot and therefore refusing to "fight my own government") and adding: "Thing is, if I stay here, if I stay silent, then it's as good as saying I condone what they're doing. I hafta make some kind of statement. So I'm goin'."[54]

By leaving the country—for Paris, like the expatriates of old he read about as a kid—Ben feels he is avoiding the feeling of acquiescence and engaging in his own kind of protest, albeit a passive one. This is not enough to satisfy Sue, or Cap, or even Cee, but it is the only way Ben can reconcile his conflicting ideals—and avoid fighting his friends, which may be the desire underlying much of Ben's behavior through this episode. We see this when Ben gets to France and meets "Les Heroes de Paris," who fight ordinary supervillains—with Ben proclaiming "*it est temps de battre!*"—followed by a relaxing meal, conversation, and laughter. When they ask why Ben is tearing up, he replies "I'm okay, it's just…it's just like the old days, back when there weren't all these stupid conspiracies and you knew who the good guys were, and the bad guys, and there wasn't this…this…freaking civil war!"[55]

When Johnny visits to asks Ben to come back, saying vaguely that "we need you," Ben simply says he'll think about it.[56] But during the climactic battle between the two sides in the Civil War, Sue is surprised to see Ben, who says "ya really think I wuz gonna sit this one out eatin' croissants? Get your act together, Suzie! We got people ta protect!"[57] We don't know exactly why he decided to return, but protecting people from the fallout of the battle, rather than to support or oppose registration, seems plausible. As we recounted earlier, Captain America eventually stands down for just this reason, and when Johnny says afterwards that he "never

149

thought I'd see the day when Cap would quit a fight," Ben says, "If you think he quit, you don't know him at all."[58]

Ben also may have decided to come home because he needed his family. As much as he is upset by how registration tore the hero community and the country apart, he is more deeply affected by what it is did to the Fantastic Four personally, driving a wedge between Reed and Sue as well as between each of them and Ben. We discussed in chapter 5 how Ben has a different perspective on the Fantastic Four as a family because he is only one of the original four who is not related by blood or marriage, and sometimes feels they only keep him around out of pity.[59] Because of this, he has a unique reason to fear the break-up of the team: the others will likely stay in touch because they're a "real" family, but he can't be sure where this will leave him. No one needs his family more than the man who sees himself as a "monster"—even when that monster ends up being the most powerful voice against fighting and violence through this entire episode, which remains to this day the most morally substantial event in Marvel Comics history.[60]

[1] *Fantastic Four*, vol. 1, #141 (December 1973).

[2] The second superhero Civil War, which started appropriately enough in *Civil War II* #1 (August 2016) and had nothing to do thematically with the first, occurred when Reed, Sue, and the kids were rebuilding the multiverse following the second Secret Wars event, and Ben and Johnny were only marginally involved.

[3] For more on the issues facing Cap, Iron Man, and Spidey, see my book *A Philosopher Reads Marvel Comics'* Civil War: *Exploring the Moral Judgment of Captain America, Iron Man, and Spider-Man* (Ockham Publishing, 2016).

[4] *Fantastic Four*, vol. 1, #334 (December 1989).

[5] From his "General Defense of the Constitution," a speech delivered on June 6, 1788, which can be read at https://founders.archives.gov/documents/Madison/01-11-02-0062.

[6] *Fantastic Four*, vol. 1, #335 (December 1989). If you remember this as Spock's famous dying words from the 1982 film *Star Trek II: The Wrath of Khan*, you're not alone: Ben points this out too. (There's a big difference here, though: Spock used these words to explain *his own* noble sacrifice, not a sacrifice he was forcing others to make on his behalf.)

[7] Ibid.

[8] *Fantastic Four*, vol. 1, #336 (January 1990).

[9] Gyrich's illustrious tenure began in *Avengers*, vol. 1, #168 (February 1978), and the hearing began in vol. 1, #190 (December 1979). And don't get me started on his part in replacing Steve Rogers with John Walker as Captain America (as seen in *Captain America*, vol. 1, #333, September 1987).

[10] *Fantastic Four*, vol. 1, #336.

[11] Ibid.

[12] *Civil War* #1 (July 2006).

[13] *New Avengers: Illuminati*, vol. 1, #1 (May 2006). As it happens, immediately after the Illuminati meeting, Tony appears before Congress, with Peter Parker at his side, to argue against registration while he could. He made many of the same arguments Reed made at the Fantastic Four's hearing, including citing "forty-seven occasions on which super heroes prevented the entire North American continent from being vaporized, conquered or nuked back to the Stone Age" (*Amazing Spider-Man*, vol. 2, #530, May 2006).

[14] *New Avengers: Illuminati*, vol. 1, #1.

[15] *Fantastic Four*, vol. 3, #536 (May 2006).

[16] *Civil War* #1. Sue apparently forgot about her children, who are often in danger due to their public status, as mentioned in chapter 2.

[17] *Civil War* #2 (August 2006).

[18] *Fantastic Four*, vol. 3, #543 (May 2007), "C'mon, Suzie, Don't Leave Us Hangin'."

[19] *Civil War* #3 (September 2006).

[20] *Amazing Spider-Man*, vol. 2, #533 (August 2006), after the unmasking at the end of *Civil War* #2.

[21] *Fantastic Four*, vol. 3, #538 (August 2006).

[22] *Fantastic Four*, vol. 3, #540 (December 2006). She actually refers to "your fascistic plans" in a letter informing Reed that she's leaving him and joining Captain America's side to fight registration (*Civil War* #4, October 2006).

[23] *Fantastic Four*, vol. 3, #540.

[24] For Hart's legal positivism in general, see his book *The Concept of Law* (Oxford: Clarendon Press, 1961).

[25] Fuller's version of natural law, focusing on what he called the *inner morality of law*, appeared in his book *The Morality of Law* (New Haven, CT: Yale University Press, 1965). For more on the debate between him and Hart, see Peter Cane, *The Hart-Fuller Debate in the Twenty-First Century* (Oxford: Hart Publishing, 2010).

[26] *Fantastic Four*, vol. 3, #540; this exchange also appears in *Amazing Spider-Man*, vol. 2, #535 (November 2006), also written by J. Michael Straczynski.

[27] There is a massive philosophical literature debating the obligation to obey the law, and Reed's argument is just one of those supporting such an obligation. On this debate, see Massimo Renzo and Leslie Green, "Legal Obligation and Authority," in Edward N. Zalta and Uri Nodelman (eds.), *The Stanford Encyclopedia of Philosophy* (Spring 2025 Edition), at https://plato.stanford.edu/archives/spr2025/entries/legal-obligation/.

[28] *Fantastic Four*, vol. 3, #540. This also resembles Captain America's famous answer to Spider-Man's question about how he manages to maintain his principles in the face of widespread opposition: "Doesn't matter what the press says. Doesn't matter what the politicians or the mobs say. Doesn't matter if the whole country decides that something wrong is something right. This nation was founded on one principle above all else: the requirement that we stand up for what we believe, no

matter the odds or the consequences. When the mob and the press and the whole world tell you to move, your job is to plant yourself like a tree beside the river of truth, and tell the whole world—'no, *you* move'" (*Amazing Spider-Man*, vol. 2, #537, February 2007).

[29] Dr. King's letter is available at https://www.africa.upenn.edu/Articles_Gen/Letter_Birmingham.html.

[30] *Fantastic Four*, vol. 3, #540.

[31] Ibid.

[32] *Civil War* #4. (Ben was particularly close to Foster, who appeared in many issues of *Marvel Two-in-One*.)

[33] Ibid.

[34] *Fantastic Four: Foes* #2 (April 2005).

[35] This was a clear analogue to Guantanamo Bay, where the United States held terror suspects after the September 11 attacks; indeed, the entire "Civil War" storyline was a metaphor for post-September 11 law in the United States, such as the PATRIOT Act, which critics argued went too far in allowing government surveillance and curtailing civil liberties in the name of fighting terrorism. For more on these parallels, see several of the chapters in Kevin Michael Scott (ed.), *Marvel Comics'* Civil War *and the Age of Terror: Critical Essays on the Comic Saga* (Jefferson, NC: McFarland & Company, 2015).

[36] *Fantastic Four*, vol. 3, #543, "C'mon, Suzie, Don't Leave Us Hangin'."

[37] *Civil War* #4. By the way, that isn't Matt Murdock in the red union suit but Danny Rand, the Immortal Iron Fist, who posed as Daredevil during the Civil War because Matt had to go to jail. (It's a long story—see *Civil War: Choosing Sides* #1, December 2006, "Choosing Sides.")

[38] *Fantastic Four*, vol. 3, #542 (March 2007).

[39] *Fantastic Four*, vol. 3, #542 (where the rest of Reed's conversion with the Mad Thinker is from). Psychohistory was introduced by Asimov in *Foundation* (New York: Del Rey, 1951), the first novel in the legendary *Foundation* series.

[40] *New Avengers*, vol. 3, #3 (April 2013).

[41] *Civil War* #7 (January 2007).

[42] Ibid.

[43] *Fantastic Four*, vol. 3, #543, "C'mon, Suzie, Don't Leave Us Hangin'."

[44] *Fantastic Four*, vol. 3, #546 (July 2007).

45 *Fantastic Four*, vol. 3, #553 (March 2008).

46 *Fantastic Four*, vol. 3, #538.

47 Ibid.

48 For more on Zinn's thinking, see https://www.howardzinn.org/collection/dissent-in-pursuit-of-equality-life-liberty-and-happiness/. Captain America exemplifies this view, as seen in chapter 7 of my book *The Virtues of Captain America: Modern-Day Lessons on Character from a World War II Superhero*, 2nd ed. (Hoboken, NJ: Wiley & Sons, 2024).

49 *Fantastic Four*, vol. 3, #538.

50 Ibid. However, in *Civil War* #3, we do see Ben helping Tony and his allies round up unregistered heroes, with Ben taking down the Young Avenger named Hulkling while asking, "I don't wanna fight you guys, Hulkling! Why can't you just do like you're told, huh?" This momentary cooperation is never explained, but it does reflect Ben's resentment at having to fight his friends, as well as his general support for following the law.

51 *Fantastic Four*, vol. 3, #538.

52 *Fantastic Four*, vol. 3, #539 (October 2006).

53 Ibid.

54 *Fantastic Four*, vol. 3, #540.

55 *Fantastic Four*, vol. 3, #541 (February 2007).

56 *Fantastic Four*, vol. 3, #542.

57 *Civil War* #7.

58 *Fantastic Four*, vol. 3, #543, "C'mon, Suzie, Don't Leave Us Hangin'."

59 *Spider-Man/Fantastic Four* #4 (December 2010).

60 As of this writing, the "One World Under Doom" event has just begun, but based on the early issues—*One World Under Doom* #1 and *Fantastic Four*, vol. 7, #29, both April 2025—it looks like "Civil War" may have a challenger in this regard.

Chapter 7

Galactus and the Silver Surfer

Of all the threats the Fantastic Four has encountered in their long history, none looms larger—literally—than Galactus, the Devourer of Worlds. Ever since he first arrived on Earth in 1966's *Fantastic Four* #48, Galactus has been a unique presence in the Four's world as well as the Marvel Universe as a whole. Although he represents an existential threat to everyone on the planet—not to mention all planets in the universe— he is not just another nefarious supervillain the team has to defeat every couple of years. As Reed himself once told him, "I have never thought of you as an enemy—not as evil!"[1]

What exactly is Galactus, then? We know *who* he is: Galan, the last survivor of the previous universe, who survived its collapse to be reborn alongside the new universe as Galactus during the Big Bang.[2] But this doesn't tell us *what* Galactus is. Is he a necessary, elemental force of nature, as he is often described—and if so, what does this mean? More important, what does this imply about his status as a moral agent responsible for his choices and actions? We'll see in this chapter that the evidence in the comics is ambiguous at best and confusing at worst, but a more coherent picture presents itself during an intergalactic criminal trial—one at which Galactus is not the defendant.

Also, how can we talk about Galactus without turning an eye to his long-serving herald, the Silver Surfer, who eventually rejects his master's purpose and his authority? How complicit is he in Galactus's actions and how much responsibility does he share for them (if any)? Finally, what role does Alicia Masters play in the Silver Surfer's life and the search for his dormant humanity?

Is Galactus "Above Morality"?

When Galactus makes his first visit to Earth, preceded by his herald the Silver Surfer, it is Uatu the Watcher who explains his mission and nature to the Fantastic Four: "Galactus, who drains entire planets of their elements, and then leaves them dry, unable to support life!"[3] Galactus is more accurately described as getting his sustenance by draining a world's energy, which is more plentiful on planets teeming with life, especially those with developed societies—hence his threat to living beings throughout the universe. As he tells Uatu himself in the next issue while defending his plans for Earth, "This planet contains the energy I need to sustain me! I shall absorb it at will…as I have done for ages, in countless galaxies across the cosmos!" Uatu pleads the case for Earth's inhabitants, but Galactus says "that can be of no concern…to Galactus!"[4] (Galactus has a habit of speaking in the third person, much like the Latverian dictator we will turn to in the next chapter.)

It is notable that Galactus says the loss of life "cannot," rather than "does not," concern him. Although this may just be a reflection of his hunger that must be sated, it may also indicate his relationship to ethical concerns in general. We see this after the Silver Surfer meets Alicia Masters and learns about beauty, compassion, and the nobility of humankind, and he is inspired by this new knowledge to confront his master. As he watches, Uatu wonders, "How can the silver one convince his master? Galactus is not evil! He is above good…or evil! He does what he must…for he is Galactus!"[5]

156

The idea that Galactus is "above" or separate from the demands of morality is reiterated many times in the comics, including most times the team encounters him. At various times, Galactus himself proclaims that "Galactus is beyond mere moral concepts" and "Galactus is above mere morality.... Galactus is amoral."[6] Another time, he claims that "evil is a concept I cannot even comprehend, except with great difficulty," which, given his inestimable intellect, implies that good and evil, and perhaps morality in general, are alien to him on a conceptual level. This could explain why, when Reed argues for the value of the lives that Galactus will end, the Devourer responds that "argument is useless, Earthling. Our points of view are too totally different."[7] Galactus may simply lack the moral vocabulary or mental architecture necessary to discuss, or even think about, good and evil or right and wrong.

However, Galactus demonstrates on many occasions that he is capable of moral sentiments, hardly the sign of someone who cannot even comprehend ethical concepts. Despite his protestations that he "cannot" feel concern for the lives he ends, or that "emotion is for lesser beings," he expresses regret when, during his first visit to Earth, he explains to Uatu that "it is not my intention to injure any living being! But...I must replenish my energy! If petty creatures are wiped out when I drain a planet, it is regrettable...but unavoidable!"[8] When the Silver Surfer later rebels and Galactus considers killing him, he says, "I regret what I must do! For, of all who live, I have cherished you the most!"[9]

Galactus also finds it in himself to admire the courage and nobility of human beings, which reflects an appreciation, if not necessarily an embrace, of moral virtue. Despite occasionally dismissing humans as "so small—so weak—their lives so brief," and asking himself, "why do they so desperately cling to their brief moments on Earth?", when the Fantastic Four stand up to him on Earth, and Uatu and the Silver Surfer argue the merits of humanity, Galactus concedes that "at last I perceive the

157

glint of glory within the race of man!"[10] Perhaps due to his repeated encounters with the best humanity has to offer, Galactus starts to feel enough regret over his actions to pain him, saying at one point that "my deeds weigh upon me, and so does my very sanity totter upon a razor's edge."[11]

In one long and eloquent response to one of Reed's appeals on behalf of humanity, Galactus suggests that he naturally feels compassion, but has to suppress such thoughts to do what he must to survive:

> Speak to me not of humanity, Reed Richards! You talk of color to one struck blind. My humanity is lost in the swirling mists of time. Yes, once even Galactus was a man, a mere mortal such as you, though memories of that life are but a dim and dying pain within my heart. The past is done and gone, and mourn it though we may it cannot be retrieved. So do not speak to me of four billion lives. Galactus has seen the end of forty times four billion worlds! Must we know grief for each of these? Had he but tears to cry, Galactus would weep oceans in their memory, and in the end they would still be dead, and madness would at last have claimed me. So do I turn my thoughts ever from that path, for one foot set upon it…and is a journey thus begun, from which no creature ever could return.[12]

Afterwards, Doctor Strange uses the Images of Ikonn (as you do) to confront Galactus with the ghosts of the untold trillions he has killed. When Galactus passes out and collapses, Reed pronounces that "his mind must have closed completely to escape madness!"[13]

If Galactus is capable of comprehending and appreciating ethical concepts such as regret and compassion, might there be something about his very nature that prevents him from *acting* according to moral imperatives? One clue is that, whenever anyone proclaims that Galactus is not bound by ethics, they often follow it by saying he has no choice in what he does. After he proclaims that he is "above mere morality" and "amoral," he goes on to say that "Galactus does what he must do in order to survive!"[14] Uatu recognizes this too: as he said above, "He does what he must…for he is Galactus!"[15]

Galactus also ties his lack of choice to his fate or destiny, such as when he tells the Fantastic Four that, after searching in vain for alternative sources of energy that did not involve ending so many lives, "so I have gone forward, doing that which a merciless fate has decreed I do." Later in the same issue, he tells Reed that "it is my destiny to devour worlds. Being Galactus, I cannot do otherwise." Even Reed agrees: When an alien named Gorr calls Galactus an "inhuman monster," Reed says that he is "more like an elemental force, Gorr—an earthquake or a tidal wave, smashing all in its path, with neither ill will nor compassion."[16]

What does it mean to say Galactus has no choice? Sometimes he makes himself sound like an animal or beast, creatures who lack the necessary rational faculties to be held morally responsible for their choices. For example, he tells the High Evolutionary, who begs him to spare his world of Counter-Earth, "I hunger. And when I hunger…I feed," no different from a wild animal.[17] We saw above that he references the survival instinct, which he also cites when he explains how his regret tortures him: "Galactus does what Galactus must to survive. Still my deeds weigh upon me, and so does my very sanity totter upon a razor's edge."[18] Even Captain America, in arguing for Galactus's life when the heroes have a chance to simply let him die, argues that "Galactus is a living, sentient being. And he does not act out of evil intent. He does what he must, simply to survive, just as we would."[19]

Galactus himself makes a similar argument when he explains that he has been focusing on worlds in which life has just begun, before it has developed to the point where its inhabitants have become self-aware. He challenges Reed and the rest of the team to disagree:

Nor should any of you judge me, as I sense you do…For, most beings are fortunate enough never to have to face the unpleasant, numbing truth about themselves: That, given the choice between survival and extinction…most would do precisely the same as I! But, that is something which few will believe—till they have stood face to face with themselves, and blanched with horror at what they see.[20]

This statement—again, quite an eloquent one—makes clear Galactus's own dilemma in which his hunger and fear of death force him to kill others, even as he tries to minimize the impact of satisfying his tremendous needs. In fact, he made a similar argument in much simpler terms when he first came to Earth, asking the Silver Surfer, "Do not the humans themselves slay the lesser beasts for food…for sustenance? Galactus does no less!"[21]

However, the fact that Galactus *can* try to steer his hunger away from planets with more developed societies means that he *does* have choice in how he satisfies it and fulfills his "destiny." Although he must eat—as must we all—he can choose to do it in more ethical ways, just like those of us who choose not to eat food from certain sources or farmed in certain ways.[22] So, his claims that survival or destiny prevent him from making choices and therefore set him above morality are hollow—as demonstrated most obviously by his repeated decisions to spare the Earth as he searches the universe for sustenance.

This choice provides even more evidence that Galactus has the capacity to make moral decisions regarding his hunger—in this case, to make promises and stand by them, even when they stand in the way of the feeding which is necessary for survival (or fulfilling his destiny). Holding yourself to promises is a basic ethical act in terms of all three major schools of ethics, and keeping your word even when it is in your interests to break it is a clear signal that you are an ethical or good person.[23]

At the end of their first encounter, when Reed threatens Galactus with the all-powerful Ultimate Nullifier—which Uatu sent Johnny to "borrow" from Galactus's ship—Galactus acknowledges the courage of humanity and demands "the human surrender his weapon, and I shall tarry here no longer." In case Reed were tempted to hesitate, Uatu urges him on: "Do as he says, mortal! The promise of Galactus is living truth itself! His word can never be questioned!"[24] This is an odd thing to say about someone who is "above morality" and acts "only as he must to survive," and shows that Galactus is not only capable of experiencing moral sentiments but acting on them as well.

Galactus continues to make deals with Reed, even in the same issue in which he proclaims he is "beyond moral concepts" and Reed admits that "Galactus gives no guarantees."[25] Later, Galactus tells Reed that "Galactus's word is Galactus's bond," adding dramatically that "when a being must roam the starways alone, for all time…what else has he?"[26] The richness of his moral sense is on display after Frankie Raye, Johnny's girlfriend at the time, agrees to become his new herald in exchange for sparing the Earth. As he explains,

> True also was my vow, my pact with her. The woman is my herald and so shall Earth remain inviolate. Yet, perhaps there is another reason I stay my hand. A deeper, truer reason. Perhaps it is because you risked all to save me, when it would have been easy to do otherwise. Perhaps Galactus has learned an important truth this day. Earth shall never more need fear me…for perhaps here, on this tiny whirling note alone in all the cosmos has Galactus truly found those he might dare name…friends.[27]

Besides the principle of keeping his word, and the acknowledgment and admiration of the Fantastic Four, Galactus also reveals that he values friends—not in a transactional way, but in the perfect sense that Aristotle wrote about, a coming together of equals who respect each other's good character.[28] Again, this is not something that someone who is "above morality" would feel or say!

The Purpose of Devouring

We get the most complete answer to *what* Galactus is when Reed Richards is put on trial by an assortment of alien beings from across the universe whose worlds perished at the hands of the Devourer. His crime? Saving Galactus's life when he was dying, after which he resumed consuming worlds, including the Skrull Throne-World. Reed admits he saved Galactus's life but argues that it was not wrong to do—not because his was a life deserving of being saved, which he (and Cap) argued at the time, but because Galactus is an essential aspect of the universe that must be allowed to exist, despite the catastrophic devastation he causes. In this sense, the trial focuses less on Reed than Galactus himself, and in the process reveals more about his nature and behavior than ever before.

We get our first glimpse of this just before Galactus consumes the Skrull Throne-World. He is speaking with Death, the living embodiment of…well, death…and asks her if he should die rather than continue killing entire populations of the worlds he devours, based on the compassion he has begun to feel for his victims. Death tells him that "your newfound conscience clouds your reason" and then goes on to explore their partnership as "the shepherds who guide [the cosmos] to its proper purpose. Or, more precisely, it is a tangled garden you and I must ever weed." She makes clear the essential nature of what he does: "Yours is quite possibly the most important role. Do not shirk it, lest the universe fail at the last." Galactus accepts this, conceding: "No more to debate the correctness of what I do. Such terms have little meaning now."[29]

This suggestion of a universal purpose for Galactus to fulfill elaborates on his earlier claims that fate or destiny have doomed him to eternal hunger, giving the concepts meaning as well as moral relevance. The idea that there is purpose to the universe as a whole, as well as our lives as individuals, is central to the philosophical concept known as *teleology*, based on *telos*, the Greek word for a purpose or goal. In terms of ethics, an aspect of teleology can be found within all three approaches we introduced in chapter 1. The *telos* of utilitarianism is clearly the happiness or well-being of all, while the *telos* of deontology could be understood to be justice or "right" (in a general sense). In Aristotle's conception, virtue ethics is based on the goal of *eudaimonia*, his word for a deep, lasting sense of flourishing that transcends the momentary pleasures or satisfaction that some utilitarians focus on.[30]

We can also take a broader teleological point of view to existence as a whole, in which all things have a function that contributes to the purpose or *telos* of the universe itself. This is often associated with a religious worldview, in which events are attributed to God's plan, but not necessarily, such as when people say that an event or coincidence was simply "meant to be." Even so, the question remains of *who* "meant" for these things to "be," whether the answer is a personal deity or an impersonal concept such as nature or the universe itself.[31]

The most powerful beings in the Marvel Universe regard its *telos* in this last sense. As Uatu says before Reed's trial, "Galactus has a purpose. There is an order of things in this universe. One such as he would not be permitted to exist unless he had a place in it."[32] Note that Uatu only says there is "an order" to the universe, not what it is, much less its meaning or purpose. Simply acknowledging that there *is* a purpose to the universe allows him to conclude that Galactus must be important to it, given his continued existence amidst the tremendous suffering he causes.[33]

Reed makes another version of this argument at his trial as part of explaining why saving Galactus's life was not a crime. He starts by recounting what Uatu told them years ago, that Galactus is neither good nor evil, and concluding that he must then be neutral. He then cites the catastrophic effect on life Galactus has throughout the universe and questions how "can any rational man judge that to be neutral?" Here, Reed seems to confuse the effects of Galactus's actions, which cannot be called neutral, to Galactus's own moral status, which is more complicated, given the survival imperative we discussed earlier. If he effectively has no choice, like an animal or beast, or is considered an impersonal force, like "an earthquake or a tidal wave," then morally he could be considered neutral, aside from the devastating effects of his actions.

Nonetheless, Reed proposes an answer to his own question, borrowing a line from another prominent human scientist:

> Albert Einstein once said that "God does not play dice." He meant that there is an order of things in the universe. And it does not require any belief in a supreme being to realize that Galactus must somehow be part of that order—and, I suspect, an important part. For if he is truly to be considered neutral then the apparent evil of his actions, must, in the end result, not be evil. And so, they must be part of some greater good. I cannot believe he would be allowed to exist, if this were not the case.[34]

In response to this, the empress of the Shi'ar Empire, also known as Majestrix, accuses him of "arithmetic," by which she may mean "sophistry" in the sense of making clever yet fallacious arguments that are meant to seem correct if you don't think about them too deeply. (Philosophers are all too well accustomed to this accusation!) When she asks him for proof, Reed says, "Ultimately I have no proof, Majestrix. I have only logic…logic and faith."[35] The reliance of Reed's argument on logic is obvious, but faith is necessary as well—not faith in a deity, necessarily, but in an order or purpose to the universe, which can never be demonstrated or proven scientifically.

Uatu pays Reed a backhanded compliment of sorts when he asks the court to "measure the power of the intellect of his lone Earthman. For he has reasoned order out of chaos. And he reasoned correctly," as confirmed by a sudden visitor to the trial: Odin, the All-Father of Asgard. (Uatu sent Johnny to fetch him, just as he sent him after the Ultimate Nullifer the first time Galactus came to Earth.) Odin recounts Galactus's origin, explaining that "the sentience of the universe" whispered to him as he transitioned from one universe to the next, and continued to expound on his purpose in the new universe:

> Thus was born into the new universe a new natural force. Like the solar wind, like the super-nova…like the roiling seas that tested our Viking worshippers, tested them, and made them strong. Such is the function of Galactus. To each world in time he comes and his very coming is a test. Those that pass the test are strengthened by it, and made more worthy of that great fate which is the promised end of our universe. Those that fail, fail totally, and are forever expunged, wiped from the slate of time and space.[36]

This aligns with Death's comments above that Galactus serves to "weed" the "tangled garden" of the universe, culling worlds that are weak and making the strong ones even more so. At its most basic this is "survival of the fittest" of worlds, an intergalactic version of *social Darwinism*, but missing clarity regarding what makes a world "strong" and allows them to pass "the test"—other than Reed's successful attempts to turn Galactus away from Earth—or why this culling is necessary (and what would happen in its absence).

Having spoken, Odin pronounces Reed innocent of any criminal wrongdoing and calls an end to the trial. Galactus then appears, assuring the frightened attendants that he is no threat and proclaiming his desire to "bring instead justice for that mortal I name friend. Reed Richards is a noble spirit, untainted by the pettiness of fear and hate. His deed was honorable and good."[37] His endorsement likely means little to the gathered survivors of his hunger, but it does serve to affirm his admiration and fellow-feeling for Reed.

Finally, Galactus and Uatu summon Eternity, the embodiment and representation of the universe, who proclaims: "Let the cosmic truth be known!" Suddenly everyone present is mesmerized as Eternity lets them experience Galactus's life as well as that of "the countless billions of the universe gone." He also gives them knowledge of what Reed took on faith:

> through it all they feel an overwhelming sense of purpose, a sure knowledge that there is a destiny to the universe—a grand and glorious destiny. And with it comes a pain of realization—the image of a universe shorn of Galactus, and, as a consequence, that great destiny so suddenly snuffed out. Like a lone candle in a cold night wind. To all mortals present is this cosmic truth made plain.[38]

Everyone present now knows that Galactus plays such an important role in the purpose of the universe that, without him, that universe would perish, although it is still not explained why or how. Galactus is explained simply to be the universe's apex predator, one who causes tremendous pain and death but is essential to the operation and continuation of the ecosystem.

In the end, it is this purpose, goal, or *telos* that is put forward to justify Galactus's actions. He is limited by this purpose in how much compassion he can show for those he consumes, for he still must consume, but he does have some degree of choice in how he fulfills his purpose. As we have seen, to ensure his own survival he must not only consume worlds, but he also has to put out of his mind the suffering he causes by doing so—like soldiers who must kill enemy combatants to serve their country, but cannot think too much about what they're doing, for the sake of their own sanity.[39] Seen this way, Galactus lives a tragic existence, condemned to committing atrocious acts that earn the hatred of the entire universe, all to serve a purpose he did not choose.

The Tragic Choice of the Silver Surfer

No discussion of Galactus would be complete without his favorite herald, the Silver Surfer. He was born Norrin Radd on the world of Zenn-La, home to a society so developed that its people had grown lazy and complacent, among whom Norrin was alone in his desire to learn and explore—and when the Devourer came for Zenn-La, Norrin alone had the initiative and spirit to confront him. When he argues that "you dare not slay an entire race," Galactus responds as we have come to expect: "I have no wish to harm any who exist…But, think you this…If your own life depended on stepping on an ant hill—you would not hesitate!"

Norrin pleads for his own world—and the woman he loves, Shalla-Bal—arguing that there are other worlds with no intelligent life and begging him to "find a world such as that…do with it what you will…for, even ants have a right to life!" Galactus says there is no time, but "had I a herald…to probe the universe for me…then many worlds such as this would I spare!" Norrin offers himself up: "Let me probe the heavens…scan the starways…roam the endless cosmos for you!" Galactus warns that the role will be "forevermore," and Norrin accepts, saying that "my fate is of little consequence…if it can save the world that gave me birth."

"Mighty Galactus," Norrin proclaims, "do but spare Zenn-la…and I am ever yours…to command!" Galactus encloses Norrin's body in "a life-preserving silvery substance of my own creation" that protects him from the extreme conditions of space, gives him "an indestructible flying board…yours to control…with but a single thought," and proclaims that "now, and forevermore…you are truly…the Silver Surfer!"[40]

With this act, Norrin makes a noble sacrifice to save his love and his world, never to see either again (as far as he knows), with the one "silver lining" being that he gains the power to explore the mysteries of the universe (a drive he shares with a certain Earthman with silver only on his temples). But he also strikes a morally questionable bargain, agreeing to find other worlds for Galactus to consume in exchange for sparing *his*. He does promise to seek out worlds "where no intelligent life exists," but why should intelligent life be privileged over nonintelligent life, especially if, as Norrin says, "even ants have a right to life"? On one of his first visits to a candidate world for Galactus, he finds a primitive species and decides "I cannot summon Galactus here, where life abounds! Though they be simple, aimless creatures…they think…they breathe… they feel! This, they must not perish from this land!"[41]

We can easily understand why Norrin would want to save his world at the cost of condemning another; in chapter 1, we saw Reed Richards and the Illuminati struggle with this during the incursions. However, even if hard choices must be made regarding which worlds to save, the choice to grant more value or consideration to intelligent life needs justification. In terms of moral status, the deontologist Immanuel Kant reserved his incomparable and incalculable sense of *dignity* for rational beings. While he argued that we owe a certain amount of kindness and consideration to nonrational beings such as animals—as would many virtue ethicists—this did not rise to the level of equal status that would protect them from being means to the ends of humans (such as for food).[42]

A utilitarian may suggest that more intelligent beings make a greater contribution to overall well-being and happiness for themselves and others. For instance, John Stuart Mill famously wrote that

> It is better to be a human being dissatisfied than a pig satisfied; better to be Socrates dissatisfied than a fool satisfied. And if the fool, or the pig, are a different opinion, it is because they only know their own side of the question.[43]

Mill based this on his idea that there were important qualitative differences in the pleasures available to beings with different cognitive and moral capacities, which would support Norrin's belief that more intelligent life was more worthy of protection (while not dismissing entirely the loss of less intelligent life).

In the beginning of his time as herald, the Surfer avoids even this question, finding uninhabited worlds for his master to consume. But it does not take long for Galactus's need for energy to demand that his herald find inhabited worlds, or else he will return to Zenn-La and doom its population (including Shalla-Bal). Norrin fully appreciates the tragic dilemma before him: "So, which billions do I condemn to death to save the woman I love? I see the goodness in many worlds…and the potential in others. Old gods of Zenn-La, help me! I…I cannot choose." He soon finds a world inhabited by insectoid beings, who are

> polluting their own planet to the point of ensuring their own extinction. They are too primitive to climb out of their cycle of war and hate. Yes, this species would not be missed. It would almost be

a mercy to the universe to wipe them out before they find a way to infest other worlds.[44]

We see his thinking here: he regards this species as doomed to self-destruction as well as threatening harm to other species, invoking Galactus's mission of "culling" the weak worlds in favor of the strong as an act of "mercy to the universe."

After he summons his master, however, the Surfer learns that there is an advanced civilization under the surface of the planet, comprised of beings that fled their savage members and created a society of beauty and serenity, relying on the savages on the surface to (unknowingly) protect them from invaders. When Galactus arrives to feed, Norrin argues for the value of the lives on the planet, arguing that "to know that I ended their race…it is driving me mad!" Galactus calls him naïve and argues that "these beings die for highest of callings—to keep me alive. Such is the way of things. Such has been prophesied." Because he cannot have his herald go mad, Galactus removes the memory of this world from Norrin's mind, leaving him free to seek out another world of violent "insects," Earth, thinking to himself that "the universe would not miss them."[45]

Years later, after leaving Galactus's service, the Surfer learns that there is much more he "forgot." The ghost of a mass murderer confronts Norrin with his own complicity, telling him that "you were the herald of Galactus. You led him to worlds teeming with life. You stood by while he consumed those worlds. The deaths of countless billions rest upon your head." When Norrin realizes what he had done, he falls to his knees saying, "my…past is…an obscenity." He assumes that he made himself forget these horrible acts: After he is tortured by visions in which he is overwhelmed by the countless beings he helped his master slaughter, he pleads that "I was blind before! I did not see with caring eyes! My crime was ignorance!"[46]

However, the Surfer visits Galactus soon afterwards and recounts this experience, telling his former master that "I aided you in the destruction of hundreds of worlds, abetted the deaths of millions of poor souls. Yet I've never felt any great guilt over this matter. How can that be?" Galactus cites the Surfer's "penchant for righting wrongs and protecting the weak" and explains that Norrin Radd "was an honorable man. He would not have been capable of carrying out certain desires of mine…without undergoing delicate personality alterations." The Surfer is outraged, accusing his former master of altering "the essence of me" and demanding that his "unaltered" moral character be restored: "Undo your handiwork, mighty Galactus! Allow me to be the man I should be!"[47]

Galactus warns that "the soul can be a merciless tormentor" before transforming the Surfer, who once again hallucinates about the deadly impact of his past actions, thinking that "my life is exposed for the sham it truly is. The mask of self-righteous virtue is torn from my face." When he rouses, Galactus offers to reverse the change, but the Surfer declines, saying,

> I've a past and sins I must learn to accept and live with…take responsibility for. Too long have I hidden away in the cozy harbor of self-deceit. Never again. I will either come to terms with my soul's burden or die trying. A man can live no other way and remain a man.[48]

Like many others we have discussed in this book, Norrin feels more responsibility than he should. In his case, his heinous acts in assistance to the Devourer were done under unwanted mental interference, and had Galactus not altered his personality—his "moral center," as one source puts it, and the virtues Galactus found inconvenient—he may never have gone along with them.[49]

Surfing a New Path, Thanks to Alicia

Regardless of what Galactus did to suppress his moral character after the episode with the insectoid world, the Surfer's better instincts were awakened when he first visited Earth.[50] After a violent confrontation with the Fantastic Four, Norrin finds himself at the skylight of Alicia Masters' studio. After falling through, she tends to him, hearing "a certain nobility in your voice"—a concept of which he claims ignorance—and feeling "unimaginable loneliness" in his face.[51]

When he explains why he and his master are on Earth and that "it is only he that matters," Alicia pounds her fists into him, pleading what he used to know:

> No! No! We all matter! Every living being...every bird and beast...this is our world! Ours! Perhaps we are not as powerful as your Galactus...but we have hearts...we have souls...we live... breathe...feel! Can't you see that? Are you as blind as I?

Her words awaken some of moral sensitivity that Galactus suppressed; he expresses surprise at her courage and, after touching her face, he says "there is a word some races use...a word I have never understood...until now! At last I know...beauty!"

Alicia implores him to look at the people outside her window, saying "each of them is entitled to life...to happiness...each of them is...human!" The Surfer dismisses the meaning of humanity but acknowledges that he feels another new sensation: pity. When she says he has the power to save us, he says defying Galactus is "unthinkable," after which she asks how "you could stand by and see a world destroyed? How...how could I have been so wrong about you...when I sensed nobility...when I thought you possessed...compassion?" Norrin admits she might be right, and flies away saying, "perhaps for the first time within memory...I have found something worth protecting!" The words "within memory" are crucial here, because Galactus removed the memories of his past concern for the civilized members of the insectoid world he previously visited.

When the Surfer finds Galactus preparing to absorb Earth's resources, he shouts to him, "For the first time I realize the dreadful enormity of what you plan to do! You must not tamper with other worlds! You cannot destroy the entire human race!" After Norrin attacks him, Galactus accuses his herald of betrayal, but Norrin reveals his awakened moral sense when he says that "I should betray myself if I did not fight to prevent the annihilation of a people. For here...on the lonely little world...I have found what men call...conscience!" When Galactus threatens to kill him, the Surfer says that "no matter what my fate, I face it without qualm! For I have learned from the humans how glorious it can be to have a cause worth dying for!"[52]

As we know, Galactus agrees to leave Earth only after Reed threatens to use the Ultimate Nullifier, but before he does, he rejects the Surfer as his herald and traps him on Earth within an impassable energy barrier. As Norrin tells Alicia, "There is still so much I do not know about Earth...about mankind...! But now, I have the rest of my life to learn...for, in finding a conscience...I have lost...the stars!"[53] However optimistic he may have sounded, his subsequent time on Earth is filled with disgust at the inherent anger and violence of mankind, both toward each other and outsiders such as himself, regardless of how much he tries to help them. He also experiences tremendous loneliness and sadness over his former world and his lost love, Shalla-Bal, and many of his adventures are focused on breaking through Galactus's barrier and getting back to them.[54]

Years later, after finding a way through the barrier and soaring through the stars on his own heroic mission—for a time accompanied by Alicia—the Silver Surfer faced the Annihilation Wave, a massive invasion led by Annihilus, ruler of the Negative Zone.[55] After seeing the massacre left by the invaders, the Surfer compares it to what he used to do for Galactus: "I would survey the world. I would call the Devourer to feed. And Galactus would feed. But there was no malice in the act." He remembers when Alicia asked how he could watch as a world was destroyed when she sensed such nobility and compassion in him, and says to himself about the Annihilation carnage: "No, not the same. This is worse. So much worse...There is no meaning in this!" Both statements evoke Galactus's purpose in the universe, which gave meaning to both their "culling" of the universe and the way they went about it, with the Surfer arriving beforehand to warn the inhabitants and giving them a chance to make their peace and say goodbye.[56]

Soon, Galactus summons the Surfer and asks him to rejoin him, as both herald and partner, to fight the Annihilation Wave; he feels that, unlike his more obedient heralds, Norrin's integrity may serve them all in the coming battle. Norrin demurs, mourning the lives lost under their previous time together, but Galactus only sees a herald who has lost his will, for which he blames himself—and Alicia. "This is my doing. I let an Earth woman condemn you to her world's madness," he says, followed by an offer: "I can give you conviction. Conviction—and the power to see it through. I can undo what was done in anger. I can restore you," offering to grant him new power and taking away his sense of remorse. Like before, the Surfer rejects the last part, telling Galactus, "No, give me the will to do what must be done. Let my remorse define me," wanting to retain his humanity to ensure he does not go far in serving the Devourer, especially when their shared purpose turns towards war and violence.[57]

And it does, as the Silver Surfer, once again the herald of Galactus, goes on a mad rampage against Annihilus's fleet, destroying numerous spaceships (and their crews). But he stops short of killing their leader, Ravenous. When Galactus asks why, the Surfer says, "I am not a killer." When Galactus points out, "Yet you, once again, serve Galactus," Norrin repeats, with added emphasis: "*I* am not a killer."[58] Although he destroyed many anonymous enemies in the field of battle, Norrin presumably saw a way to avoid killing one enemy face-to-face, showing Galactus that he retains his disobedient streak in service of some degree of moral restraint.

As he leaves to find new worlds for Galactus to consume, the Surfer thinks to himself, "Now I set down a familiar path. There will be more destruction. But there will also be purpose. And meaning. I will steer Galactus clear of Annihilus…and lives will be saved."[59] This statement elaborates on his earliest conception of his mission: to find a way to sate the Devourer's hunger in a way that minimizes the necessary loss of life. This focus on life is confirmed when the Black Panther uses a simulated energy burst to attract Galactus's herald, who resents being tricked. When the Surfer, in his anger, asks T'Challa why he shouldn't kill him, the Wakandan king responds that "it's not in your nature," and when Norrin reiterates he's the herald of Galactus, T'Challa affirms that this is "a responsibility you took on to preserve life."[60]

This is also what the Surfer says when he next meets the Thing soon after the Annihilation incident. In a conversation we touched on in chapter 1, Ben says, "I don't get it, Surfer. You're one o' the good guys. What would make you go back to workin' for that piece of crap?" The Surfer confirms that, "as you say, friend Grimm, you don't get it," and then explains that "good and evil are far more complex concepts than you would have them be. Sometimes to save lives, one must commit acts that in other contexts one would find reprehensible." When Ben restates this as "the ends justify the means, huh?" the Surfer says sometimes they must, referencing what many people, hero or not, learn when they face a tragic dilemma from which they cannot escape with clean hands.[61]

Finding New Purpose

Some time later, after reality itself was destroyed and reborn in a reiteration of the universal death and rebirth that created him, Galactus is approached by a team of heroes known as the Ultimates, including the Black Panther, Carol Danvers (Captain Marvel), and Adam Brashear, the scientific genius known as the Blue Marvel. They suggest an audacious plan to transform the Devourer of Worlds into the Lifebringer, Seeder of Worlds, which he accepts, after which Galactus begins his new life by restoring the worlds he had consumed over his eons of existence.[62] It does not take long for the other cosmic entities in the universe to question his new status, given the importance of the role he once held, as made clear during Reed's trial.

Appropriately enough, the cosmic entities put Galactic himself on trial, with the Living Tribunal—the universal personification of law and judgment—accusing him of "distorting the great balance that maintains reality." Lord Order argues that Galactus threatens "the balance" by deserting his "vital role in the multiverse," and Lord Chaos follows, saying Galactus now "undoes his work! Builds what was broken! Brings life to what died! Gleaming blight! Reversal of sweet destruction!" The Living Tribunal hears these arguments but judges them "irrelevant," and allows Galactus to continue seeding the worlds he once destroyed. "A new balance," it says, "for a new cosmos. What was is over. What will be has yet to become. Until more is known…can set no precedent."[63]

But even this new purpose is not to last. Eventually, the Silver Surfer returns to his former master to ask him to devour again, but for good reason. "I know you have struggled mightily to bring life to the galaxy,"

176

Norrin begins. "I am proud to see you atone for our shared legacy of destruction, but now all life as we know it is imperiled by a heinous evil," whom Galactus can destroy by consuming a world (thereby destroying the "heinous evil"). He finally asks, "What say you, Galactus the Life-bringer? Will you consume one world…to save the entire galaxy?"[64] After responding with a Galactus-sized "NO," he says the Surfer should "not ask me to consume a planet for any reason. The burden would weight on me for all eternity…and the cost would not be mine alone."[65]

By the end of the story, however, Galactus does revert to his former self and devours the planet in exchange for the Silver Surfer resuming his position as herald. We don't know exactly what transpired between them to bring about this change of heart, but perhaps Galactus realized that, in the interest of saving life, he had to consume once again—even though, once he did, his change would be permanent. That said, he does continue to devour worlds in the interest of life, such as when he consumes five incredibly energy-rich worlds the Surfer had long hidden from him in order to battle the Black Winter, the force that destroyed Galan's universe.[66]

Very recently, Galactus and the Silver Surfer have had perhaps the most drastic change of purpose yet. After (yet) another massive cosmic conflict—this one due to malfeasance by the Watchers countless eons before—the known universe expands tenfold.[67] Having merged with the Asgardian Destroyer to help win the battle, Galactus emerges reborn, and the "three faces of existence"—Eternity, the Griever, and the Never Queen—are curious about the role he now plays in "the grand design." The Surfer asks Galactus if he hungers, to which the former Devourer and Lifebringer replies, "Yes. For knowledge of these new borderlands. And I require…a herald." Norrin declines, but agrees to be his companion, and together they leave to explore a universe now much larger than ever.[68]

Will exploration, which was Norrin Radd's original dream long before the Devourer came to Zenn-La, remain Galactus's purpose going forward? Already, he has been called by a multiversal assortment of Avengers to consume Doom the Living Planet—it's a long story—to save all the universes, being declared an honorary Avenger in the process.[69] So it would seem that devouring worlds, not just knowledge, is never too far from Galactus's nature or his purpose, although in recent years this seems to be geared more to consuming worlds to advance another goal rather than simply to survive or "weed" an unruly universe. Perhaps he needs a more direct and urgent reason to feed in full awareness of the incalculable harm it does—which suggests a part of the Lifebringer survives in Galactus to this day.

[1] *Fantastic Four*, vol. 1, #243 (June 1982).

[2] Galactus's origin was first presented in its complete and canonical form in *Super-Villain Classics* #1 (May 1983), consolidating and updating several contradictory accounts up to then.

[3] *Fantastic Four*, vol. 1, #48 (March 1966).

[4] *Fantastic Four*, vol. 1, #49 (April 1966).

[5] *Fantastic Four*, vol. 1, #50 (May 1966). In response, Ben comments, "just when we need all the help we can git, Baldy decides ta turn philosopher!" (Hey, we're helpin' heah!)

[6] *Fantastic Four*, vol. 1, #123 (June 1972) and #211 (October 1979).

[7] *Fantastic Four*, vol. 1, #173 (August 1976).

[8] *Fantastic Four*, vol. 1, #50 and #49.

[9] *Fantastic Four*, vol. 1, #50.

[10] *Fantastic Four*, vol. 1, #123 and #50. See also *Fantastic Four*, vol. 3, #523 (April 2005), when Galactus is made human and, although initially skeptical, comes to appreciate the value of humanity through interaction with the Fantastic Four (and Alicia, who did the same for the Silver Surfer years earlier).

[11] *Fantastic Four*, vol. 1, #243.

[12] Ibid.

[13] Ibid. Another time he says to himself, about the man he once was, "I had prayed it might be so. But now his ghost returns, and with it comes that specter that one such as Galactus cannot dare face—compassion" (*Fantastic Four*, vol. 1, #257, August 1983).

[14] *Fantastic Four*, vol. 1, #211.

[15] *Fantastic Four*, vol. 1, #50.

[16] *Fantastic Four*, vol. 1, #173. This is not Gorr the God-Butcher, whom fans of Thor will know well and who plays an important role in the saga discussed in my book *A Philosopher Reads... Marvel Comics' Thor: If They Be Worthy* (Ockham Publishing, 2022).

[17] *Fantastic Four*, vol. 1, #175 (October 1976).

[18] *Fantastic Four*, vol. 1, #243.

[19] *Fantastic Four*, vol. 1, #244 (July 1982).

[20] *Fantastic Four*, vol. 1, #173.

[21] *Fantastic Four*, vol. 1, #50.

[22] Even Galactus's choice to consume worlds with less developed life resembles defenses of eating animal meat based on their lack of sentience—although this begs the question of why sentience is relevant. For more on these issues, see Peter Singer and Jim Mason, *The Ethics of What We Eat: Why Our Food Choices Matter* (New York: Penguin Random House, 2007), and Tyler Doggett, "Moral Vegetarianism," in Edward N. Zalta and Uri Nodelman (eds.), *Stanford Encyclopedia of Philosophy* (Fall 2023 Edition), at https://plato.stanford.edu/archives/fall2023/entries/vegetarianism/. Of course, as one alien creature asks when considering Galactus's actions, "do we not also destroy life when he feed? Even those of us who eat only plants" (*Fantastic Four*, vol. 1, #261, December 1983).

[23] For a thorough overview of the moral philosophy of promises, see Allen Habib, "Promises," in Zalta and Nodelman (eds.), *Stanford Encyclopedia of Philosophy* (Winter 2022 Edition), at https://plato.stanford.edu/archives/win2022/entries/promises/.

[24] *Fantastic Four*, vol. 1, #50.

[25] *Fantastic Four*, vol. 1, #123.

[26] *Fantastic Four*, vol. 1, #175, in which he also says, when pleased that a world resists him, "Most worlds fall before the scythe with an ease which fills me with ennui." These statements reveal an underlying existential angst to the Devourer of Worlds that is beyond the focus of this chapter. This is most evident in issue #123, when he says that "for untold ages, beyond the scope of my own memory, I have wandered the cosmos, alone and unloved! My life has lost all meaning!", adding that "the conquest of life has afforded me no joy." These concepts come from the branch of philosophy known as *existentialism*, for which a good introduction is Sarah Bakewell's *At the Existentialist Café: Freedom, Being, and Apricot Cocktails* (New York: Other Press, 2016).

[27] *Fantastic Four*, vol. 1, #244.

[28] Aristotle discusses friendship at length in Book VIII on his *Nicomachean Ethics*, at https://classics.mit.edu/Aristotle/nicomachaen.html. For a quick summary, see Emily Katz, "Three Lessons for Aristotle on Friendship," *The Conversation*, May 17, 2023, at https://theconversation.com/three-lessons-from-aristotle-on-friendship-200520.

[29] *Fantastic Four*, vol. 1, #257.

[30] Aristotle expounds on this in Book 1 of his *Nicomachean Ethics*.

[31] This is related but not the same as the *teleological argument* for the existence of God, on which see Del Ratzsch and Jeffrey Koperski, "Teleological Arguments for God's Existence," in Zalta and Nodelman (eds.), *The Stanford Encyclopedia of Philosophy* (Summer 2023 Edition), at https://plato.stanford.edu/archives/sum2023/entries/teleological-arguments/.

[32] *Fantastic Four*, vol. 1, #261.

[33] Again, this is similar to arguments in theology and the philosophy of religion for why God allows suffering, also known as the "problem of evil." For more, see Michael Tooley, "The Problem of Evil," in Zalta (ed.), *Stanford Encyclopedia of Philosophy* (Winter 2021 Edition), at https://plato.stanford.edu/archives/win2021/entries/evil/.

[34] *Fantastic Four*, vol. 1, #262 (January 1984). The usual source of this quote is a 1926 letter to Max Born, included in Irene Born (trans.), *The Born-Einstein Letters* (New York: Macmillan, 1971), p. 91.

[35] *Fantastic Four*, vol. 1, #262.

[36] Ibid.

[37] Ibid. For his part, Uatu merely says, "So speaks Galactus. So speaks the cosmic truth!" This aligns with what he said after Galactus demanded the Ultimate Nullifier in exchange for leaving Earth on his visit, but it also sounds a little subservient to me (especially for one who faced Galactus down in that earlier episode).

[38] Ibid.

[39] This can lead to *moral injury*, similar to post-traumatic stress disorder (PTSD), for many soldiers; for more, see Nancy Sherman, *Afterwar: Healing the Moral Wounds of Our Soldiers* (Oxford: Oxford University Press, 2015).

[40] All of this is from *Silver Surfer*, vol. 1, #1 (May 1968), "The Origin of the Silver Surfer!".

[41] Ibid.

[42] This has been questioned by Kantian scholars such as Christine Korsgaard; see her book *Fellow Creatures: Our Obligations to Other Animals* (Oxford: Oxford University Press, 2018).

[43] John Stuart Mill, *Utilitarianism* (London: Parker, Son & Bourn, 1861), chapter 2, available at https://www.utilitarianism.com/mill2.htm. For more on Mill's utilitar-

ianism, which was much more nuanced than Jeremy Bentham's original formulation, see David Brink, "Mill's Moral and Political Philosophy" in Zalta and Nodelman (eds.), *Stanford Encyclopedia of Philosophy* (Fall 2022 Edition), at https://plato.stanford.edu/archives/fall2022/entries/mill-moral-political/.

[44] *Silver Surfer Annual*, vol. 8, #1 (2018).

[45] Ibid.

[46] *Silver Surfer Annual*, vol. 3, #3 (1990), "Shades of Guilt."

[47] *Silver Surfer*, vol. 3, #48 (April 1991).

[48] Ibid.

[49] *Annihilation: Silver Surfer* #1 (June 2006), in a informational page at the end.

[50] Although that story implies he visited Earth next, we have to assume that the "hundreds" of worlds were consumed in between.

[51] *Fantastic Four*, vol. 1, #49 (including the rest of the Surfer's initial encounter with Alicia).

[52] *Fantastic Four*, vol. 1, #50.

[53] Ibid.

[54] This next stage in Norrin's life begins in *Silver Surfer*, vol. 1, #1.

[55] Norrin returned to Earth to reclaim his lost humanity, only to find the Fantastic Four believed to be dead after the battle with Onslaught, and sought out Alicia instead (*Silver Surfer*, vol. 3, #123, December 1996); their time together ended after he felt new responsibility after the apparent death of Galactus (*Galactus the Devourer* #6, March 2000).

[56] *Annihilation: Silver Surfer* #1.

[57] *Annihilation: Silver Surfer* #3 (August 2006).

[58] *Annihilation: Silver Surfer* #4 (September 2006).

[59] Ibid.

[60] *Fantastic Four*, vol. 3, #550 (November 2007).

[61] *Fantastic Four*, vol. 3, #545 (June 2007).

[62] *The Ultimates*, vol. 2, #2 (February 2016).

[63] *The Ultimates 2*, vol. 2, #2 (February 2017).

[64] *Infinity Countdown* #3 (July 2018).

[65] *Infinity Countdown* #4 (August 2018).

[66] *Thor*, vol. 6, #1 (March 2020). And his new herald for this mission? None other than the Odinson himself, who kills Galactus afterwards, leading the Surfer to admit "there is a part of me that feels…mournful…for Galan. To know that his journey began such as mine" (*Thor*, vol. 6, #6, October 2020).

[67] For background, see *Fantastic Four: Reckoning War Alpha* #1 (April 2022).

[68] *Fantastic Four*, vol. 6, #45 (September 2022).

[69] *Avengers*, vol. 8, #66 (May 2023).

Chapter 8
Doctor Doom

Doom! That lone ominous word signals one of the greatest threats the Fantastic Four has ever faced, perhaps not on the existential scale of Galactus, but in a way all the more frightening because of its down-to-earth nature. In many ways, Victor von Doom is the mirror opposite to the Fantastic Four—especially Reed Richards, both of them endowed with an extraordinary mind that enables them to achieve things unimaginable to most people. Reed uses his abilities to help mankind through exploring new worlds and developing new technology; Doom too believes he is using his mastery of science and magic to help mankind, but he sets out to do so by conquering and ruling it.

In this chapter, we'll explore Victor von Doom's background to see what it is about his early life experiences that led him down such a different path than Reed and to use his gifts in such a radically different way. We start with his feelings about his appearance, which are a reflection of his deeper and more widespread insecurities and the vanity he uses to cover them up. These are grounded both in tragic events during his childhood, for which he blames mankind, and his disastrous time at college, for which he blames Reed. From this we'll move on to his obsessive competition with Reed (and Reed's compassionate response) before we address Victor's ethics, including his claims to want to save the world by ruling it and to be a man of honor, both of which are revealed to be compromised by his own ego and ambition.

Humble Beginnings

When we and the Fantastic Four first meet Doctor Doom, Reed recognizes him as his classmate Victor from college, whose experiments with magic caused an explosion on campus that disfigured his face and got him expelled, leading him to wander the world "seeking forbidden secrets of black magic and sorcery!"[1]

Over time, we learn much more.[2] Victor is the son of Werner and Cynthia von Doom, members of a Romani community called the Zefiro who lived in the Eastern European country of Latveria, where they were persecuted by its ruler, King Vladimir. Cynthia sold her soul to the powerful demon Mephisto to boost her already formidable skills with sorcery so she could strike back against the king. However, she lost control of her power, resulting in the death of many local children, and after she was killed by a guard, her soul was claimed by Mephisto. Werner was a doctor who was later asked by the king to heal his dying wife, and when he could not, he and Victor fled into the mountains. They were later found, nearly frozen to death, by their friend Boris, who brought them back to their camp, but Werner died soon afterwards.

Victor was tormented and enraged by what he considered the murder of his parents at the hands of the king and swore his revenge, not just on him but on all of humanity "for its crimes against the name of Doom!"[3] Despite his mother's wishes that he never take up the dark arts, Victor discovered her mystical artifacts and began training himself in their use, while at the same time becoming an expert in the sciences as well. Eventually, he attracted the attention of the American government, who offered him a scholarship to Empire State University, where he met a young Reed Richards and his roommate Benjamin Grimm.

After inspecting Victor's work one day, Reed noticed an error in the calculations and tried to warn him, but Victor rejected the advice and went through with his experiment, which resulted in the explosion that scarred his face and led to his ejection from the university. Victor then fled to the mountains of Tibet where a school of monks crafted armor for him, including a mask which he insisted he wear before it was cooled, resulting in even worse scarring to his face and reinforcing his refusal to let most people see him without it. Now demanding to be called Doctor Doom, Victor returned to Latveria to lead an uprising against the king and install himself as the new ruler, a position from which he then launched his plans to defeat the Fantastic Four and take over the world.

Although he is master of both science and sorcery who rose from meager beginnings to rule his country, Victor is wracked by a deep insecurity that explains much of his subsequent behavior and unsavory character traits. We'll leave it to psychologists to explain the roots of his insecurities, although for our purposes it suffices to assume that they stem from the persecution his people suffered in Latveria and the loss of both his parents at a young age—not to mention his college accident, for which he blames Reed Richards, regarded as the "star" genius of Empire State University and later an admired and respected superhero and inventor. As we'll see later, much of what Victor does and says is driven by "competition" with Reed, an obsession that defeats his own plans just as often as the Fantastic Four does.

Do the Scars Doom the Man?

The most obvious source and visual representation of Victor's insecurity is his face, which is stressed from the first complete account of his origin. After his bandages are removed following the accident, he smashes the mirror when he sees himself, pronouncing himself ugly and deciding that "my face is too horrible! No other eyes must ever gaze upon it! I'll hide from the sight of mankind...somewhere...somehow!" After he dons his mask in Tibet, he announces a transformation that extends well past his appearance:

> Never again will mortal eyes gaze upon the hideous countenance of Victor von Doom! From this moment on, there is no Victor von Doom! He has vanished…along with the handsome face he once possessed! But, in his place, there shall be another…wiser… stronger! More brilliant, more powerful than ever before! From this moment on, I shall be known as…Doctor Doom![4]

In the same issue, Victor's story continues in the modern day as he arranges for the Fantastic Four to be invited to the Latverian embassy and then traps them after spiking his "specially prepared berry drink" with a hallucinogen. While celebrating his impending victory, he asks himself, "But what does it mean? Will I be any happier once I've defeated the Fantastic Four?" His conclusion has little to do with his foes: "No victory…no triumph can ever restore my normal face to me! No conquest can make me the man I once was!" He decides to remove his mask but then hesitates to look at his own face, and when he does he finds that "it's even worse than I remembered!" He covers his face while he destroys the mirror, shouting, "I can't bear it! I must destroy it! Drive it from my sight…from my mind!" Ironically, the noise of the mirror breaking draws the Fantastic Four's attention to his presence, leading to a battle that ends when Reed uses Doom's own berry drink to make him think he defeated Reed and banished him to limbo. Afterwards, Victor tells the others to leave, saying that "in my moment of supreme triumph, I can afford to be forgiving!"[5]

Victor's marred face continues to torment him long after this early tale. Later, during a climactic battle inside a crystal complex, Reed detaches Victor's mask and subjects him to what Victor calls "millions of grotesque reflections of my face!" This is too much for him, and the exposition tells us that he "falls whimpering like a mindless cur to the ground, groveling out of control in a painful, contorted rage."[6] Many years later, to less visceral but more meaningful effect, Sue renders Victor's mask invisible while he is proclaiming his victory over the Fantastic Four on an interplanetary video broadcast, revealing his true face to the entire world while thinking to herself, "you wanted every eye in the galaxy on you, Victor. Well…is it everything you hoped for?"[7] After the team escapes, Doom searches televisions signals from around the world for mentions of him, hearing numerous accounts of "horrifying," "haunting visage," and "may actually pity him now," as well as claims that the "Fantastic Four played him" and he's "no match for Sue Storm." Predictably, he destroys the wall of screens before walking away.[8]

The nature of Victor's scars following the accident remains unclear to this day. Sue speaks for the readers when she wonders,

> There are so many contradictory stories of how he was scarred so hideously! Was it the result of his own carelessness in a laboratory experiment which went awry while he was still in college? Or, was it caused by impatience because he refused to wait for his still-molten mask to properly cool before being placed on his face? I doubt the world will ever know the real truth![9]

The implication here is that the initial scar was minor, but Victor's vanity led him to reject any flaw in his handsome face, no matter how tiny, so he ruined it completely by putting on the mask before it had cooled. When Victor's Doombots implant his memories in young Kristoff, his presumed successor, it shows some burnt skin on the left side of his face, extending from the top of the cheek to his chin—so even in his own memories his scars are much less than his reaction would suggest.[10] In this interpretation, his revulsion of his "ugliness" was actually remorse for the loss of his "perfect" handsomeness, which in his mind matched his unparalleled intellect and ambition.

Also, Victor fears that his scarred face—especially after he put the mask on—will prevent him from experiencing romantic love. Early on, he plots to strike the Fantastic Four through Alicia Masters, who had just started seeing Ben at the time, but he "cannot comprehend how one as lovely as Alicia can feel affection for the grotesque Thing!" He removes his mask but hides his face from a mirror as he says:

> How ironic it is that even a gargoyle such as the Thing can find love—even he can mingle with normal people! And yet I—and I alone, dare not expose my face to the view of other humans! I alone must hide like a dark wraith from the sight of my fellow man![11]

Then he asserts that "I shall have my revenge—upon the entire human race—beginning with Fantastic Four." This suggests that his vengeful mission is motivated primarily by the rejection he feels, even though it was he who rejected humanity after the accident when he withdrew from society and adopted the guise and name of Doctor Doom.

If Victor cannot find love it is not necessarily because of his appearance. When young Victor finds his mother's mystical artifacts and swears to use them to get his revenge on mankind, his first love Valeria urges him to "abandon this madness" and remember the promises they made to each other. When he refuses, she is forced to admit that "the man I once loved...the man whose children I once longed to bear...is dead." He proclaims that he "has no need for love, be it from woman or child! I am absolute!"[12] When he later has a chance to reunite with Valeria as adults, however, he wonders, "could she bear to look on a face disfigured by a fiery explosion...look on it without revulsion, without sheer, shameless loathing?" He removes his mask and shouts "No! How could she...when even I am driven to madness by the sight?"[13]

When they are at last reunited, Valeria does reject him, not for how he looks, but for his cruelty and resentment at the world. "Tell me you would renounce your towering ambition...for the girl you once loved!" He says nothing, which she takes as his answer, with the exposition describing Victor as "knowing, at long last, that it is not his burnt, scarred face...his grim, metal mask...which are now and forever his merciless prison...but the man himself...the tortured, twisted being whom the world calls only...Doom!"[14]

It is not just the love of a woman like Valeria that Victor craves—despite his protestations to the contrary—but the love and admiration of mankind that he has lacked since he and his fellow Romani were hounded by the Latveria monarchy. This is especially tragic because, in his heart, Victor believes that his never-ending quest for power and conquest are ultimately for the good of humanity, who would truly prosper only under his rule (as we discuss further below). Recently, when he acts alone to destroy a black hole on the moon that threatens all life on Earth, he thinks to himself that "I will be their hero. I will no longer be seen as their tormentor. I will atone. I will be loved. And then I will rule all of Earth with great humility."[15]

More than the love of anyone else, Victor needs to find a way to love himself. At one point, he goes so far as to create a clone of himself to succeed himself as ruler of Latveria, but with the powers of the Fantastic Four to boot. When the clone develops rocky skin like the Thing, Victor rejects him, saying that "your face is almost as horrible as my own," and they begin to fight. The clone argues that he is the same as Victor, only "before the accident which drove you mad" and therefore lacking "your outrage...your hate...or your insanity!" He accuses Victor of hating what he is and where he came from and hiding "your battle-scarred face with an even more hideous mask," and says that the fact that he has Victor's "perfect mind" and "perfect face" only reinforces "the hideously deformed mockery that you see yourself to be" before accusing him of losing his humanity when he created him as his replacement.[16] More recently, Victor's advisor Boris asks him if he loves himself, to which Victor evasively replies, "I'm the living salvation of the human race." When Boris presses the issue, asking "but is there love in that self-adulation?", Victor only demands he kneel before him, even though Boris is frail and dying.[17] As above with Valeria—who is, incidentally, Boris's granddaughter—Victor's silence reveals his answer.

We discussed self-hatred and self-loathing at length in reference to Ben Grimm in chapter 5, and the similarities and differences in how he and Victor express it are fascinating. We saw above an early indication of how Victor compares himself to Ben in that they are both considered hideous by society, yet Ben walks freely, is adored by society (for the most part), and is beloved by Alicia. Later, when Ben starts wearing a metal helmet after his face is scarred in a fight with Wolverine—an obscure and minor character, don't worry if you've never heard of him—Doom tells him, "If any one man could fully sympathize with your plight...it is I! For I too am prisoner behind an iron mask!"[18]

Whereas Ben internalizes his resentment about his tragic fate, Victor holds his against humanity as a whole; and while Ben is a hero who regularly risks his life to save others, Victor paints himself as a hero for trying to save humanity from itself by conquering it. The one thing they have in common is blaming Reed, and even this points out an important difference. For the most part, Ben has forgiven Reed for the accident—for which his responsibility is questionable, as we discussed in chapter 2—as well as his failures to cure him, and still counts him as his best friend. In contrast, Victor holds Reed accountable for his own mistake that caused the explosion and almost everything bad that happened to him afterwards (as we will discuss later), and despite Reed's repeated attempts to reach out, Victor still counts him as his greatest enemy.

There are times, however, when Victor seems to have reconciled himself to his face he lets no one see and the mask by which he is known to the world. Recently, after some time away from Latveria, Victor returns home, dressed in nothing but frayed robes. A local woman named Zora welcomes him home and begs him to once again be their savior and overthrow the current rulers, but he only shows her his face and asks, "is this the face of a savior?" She removes the faceplate from a nearby fallen Doombot and lifts it to him, calling it "your true face" and, for Latverians, "the face of hope." Victor thanks her for reminding him that "there is the visage I was born with. The one fate would keep forcing upon me. But this is the face I chose."[19] After granting Zora power and renaming her Victorious, they later join a work crew rebuilding Mount Doom after it was destroyed in a battle with the Fantastic Four. Because of the heat, Victor removes his cloak and tunic, and a woman asks why he keeps his mask on in the heat, saying they all love him and don't care about his face (after Sue exposed it for all to see). Victor explains that "this mask *is* my face. The face I have made for myself."[20]

His Greatest Fear

Even if he has accepted his appearance and embraced the "face he chose," this does not seem to have resolved any of Victor's other insecurities.[21] They are too many to list here, so I will focus on the ones that reflect his fear of appearing weak, both to others as well as to himself, which can be understood to reflect insecurity about his own strength in all its forms (like we discussed in chapter 3).

One manifestation of this fear is Victor's rejection of any concern from others. For example, when his ship is shot down on the Beyonder's world at the beginning of the first "Secret Wars" episode, Captain America extends a helping hand despite his fellow heroes' objections, but Victor turns him away, saying, "Doom…needs the aid…of no man." He also mistakes concern for pity, which we see when he next turns to the collected heroes and asks, "Is that pity I see in your eyes, Captain America? And yours, Richards?" before he attacks them for little apparent reason other than to show he can.[22]

Later in the same story we also see Victor deny that he can feel fear. After he sneaks onto Galactus's ship to find a weapon to use against the Beyonder, he wonders how long it will take for Galactus to notice his presence. He asks himself, "am I afraid?" but quickly answers, "No! No, it is merely excitement! Fear is more lesser men!"[23] Although it is well known among heroes that fear is something to be overcome, Victor sees it only as a weakness that brings shame to one who imagines himself above all human frailties. He shows a more virtuous courage when preparing to go into battle with Kristoff and an alternate version of Reed, who warns him not to betray them and flee, to which Victor responds simply, "Doom does not run."[24]

As we saw above, Victor often denies that he needs love or affection, as he said after being rejected by his first love Valeria. Surprisingly, this extends even to his long-lost mother, whom he spent years trying to rescue from hell after Mephisto imprisoned her there as part of their deal. During an epic quest with Doctor Strange into Mephisto's underworld realm, Victor appears to turn on Strange, exchanging his soul for his mother's. Even though she balks at this and calls him "no son of mine," Victor eventually manages to free her from hell without betraying Strange. When Victor boasts that he got what he wanted, Strange says yes, "but only at the cost of her love," and asks, "did you make that sacrifice knowingly?" As is his wont, Victor walks away without answering, but Boris confirms Strange's suspicions, telling him that "the master would want more than simply to rescue his mother. He would want to win free and clear, beholden to no one," which is apparently more important to him than his mother's love.[25]

Another aspect of perceived weakness that Victor rejects is help from others. Before they descended into hell, Victor launches an elaborate plan to secure a "boon" from Strange upon his being pronounced Sorcerer Supreme by the mystical beings known collectively as the Vishanti. After he explains his plan to rescue his mother, Strange asks him, "if you have worked so long for your mother's salvation, why did you subject yourself to the contest of the Vishanti…Why did you never simply seek me out and ask for my help?" Victor answers, "I will bear any ordeal, Strange…but Doctor Doom does not beg."[26] To Victor, asking for help means that he has made himself small to someone else, and he cannot abide that. This goes double for his greatest enemy: When Reed finds Victor buried in rubble during an attack on Latveria, he extends his hand in assistance, but Victor recoils, asking, "Are you mad, Richards?! Doom…needs no aid…from you…or any man!" After defeating their common foe, Victor lies dying and asks Reed for help, telling him that "when I am so weak…so near death…I find myself forced to rely upon your kindness…your assistance," but this is merely a ploy to take Reed with him as he dies (temporarily, of course).[27]

In general, Victor rejects any emotion or feeling that he associates with weakness. When the monks of Tibet were first dressing him in his armor and preparing his mask, they ask if any of it pains him, to which he responds that "pain is like love, like compassion! It is a thing only for lesser men! What is pain to Doom?"[28] This is reinforced after he tells Reed and Sue's daughter, Valeria—for whom he has had sincere affection ever since aiding in her birth and granting her the name of his first love—that because of her he has begun to understand compassion. After she leaves, however, he thinks of her concepts of altruism and compassion and that "neither are words in the lexicon of Dr. Doom."[29] Forgiveness is also such a term, as Victor tells the Scarlet Witch when she refuses to forgive him for using her power against the mutant population: "Your forgiveness means nothing to me—Doom does not mourn the insects he steps on."[30]

Victor also makes it clear that he has not been given anything in life, not just the assistance or aid he consistently turns away. It is important to him that everyone know he has fought and scraped for everything he has accomplished—which to a certain extent is understandable, but he takes it to absurd extremes. For example, when Reed is addressing the United Nations and Victor interrupts, demanding to speak, Reed tells him "I don't believe you've been given the floor," to which Victor responds, "I have never been given anything, Richards."[31] He also tells Charles Xavier of the X-Men that he is insulted by mutants' "pretense of superiority," explaining that they did not earn their powers but merely were born with them.[32]

On that note, Victor tells the human host to the Venom symbiote, Eddie Brock, after his ascension to the title of "King Venom," that not only are they both monarchs, but also that

> you came by that title, as I did, not through some petty accident of birth—as random and unearned as the path of a cosmic storm—but by the shedding of your blood, the sweat of your brow and the knowledge at your command.[33]

One gets the feeling that this was meant more as self-congratulation than praise for Brock, which is yet another sign of Victor's insecurity: his unparalleled vanity, which is a poor substitute for the sincere appreciation of others (or himself). He demands adulation from all around him, including his Latverian subjects, even though he knows they provide it out of fear. When Victor asks his scientist Hauptmann, "am I not the greatest military genius of all?" Hauptmann makes the mistake of saying "your brilliance rivals that of the Red Skull himself," for whom Hauptmann used to work. Victor becomes enraged, proclaiming that "Doctor Doom has no rivals! None! None!"[34] Young Kristoff makes the same mistake when he suggests that Magneto, the mutant master of magnetism, has power that rivals Victor's, prompting an almost identical response—"No one rivals Doom! No one!"—before Victor banishes the boy.[35] Victor's vanity is such that he has an employee named "the Editor" who reviews the news of his master's exploits and revises them to make him look good—including attributing any defeats or failures to his Doombots (as Victor has claimed many times).[36]

Victor is so afraid of the concept of weakness that, at one point, he destroys an entire universe whose version of Victor von Doom has overcome his insecurities and is at peace with himself and the world. When they meet, this alternate Victor admits he too was "once tortured and broken. Filled with greed, hate, and delusion," and when "our" Victor denies this, his doppelganger tells him, "don't be ashamed. This was the hardest part for me too." He shows Victor how he has saved his world but refuses to take any more credit than anyone else, which Victor finds "preposterous," saying his "humility is overwhelming. Inconceivable." The alternate Victor tells his broken self that he could have fixed his face years ago, but he chose to keep it as it was, "to show how humanity has wronged you, how it's betrayed you." Not only can he get over this, the other Victor says, but he can also forgive his Reed, who in this other universe is Victor's "oldest and strongest" friend. When this other Victor says everything about his lesser self is just "a denial of a giant wound within your soul" and "a desperate and honestly pathetic attempt to conceal your endless fear," rendering him "ludicrous," our Victor kills him and then uses the Ultimate Nullifier to destroy his entire universe, writing it off as a "repulsive and indulgent self-portrait of weakness" and claims "zero pity for the nearly infinite sentient beings within it as I extinguish them." [37] It is difficult to imagine this reaction if he has any doubt that his doppelganger was right, and he was unable to face the truth for the same fear the other Victor correctly identified in him.

"Richards!"

Although many of Victor's insecurities stem from his experiences as a Romani youth in Latveria and losing his parents in tragic circumstances, we cannot forget the obvious source and focus of much of his anger and resentment afterwards, whether deserved or not: Reed Richards. Victor has always blamed Reed for the explosion in college, convinced that he did something out of jealousy to sabotage Victor's attempt to contact his mother.

Unfortunately for Victor, this scenario plays itself out many times during their endless conflict as Doctor Doom and Mister Fantastic. When Victor is trying to save Kitty Pryde of the X-Men, Reed finds a mistake in his calculations and orders the process stopped. Victor declares such a notion impossible, and Ben reminds him of the first time Reed tried to warn him, asking "didn't you learn your lesson then?" Victor actually seems ashamed when little Franklin asks him if saving Kitty isn't "more important than bein' boss, or provin' how smart you are?"[38] Years later, when Victor prepares to drain the power cosmic from a subdued Galactus in front of the captured Fantastic Four on a live video feed, Reed tries to warn him of power surges which will not only destroy Latveria but the world. Victor is angry that Reed is "questioning my abilities? My judgment? Underestimating my intelligence—before the whole world? Before the rest of the universe?"[39] Once Sue humiliates him by exposing his face to the world, as detailed above, Reed is proven correct and frees Galactus before his energies cause any damage. Sue turns to Victor and says, "Reed did you a favor, Doom. Once again, he's cleaned up your mess," but he claims this had been his plan all again and swears (again) to kill them.[40]

Victor's paranoia about Reed comes to a head when he readies his plan to destroy the black hole on the moon that threatens the Earth (mentioned earlier). After he executes the "foolproof" plan and waits for it to work, Reed makes contact to wish him good luck. Victor says, "I don't need your concern," but Reed clarifies he's not concerned, he just wanted to wish him luck. Victor asks, "why do I need luck or childish wishes when nothing has been left to chance?" This back-and-forth goes on, with Reed trying to send good wishes and Victor questioning his "true" intentions, until Reed gives up and ends the conversation. Victor turns to his Doombots and concludes that Reed is jealous and "feels embarrassed because of his own failures," but eventually they talk themselves into the "conclusion" that Reed found a flaw in the plan that he refused to tell Victor about because he wanted it to fail. Out of sheer paranoia, Victor alters the process to disastrous effect, and blames Reed for it all: "This was Richards' plan all along, to worm into my head and corrupt my conviction...I was ready to save the world and become its hero! It would have worked! But Richards would never let that happen!" Victor lost his best chance to be recognized as mankind's true savior because he was certain Reed was out to get him once again, when in actuality he was rooting for his success and even told Captain America earlier he was relieved and grateful that Victor was handling the crisis.[41]

Many of Victor's choices are driven, not by his quest for power or world domination, but to show up Reed and prove that he's the better, smarter man. As Ben tells Sue when she asks why Victor hates them so, his hate "sort'a gives his life purpose, focus—a goal. No matter what

Doom does, he always sees Reed stealin' his thunder, denyin' him his 'proper' place in the sun."[42] We see this as Victor prepares to cure Kitty Pryde's disintegration after Reed, in a period of intense self-doubt, declined to try for fear of worsening her condition. Bragging that "Doom will succeed where Reed Richards failed," Victor shows the gathered X-Men his device, "the product of Doom's genius, improving on Richards' original conception as only Doom can, actualizing all its inherent potential along pathways that Richards, the fool, quite naturally overlooked!"[43] Yet, he cannot decide between letting Kitty die, and blaming Reed for interfering, or saving her, "especially with Reed Richards looking on! What a coup—to demonstrate once and for all which of us is truly the master." Even better, Victor appreciates the "delicious irony—to defeat my most hated rival at his own game—by playing the hero!"[44] He doesn't seem to care about any other aspect of the outcome, especially Kitty's life, which is simply a means to his end of tormenting Reed and proving that Victor is the better man.

When his superiority is challenged, Victor can't handle it. While working alongside the Fantastic Four to find a way to save the world, Victor admits he has not yet thought of a plan. When Johnny ribs him by saying, "I guess that's where Reed comes in. A man has got to know his limitations," Victor lifts him by the throat, asserting that "I am Doom, boy! I acknowledge no limitations, nor any man as my equal!"[45] Sometimes it is just a suggestion that he might not be the better man: After Victor cures temporary team member Sharon Ventura of her Thing-like appearance, his protégé Kristoff finds his achievement "miraculous" and asks in surprise, "but how could you succeed where Reed Richards has failed?" Victor tells him that he's "treading on thin ice" and explains that Richards "lacks my interdisciplinary skills," especially with respect to magic.[46]

What Victor desires more than anything is the chance to prove this to Reed directly, such as when he lures Galactus to Earth to steal his power. When Reed tells him that "there are too many variables at play. You can't have accounted for all of them," Victor replies, "perhaps you couldn't, Mister Fantastic. But then again, you are not Victor von Doom," and proceeds to do exactly what he planned.[47] He gets the opportunity to do this in a more personal way when Johnny asks him to save Sue from her dangerous pregnancy and help deliver baby Valeria into the world. Afterwards he tells Reed to "remember every time you look at your wife and daughter that Doom saved them both...when, once before, you could not," referring to Sue's earlier miscarriage.[48]

Later, Victor speaks to Valeria through a toy block, telling her that Johnny had assumed "that I could not pass up the certainty of succeeding where your father blundered," after which he informs the infant that she will be "a method by which to at last avenge myself against the indignities your family has visited upon me," despite his vow to her parents that no harm shall come to her. Ultimately, he forges a mental connection between them and reveals his true face to her; when her parents return home, they hear her utter her first word: "Doom."[49] True to his word, he and the super-intelligent girl retain a close bond from then on: For example, she asks him for help regarding a crisis (based on her future self having told her earlier that "all hope lies in Doom"), moves in with him in Latveria when she is upset with her parents, and joins with him to recruit a new Avengers team when he is "switched" into a hero during the "Axis" event.[50] Nonetheless, when Victor offers to restore Franklin's fading powers—"what his father refused to or simply cannot do"—Valeria reveals she realizes all too well what her "godfather's" true motivations are when assures her brother that Victor has "a soft spot for you and me. I genuinely think he'd never hurt us. Besides...he wouldn't pass up an opportunity to show Dad he's smarter."[51] Victor drives the same point home to Reed himself when he says to Sue in front of him: "Those children mean the world to me. I am simply doing…what his father could not."[52]

However, despite all of Victor's hatred, resentment, and incriminations, Reed still believes he has good in him. As the two battle at the end of the recent Secret Wars event, Victor tells Reed, "you think you are better than I am," but Reed denies it, saying instead, "I've always believed you could be better than what you are." After Reed prevails, he sends Victor back to Earth with his face healed, giving him one more chance to redeem himself.[53]

Reed appreciates any fig leaf from Victor, such as the time Victor invited him to dinner during the annual "Rapprochement Festival," during which "every Latverian is required to reach out to someone he has wronged. As now I reach out to you." Reed is aware Victor is distracting him while his Doombots search for a missing artefact lost in the college explosion years earlier; nonetheless, even after defeating Victor in chess he returns the missing item, an amulet belonging to Victor's mother. Victor claims that "this changes nothing between us, Richards," but Reed is every hopeful: "I think it does, just a little bit."[54] Later, when Victor prepares to marry Zora in a lavish state wedding, he asks Reed to be his best man—but not until going through the farce of a simultaneous sword fight and chess match to justify making his request, much as he did with Doctor Strange before going to hell after his mother.[55] Reed later explains to the rest of the team that Victor promises "to forgive everyone who attends for all of their past transgressions" and he finds "a clean state with Doctor Doom" to be "too good an opportunity to pass up."[56] The fact that Reed trusts Victor to keep his word, after years of betrayal, is a sign of his continuing faith in a man whose greatest exclamation of indignation is "Richards!"

After Reed appears to die (at Victor's hand), Jennifer Walters, attorney-at-law and She-Hulk, reads his will, which includes this clause: "To the man whom I once called friend…Victor von Doom…I would leave this—my class ring, from Empire State University." After Sue calms down an enraged and hurt Ben, she explains:

> You knew Reed as well as I did, Ben. You know that he always looked for the good in people…even in Victor von Doom. He never gave up hope that one day Doom might see his mistakes. That's why he gave him the ring…He hoped Doom'd see that if Reed didn't lose faith in him…then maybe he could have faith in himself.[57]

And it isn't just *this* Reed: When Victor meets a collection of Reeds from across the multiverse, one tells him that all Reeds have "always had faith. Faith that your deep intellect, your curiosity about the universe, would someday give way to a revelation…that preserving life, helping others not in service of ego, is what your place in this universe is about."[58]

Later, Reed tells Ben the same thing, that Victor is a genius and "you don't get to be a genius without curiosity," although Victor "would say his searching was about power, but that can't be the whole truth of it." In the spirit of excessive responsibility that we discussed in chapter 2, Reed worries it is his presence that distracts Victor from the pursuit of higher ends, explaining that he found a universe where the four of them never became the Fantastic Four and Victor was an upstanding man, with whom he became long-lasting friends. This is why he restored Victor's face at the end of the Secret Wars and then disappeared with Sue and the kids, leaving all to believe they were dead, in the hopes that Victor would find his higher calling. Indeed, during that time, Victor literally becomes a hero as he takes up the identity of Iron Man after Tony Stark's death.[59] Even Ben has to acknowledge that Victor tried to do good for a while before reverting to his old ways when his face is scarred once again, and asks Reed if "Dooms are always too…Doom-y…ta really stay good?"[60]

Was Doom *Always* the Hero?

All accusations about "Doomyness" aside, Victor claims to have always been a hero, if not *the* hero. During the Rapprochement Festival, Reed tells Victor "I've never understood why you don't use your immense gifts for the benefit of mankind," to which Victor responds that "we disagree on what constitutes mankind's benefit."[61] Later, when Reed summarizes all the amazing things that happened while he, Sue, and the kids were gone after the Secret Wars—including Galactus being transformed into the Lifebringer, as discussed in the last chapter—he ends with the fact that "Doom was attempting to be a hero" as Iron Man. Victor scoffs, saying "I have always been a hero. The problem is that the four of you lack the proper perspective."[62]

To be fair, Victor has consistently claimed to want to save the world. Of course, he often says it in such a way that it hardly seems sincere, such as when he asks Captain America, with whom he has temporarily and tenuously teamed to take on the Red Skull, "is not our joint purpose to save the world?"[63] Years later, he again stood with heroes against the Red Skull—who by then had come into the possession of Charles Xavier's powerful brain—and vaingloriously asserted that "once again it falls to Doom to save the world."[64]

But there are other times Victor's intentions seem more heartfelt. As the multiverse gradually collapsed in the lead-up to the recent Secret Wars event, he worked with the all-powerful Molecule Man (Owen Reece) to devise an elaborate scheme, including time travel and inventing a new religion, to combat the (even more) all-powerful Beyonders.

When Doctor Strange questions the value of his efforts, Victor asks him, "Would it be worth it if we could avoid our certain doom? If we could save something?", after which Strange concedes his point.[65] When Reed and Victor fight at the end of the Secret Wars, Reed claims he could have found a better solution, implying that he could have saved everyone without, as Victor did, making himself a tyrannical god. Victor tells him, "Your entire life, you have been distracted with the modern concerns so precious to you and your kind. Ethics, and order, and society…when all that mattered was survival. I saved millions," before pointing out, as he usually does, that "all you could save was yourself. You couldn't even save your family."[66]

Perhaps the most profound illustration of Victor's sincere desire to save the world, even if it means conquest and rule, takes place during his attempt to steal the vibranium stores from deep within the Black Panther's nation of Wakanda. As T'Challa explains to the Fantastic Four, the vault is protected by a series of complicated locks, with the last one being "a kind of psycho-spiritual polygraph" that "forces a person to reveal his true self. Any trace of guile, and hint of duplicity or evil intent triggers a ring of disintegrators." This test is conducted by Bast, the Panther God itself, before whom Victor strips off his mask and armor and offers himself for judgment, saying "I know who and what I am. Look into my soul, cat god. Look and see the truth that is Doom."[67]

Although Bast calls him a monster, Victor claims he has done no worse than Wakandans in defense of their people, calling the losses "ephemeral by-products of destiny" and sounding like Galactus when he argues that "my methods are a means to an end, no different than pruning weeds in order to let an orchard flourish." He says Reed and T'Challa never bothered to ask him why he does it: "Love. Measure my crimes against what mankind does to itself, and I am a saint." Similar to how Reed explored the multiverse to find ways to prevent tragedies and found that only he could do it (as discussed in chapter 2), Victor explains that he has used magic to see what lies ahead for humanity: "Ten thousand futures have I looked at. A hundred thousand. And in only one does mankind finally unite, and flourish...and survive. Only one. Doomworld."

The Panther God summarizes what Victor would do—"slaughter millions to save billions," "rewrite history," "wreck nations," and accept being called "a tyrant and murderer"—all in the sincere belief "that this is the only path to salvation for all mankind. You believe that with your whole heart. Everything that you have ever done—your plots and plans and twisted excesses—all serve this own goal." Bast then agrees with Victor's analysis of various future paths for humanity and reluctantly concludes that "though your methods are abhorrent and bile, your intent is pure. You have passed the test," and grants him the vibranium.

In this episode, Victor is shown to be the nightmare version of a utilitarian, accepting no limits in his pursuit of what he takes to be the only way to save mankind: conquering and ruling it. He is certainly consistent in this, such as when he tells Johnny during one battle that

> you foolishly attack me because you erroneously believe me malevolent! But my most fervent desire has always been to bring peace and prosperity to the entire universe—as I have done to my beloved kingdom of Latveria!

When Johnny points out that he rules Latveria as a dictator over a fearful people, Victor replies that "paradise is not without cost."[68] We could point out many practical issues with this, such as the veracity of his estimations of mankind's future and what alternate paths for humanity he rejected as not representing "true" peace and unity. But the chief concern with Victor's "sincere intent" is that it fails to give any weight to the significant costs of his plans, the vast majority of which will be born by others, especially the untold numbers of lives that would be lost to secure "paradise" for the survivors.

Questions of Honor

Despite his utilitarian mission for the world, Victor has quite a different idea about his personal ethics—or, at least, he wants others to think he does. He prides himself on being a man of *honor*, which to him means possessing the noble virtues of honesty, fairness, and integrity befitting a king. Acting on virtues such as these would have the effect of placing limits on his pursuit of his ultimate goal of saving the world through conquest and rule, so it is not surprising that he regularly compromises them when it serves his interests, which contradicts the very concept of honor.

For example, Victor often claims to be honest: As he tells the Molecule Man while weaving their plan against the Beyonders, "Doom does not lie. Not now. Not ever."[69] After his scientist lackey Hauptmann interferes in a plan to defeat the Fantastic Four, Victor lets them go from his castle out of frustration, telling Sue and her temporary teammate Crystal where they can find the others. When Crystal asks Sue why they should believe him, Victor answers for her, saying "though Dr. Doom is capable of many things—the master of Latveria does not lie!"[70] Another time the team confronts Victor, Sue wonders if Victor is telling the truth, to which he replies dramatically, "Of course I speak the truth! Victor von Doom has no use for petty falsehoods. What is a paltry mistruth in the grand arena in which my life is played?"[71] Next Reed references Victor's "twisted code of honor," which is a welcome evolution from his initial trust in him, saying upon their first encounter as Mister Fantastic and Doctor Doom that "despite his other faults, Doom is not a liar! He will keep his word!"[72]

However, when it suits him, Victor does lie, and sometimes in the most shameless fashion imaginable. There may be no better example than when he takes Franklin into hell and the Fantastic Four follows to rescue him. After the team defeats Victor, the three demons he bargained with for additional mystical power claim him as their own, and Victor shamelessly begs Reed for help: "Richards, please…help me…all those years ago…you tried to save me…I should have listened to you…I'm sorry…" After thinking for a moment, Reed says, "you're lying," explaining that all Victor has ever wanted was "for me to live in the shadow of your genius" and then promising to forget him instead.[73] The fact that Victor would not only lie, but also beg for help when he has so often claimed not to need it, shows that his proclaimed "honor" is little more than pride. As Scott Lang correctly tells him during one of his spells with the team as Ant-Man, "your boast that 'Doom never lies' is always the first lie out of your mouth" and that his code of honor is "only a pretense to be the man you know you're not."[74]

Another aspect of honor that Victor often claims is that his word is good and he always keeps his agreements (which can also be considered a type of honesty). Even to himself, he claims integrity in this sense, once thinking in the midst of a conflict that "Doom has given his word" and his foe should think before he "interferes in that which my honor demands I do!"[75] However, there's usually a hitch involved that allows Victor to wriggle out of any agreement he makes. When Victor traps Franklin in hell, he opens a portal in front of the Fantastic Four, showing Franklin surrounded by flames, while he holds baby Valeria in his arms. He demands that Reed surrender "and I will release your child. On that, you have the solemn word of Doom, who always honors his promises. You know this." Reed surrenders and Victor puts Valeria down, leaving Franklin in hell and torturing the four.[76] And this wasn't even the first time Victor took Franklin into hell: Much earlier, he asks Reed and Sue for permission to take him there to help free his mother, giving his "solemn oath that I will sacrifice myself before I allow him to come to any harm!" Naturally they refuse, but Victor takes him anyway and offers the boy's soul to Mephisto in exchange for his mother's, after he argues that he is "a man of stainless honor" but because Reed did not accept his offer, he is not bound by his oath.[77]

Even Victor's recent acquisition of the title of Sorcerer Supreme resulted from a promise twisted in intention. While struggling against a global vampire infestation, Doctor Strange and his fellow sorcerer (and wife) Clea approach Victor for help, which he agrees to provide only if he can use the power that comes with the title of Sorcerer Supreme. Doctor Strange is skeptical, and tells Victor, "You say that your aims are noble. Prove it. Prove that I can trust you with this power. That I've been wrong about you. I want your oath, Victor. I want your word. Once the world is saved, you will return to me what is mine." Victor replies, "You have my word. The word of Doom." Once Victor is Sorcerer Supreme, he succeeds in eliminating the vampire threat, after which Strange asks for his power back, reminding Victor of his oath. "Yes, my oath," Victor says. "To surrender the office of Sorcerer Supreme back to you once I saved the world. And I have only just begun, Stephen," leading to Victor's latest attempt to take over the world, now aided by the power of being this dimension's Sorcerer Supreme.[78]

Victor betrays his sense of honor in many other ways as well. We have already seen that he refuses to take responsibility for his own failures (when he ever acknowledges them), instead blaming Reed, Doombots, or anyone available. He claims the virtue of *magnanimity*, a generosity and largeness of spirit, when he tells the citizens of Latveria that he is abdicating the throne to his "son," who is actually the clone he created to pass his memories to (as described above) to effectively continue his own rule.[79] He also claims to honor his obligations, such the one he owes

Kristoff's mother after she died while under his protection; as he is shown caring for the boy later, the exposition says that "evil Doom may be, but also a man of honor who pays his debts."[80] But this "honorable" act is betrayed time and time again when Victor mistreats Kristoff. Once, the boy pleads for mercy for the Fantastic Four, who took him in while Victor was believed dead, and argues on the basis of honor: "They aided me! Treated me with kindness and respect! It would be improper...and dishonorable...for me to turn against them now!" Victor backhands him, warning him not to "presume on our relationship" and reminding him that "no one—not even you—may question the will of Doom!" Afterwards, Victor ponders if "that insolent child may have finally outlived his usefulness" as an heir.[81]

Victor's greatest act of dishonor, which extends for years, may be his behavior towards the people of Latveria, claiming to love and care for them while merely using their forced obedience to prop up his ego and tamp down his insecurities. This is on display starting from the earliest stories, such as when he lures the Silver Surfer to Latveria to steal the power cosmic and claims to be "but a humble servant of my people" and "the gentlest, the most unambitious of monarchs" whose "only desire is to make my people happy—and to further the cause of peace, and of brotherly love!" Even if the Surfer didn't see through him immediately, an instant later Victor berates a lab technician for merely bumping into him, making him fear "the ultimate punishment!"[82] Later he tells Alicia "I am not the tyrant others call me," but compromises his denial when he adds that "I care for the trembling toadies whom I govern."[83] The truth is revealed, however, when Victor's moral orientation is flipped during the Axis event and he proclaims to his people that he had lied to himself for years, acknowledging that "I have used this nation. Exploited her resources for my purposes. Imperiled you all," and proclaims he no longer considers himself above them and then reveals his face for all to see.[84]

In actuality, Victor's typical rule of Latveria displays many of the facets of fascism.[85] For example, fascism emphasizes the nation over the individual, with the nation represented by a central "strongman" figure to whom absolute loyalty is expected. This is seen throughout Victor's history in Latveria, even recently when he demands an oath of fealty from those who work for him and punishes disloyalty by death.[86] He goes so far as to design a machine to "destroy the subtler emotions of loyalty and price," not only in Latveria but all over the Earth, and replace them with "loyalty only to me…to Doctor Doom!"[87] Naturally, he does not earn this loyalty through admirable and honorable behavior but through fear of punishment and retribution, to the point where parents beg their children to smile because "any sign of discontent is dealt with swiftly, violently," and there is a law the forbids speaking the name "Richards" on penalty of death, making some fear even thinking it.[88]

As fascists often do, Victor lies to his people to keep them compliant as well as fearful of the outside world. Many Latverians aren't aware of his corrupt and immoral acts, focusing on the economic stability they perceived and the military prowess he displayed, and calling for his return whenever he is deposed or disappears.[89] Even when the Fantastic Four open his castle to them and reveal his torture machines and execution chamber, they walk away in disbelief—as Sue says, "it's easier to live in ignorance than in constant fear." Reed is frustrated, but as Johnny explains to him, "Doom's had unlimited control of the media in this country since I was a kid. He told folks what to think, and he told them constantly."[90]

In addition to control or suppression of the media, fascists often invent false threats that then they can claim to have defeated, earning the gratitude of the people as well as the belief that only their leaders can or will "protect" them. This includes the Fantastic Four, whom Victor teaches his people are a danger to them: as Sue acknowledges, "it's not fair to judge them. They've always seen us as a threat, because he taught them how to think, how to feel."[91] But more specifically, Victor also invents "crises" out of whole cloth, sometimes to cover embarrassments, such as his wedding ceremony to Zora, which was thrown awry when she confessed she had slept with Johnny. When Reed asks how he was going to explain the carnage that resulted from his subsequent rage, Victor explains that "clearly, Richards, this was the work of terrorists…who were targeting me and my bride on our special day," and afterwards, the state media dutifully reports "a failed attack on our capital, our citizens, and our beloved leader."[92] He even plots to create a rebellion in a neighboring country which he can then suppress, all to create a new home for the Inhumans in hopes of making them allies.[93]

Typically, fascists emphasize power and control over the institutions of government, and Victor is no different. Despite telling Sue and Crystal that Latveria has rule of law and he is subject to it as all are, when his citizens demand he follow the law and step down after his ruse with his clone was discovered, he responds, "you believe laws written on paper are more powerful than my ultimate weapons?"[94] From the latter episode, it is clear he plans to rule forever, despite claims to the contrary, and he later tells Sharon Ventura that he is considering giving up the throne, "with its trapping of nobility…and merely taking the title, president-for-life," ruling out any chance of democratic dissent.[95]

The most troublesome aspect of Victor's fascist rule of Latveria, in common with most forms of authoritarianism, is the loss of freedom among the people to grant more power to the state and its leader. As Victor says, "I insist my subjects be happy…one way or another," and openly admits that he orders them to do so.[96] After he returns to power after a period of democracy, Victor denies any "great ill" imposed on his people, saying "I demanded of them only that they be obedient and happy" and that he removed only a single freedom: "the freedom to commit evil!"[97] However, as Captain America—no stranger to fascists—says when Victor achieves ultimate power during the first Secret Wars, "freedom to do what Doom wants is no freedom at all."[98] Victor gives the Latverian people the appearance of safety, stability, and prosperity, for which they exchange their freedom; as Victor tells Ben, "you would be surprised how many of your weak-willed countrymen would eagerly embrace complete happiness in exchange for—total blind obedience!"[99]

The Summation of Doom

The dishonorable behavior Victor displays throughout his history with the Fantastic Four, not just towards the team but also his Latverian subjects, is yet another response to his insecurity and resentment towards the world for his tragic fate. Again, the parallels and contrasts with Ben Grimm are very clear: Ben was affected horribly by the accident that transformed the four adventurers, which certainly prompted an unhealthy amount of self-loathing, but he does not take that out on the world. Instead, he has dedicated himself to using his abilities for the good of mankind. In his mind, of course, Victor also helps mankind, not in the spirit of generosity (despite his claims to magnanimity) or good will, but more as a twisted form of payback, as if to say "I'll show you what's good for you"—which just happens to be his own rule.

Victor's ethical failings can also be linked to his fear of weakness and his obsession with strength. Whereas true moral strength is seen in maintaining one's principles even when it doesn't serve one's interests, Victor quickly dismisses his proclaimed "honor" when it suits him—which can be seen as a display of strength, but in a more brutish and selfish form. It is this type of strength that is also emphasized by fascists, who exercise their power through domination and cruelty rather than support and aid, which ultimately reflects their own insecurity and fear. Hypocrisy, such as refusing to follow the laws and norms that apply to everyone else, stops being a dishonorable flaw and becomes an attractive feature of authoritarians, precisely because it shows they have the power to dismiss such restrictions—restrictions that they continue to impose on others, simply because they can.

[1] *Fantastic Four*, vol. 1, #5 (July 1962).

[2] Doom's origin was first presented in *Fantastic Four Annual*, vol. 1, #2 (1964), "The Fantastic 'Origin of Doctor Doom!'" (naturally) and elaborated on many times, most notably *Marvel Super-Heroes* #20 (May 1969), "This Man… This Demon!", *Fantastic Four*, vol. 1, #278 (May 1985), *Doctor Strange and Doctor Doom: Triumph and Torment* (July 1989), and *Books of Doom* #1-6 (January-June 2006).

[3] *Fantastic Four*, vol. 1, #278.

[4] *Fantastic Four Annual*, vol. 1, #2, "The Fantastic 'Origin of Doctor Doom!'" He also regards himself as physically disfigured more generally: In *Avengers*, vol. 1, #25 (February 1966), he gives a coin to a Latverian boy with crutches, saying that "I, too, have known what it is to be… a cripple!"

[5] *Fantastic Four Annual*, vol. 1, #2 (1964), "The Final Victory of Dr. Doom!" We will discuss such claims of honor and benevolence more below.

[6] *Fantastic Four*, vol. 1, #200 (November 1978).

[7] *Fantastic Four*, vol. 6, #8-9 (May-June 2019).

[8] *Fantastic Four*, vol. 6, #9.

[9] *Fantastic Four*, vol. 1, #296 (November 1986).

[10] *Fantastic Four*, vol. 1, #278. An unpublished sketch by Jack Kirby, widely available on the internet, suggests that he had a very tiny mark on his right check, which nonetheless drove him to destroy it completely.

[11] *Fantastic Four*, vol. 1, #17 (August 1963).

[12] *Fantastic Four*, vol. 1, #278.

[13] *Marvel Super-Heroes* #20.

[14] Ibid.

[15] *Doctor Doom*, vol. 1, #9 (January 2021). Indeed, he says he will rule "with humility the likes of which the world has never seen," with no apparent awareness that bragging about one's own "great humility" contradicts the very claim to humility.

[16] *Fantastic Four*, vol. 1, #199 (October 1978).

[17] *Doctor Doom*, vol. 1, #7 (November 2020).

[18] *Fantastic Four*, vol. 1, #380 (September 1993). Incidentally, this seems to be the same mask Sue gave Ben with their first costumes in *Fantastic Four*, vol. 1, #3 (March 1962), which she tells him "even makes *you* look glamorous!"

[19] *Fantastic Four*, vol. 6, #1 (October 2018), "Our Day of Doom and Victory."

[20] *Fantastic Four*, vol. 6, #11 (August 2019).

[21] Not that the numerous times his face has been healed ever did much good either: see, for instance, *Secret Wars*, vol. 1, #11 (March 1985); *Avengers: Children's Crusade* #8 (January 2012); and *Secret Wars*, vol. 2, #9 (March 2016). Scott Lang goes as far as to suggest that Victor scars his face himself, because "it's much easier inflicting a fake imperfection on yourself than admitting to having a real one" (*FF*, vol. 2, #16, March 2014).

[22] *Secret Wars*, vol. 1, #1 (May 1984).

[23] *Secret Wars*, vol. 1, #7 (November 1984).

[24] *FF*, vol. 1, #12 (January 2012).

[25] *Doctor Strange and Doctor Doom: Triumph and Torment*.

[26] Ibid.

[27] *Fantastic Four*, vol. 1, #381 (October 1993).

[28] *Doctor Strange and Doctor Doom: Triumph and Torment*.

[29] *Fantastic Four*, vol. 5, #12 (December 2014).

[30] *Avengers & X-Men: AXIS* #3 (December 2014); Victor admitted to controlling her power in *Avengers: Children's Crusade* #8.

[31] *Fantastic Four*, vol. 3, #53 (May 2002).

[32] *X-Men/Fantastic Four* #3 (May 2020).

[33] *Venom*, vol. 5, #24 (October 2023).

[34] *Fantastic Four*, vol. 1, #85 (April 1969).

[35] *Fantastic Four*, vol. 1, #258 (September 1983).

[36] *Fantastic Four*, vol. 1, #358 (November 1991), "The Official Story."

[37] *Doctor Doom*, vol. 1, #10 (February 2021).

[38] *Fantastic Four vs. the X-Men* #4 (June 1987).

[39] *Fantastic Four*, vol. 6, #8.

[40] *Fantastic Four*, vol. 6, #9.

[41] *Doctor Doom*, vol. 1, #9.

[42] *Fantastic Four vs. the X-Men* #4.

[43] *Fantastic Four vs. the X-Men* #3 (April 1987).

[44] *Fantastic Four vs. the X-Men* #4.

[45] *Fantastic Four*, vol. 3, #25 (January 1999).

[46] *Fantastic Four*, vol. 1, #350 (March 1991).

[47] *Fantastic Four*, vol. 6, #7 (April 2019).

[48] *Fantastic Four*, vol. 3, #54 (June 2002), "A Choice of Dooms!" Sue's miscarriage was shown in *Fantastic Four*, vol. 1, #267 (June 1984), and Franklin used his power to revive that child for Sue's new pregnancy in *Fantastic Four*, vol. 3, #49 (January 2002).

[49] *Fantastic Four*, vol. 3, #68 (June 2003).

[50] *Fantastic Four*, vol. 3, #583 (November 2010); *Fantastic Four Annual*, vol. 5, #1 (2014); *Avengers World* #15 (January 2015)

[51] *X-Men/Fantastic Four* #2 (April 2020). And to drive the point home to Reed, Victor says nearly the same thing to Sue in front of him: "Those children mean the world to me. I am simply doing… what his father could not" (*X-Men/Fantastic Four* #3).

[52] *X-Men/Fantastic Four* #3.

[53] *Secret Wars*, vol. 2, #9.

[54] *Fantastic Four Special* #1 (2005).

[55] *Fantastic Four*, vol. 6, #32 (July 2021), "Duel Intentions."

[56] *Fantastic Four*, vol. 6, #33 (August 2021).

[57] *Fantastic Four Unplugged* #2 (October 1995).

[58] *Marvel 2-in-One Annual* #1 (2018).

[59] *Infamous Iron Man* #1 (December 2016).

[60] *Marvel 2-in-One* #11 (December 2018). Victor's last battle as Iron Man is in *Invincible Iron Man*, vol. 2, #600 (July 2018), after which he returns to Latveria, scarred and beaten, where he is discovered by Zora as described above (*Fantastic Four*, vol. 6, #1, "Our Day of Doom and Victory").

[61] *Fantastic Four Special* #1.

[62] *Fantastic Four*, vol. 6, #7.

[63] *Super-Villain Team-Up* #12 (June 1977).

[64] *Avengers & X-Men: AXIS* #3.

[65] *New Avengers*, vol. 3, #33 (June 2015).

[66] *Secret Wars*, vol. 2, #9.

[67] *Doomwar* #3 (June 2010), in which the rest of the episode with Bast is found.

[68] *Fantastic Four*, vol. 1, #375 (April 1993).

[69] *New Avengers*, vol. 3, #27 (January 2015).

[70] *Fantastic Four*, vol. 1, #87 (June 1969). Similarly, when Doom demands Alicia create a sculpture of him and she doubts he'll free her afterwards as promised, he

tells her, "Doom may do many things—but does not lie!" (*Fantastic Four*, vol. 1, #199).

[71] *Fantastic Four*, vol. 1, #247 (October 1982).

[72] *Fantastic Four*, vol. 1, #5.

[73] *Fantastic Four*, vol. 3, #500 (September 2003).

[74] *FF*, vol., 2, #16.

[75] *Super-Villain Team-Up* #13 (August 1977).

[76] *Fantastic Four*, vol. 3, #70 (August 2003). Part of Victor's torture of Reed apparently involves projecting all Victor's faults onto him, as recounted in chapter 2, note 45.

[77] *Fantastic Four*, vol. 1, #20 (1987).

[78] *Blood Hunt* #5 (September 2024). As I finish work on this book, Victor has succeeded in his latest world conquest, as seen in *One World Under Doom* #1 (April 2025). If you want a revised edition of this book after we see how this story ends, let the good people at Ockham Publishing know today!

[79] *Fantastic Four*, vol. 1, #197 (August 1978).

[80] *Fantastic Four*, vol. 1, #258.

[81] *Fantastic Four*, vol. 1, #409 (February 1996).

[82] *Fantastic Four*, vol. 1, #57 (December 1966).

[83] *Fantastic Four*, vol. 1, #199.

[84] *Avengers & X-Men: AXIS* #6 (January 2015).

[85] For readable introductions to fascism, see Timothy Snyder, *On Tyranny: Twenty Lessons from the Twentieth Century* (New York, NY: Crown, 2017) and Jason Stanley, *How Fascism Works: The Politics of Us and Them* (New York, NY: Random House, 2018). I discuss it with respect to Steve Rogers's conversion to the Hydra side and their subsequent takeover of the world in my book *The Virtues of Captain America: Modern-Day Lessons on Character from a World War II Superhero*, 2nd ed. (Hoboken, NJ: Wiley & Sons, 2024), chapter 7.

[86] *Doctor Doom*, vol. 1, #7.

[87] *Fantastic Four*, vol. 1, #143 (February 1974).

[88] *Fantastic Four*, vol. 1, #381; *War of the Realms: War Scrolls* #3 (August 2019), "A Rose for Victor."

[89] For example, see *Fantastic Four Annual*, vol. 1, #15 (1980), "The Power of the People," and *Fantastic Four*, vol. 1, #247.

[90] *Fantastic Four*, vol. 3, #504 (December 2003).

[91] *Fantastic Four*, vol. 3, #503 (November 2003).

[92] *Fantastic Four*, vol. 6, #34 (September 2021).

[93] *Fantastic Four*, vol. 3, #53.

[94] *Fantastic Four*, vol. 1, #87; *Fantastic Four*, vol. 1, #200.

[95] *Fantastic Four*, vol. 1, #350.

[96] *Fantastic Four*, vol. 1, #198 (September 1978); see also *Fantastic Four*, vol. 1, #258 and #380.

[97] *Fantastic Four*, vol. 1, #247.

[98] *Secret Wars*, vol. 1, #11.

[99] *Fantastic Four*, vol. 1, #380.

Conclusion

"What a revoltin' development!" I'm sure that's what the most literary member of the Fantastic Four would say when he realizes his new favorite book is coming to an end. I'm upset too, because there's so much more we could have discussed. For instance, consider the kids, Franklin and Valeria. We've seen Franklin literally create universes teeming with new life—what responsibility does he bear for their fate? How does Valeria use her genius intellect when her two chief role models are her father and "Uncle Victor"? Finally, how have Reed and Sue fared in protecting their kids from the world—as well as protecting the world from their kids?

The Fantastic Four's world in particular is incredibly rich with amazing characters, all of whom should have received a chapter. We talked about Alicia in chapter 5, but there is so much more we could have explored in terms of her relationship with her step-father the Puppet-Master, her time in space with the Silver Surfer, and the ways her blindness contributes to her life as an artist, a partner, and a mother (not to mention a superhero in her own right). Also, consider the other heroes who have spent time in the group, including She-Hulk, Crystal, and Spider-Man, each of whom changed the group's ethical dynamic of the team with their own unique moral characters. Even when not a member, Spidey was an integral part of the extended family, a close friend to Johnny and a scientific protégé of Reed who even dated Sue (once). How did the relationship between Marvel's First Family and its resident wall-crawler affect them all?

As well as other characters, there was so much more to say about the core four's ethics that I could have written an entire book about each one. How does Reed balance his passion for scientific experimentation with the responsibility to conduct research ethically? Does Sue ever cross a line in her long-simmering romantic intrigue with Namor? What does Johnny's quest for fame outside being the Human Torch say about what he values most in life? How was Ben's behavior different with his romantic partners other than Alicia, especially as it reflects his self-loathing? And let's not forget Doom, whose quest for power seems to go beyond his self-proclaimed desire to save humanity, and whose search for knowledge is motivated very differently than Reed's.

Finally, there is much more to philosophy than ethics! Just in terms of metaphysics, we could talk about time travel and its many paradoxes, alternate versions of a person and how they're related, and the nature of the multiverse itself—all of which play an essential role in the Fantastic Four's adventures. Add to that epistemology (how much can Reed actually *know*?), logic (how does Doom manage to twist every defeat into victory?), and aesthetics (why *didn't* the red costumes work?), and we see that the possibilities for deep questions about our favorite superhero family are endless.

I'm sure you can come up with your own philosophical questions about the Fantastic Four too—we've only scratched the surface here! As Reed, Sue, Johnny, and Ben go on their adventures of scientific exploration, they inspire us to launch our own adventures of philosophical exploration as well. Based on their decades of stories, we can continue to apply time-honored ideas to imaginative new examples and situations and maybe even develop new ones in the process. As long as there are new Fantastic Four adventures in any medium, there will be new opportunities for philosophical discussion—which is not a revoltin' development at all!

A Reading Guide to the *Fantastic Four*

As with most long-standing Marvel Comics titles, *Fantastic Four* has a long history that stretches all the way back to November 1961, when the first issue of the modern Marvel Universe hit the stands. The first volume of *Fantastic Four* ran continuously through issue #416 in September 1996, during which time the Human Torch featured in *Strange Tales* #101-134 (October 1962-July 1965), and his co-star for the last eleven issues, the Thing, enjoyed his own team-up title *Marvel Two-in-One* for an even one hundred issues from January 1974 to June 1983, followed by 36 issues of *The Thing* from July 1983 to June 1986. (Johnny also shared top billing with Spider-Man in the first three issues of *Marvel Team-Up*, starting in March 1972, before it mostly changed to a Spidey team-up book, occasionally featuring the Fantastic Four, separately and collectively.)

After a battle with the powerful psychic entity Onslaught, the Fantastic Four, with most of the Avengers, wound up in a pocket universe of Franklin Richards' creation for the "Heroes Reborn" period, including volume 2 of *Fantastic Four* (thirteen issues from November 1996-September 1997). After they returned to the 616 universe, volume 3 of *Fantastic Four* began in January 1998, reverting after issue #70 to #500 (its "legacy numbering," or the number the issue would have had if the numbering had been continuous since the first issue) and then lasting to #588 in April 2011, during which time a 30-issue run of a title simply named *4* (under the "edgy" Marvel Knights imprint) ran from April 2004 to July

2006.[1] The first volume of *FF* began the next month, and after the first eleven issues, the *Fantastic Four* title returned with its legacy numbering of #600.

Both titles ran concurrently until December 2012, with *Fantastic Four* ending at issue #611 and *FF* ending at issue #23, before both re-launched as the fourth volume of *Fantastic Four* and the second volume of *FF*, respectively, in January 2013. Both titles lasted sixteen issues through March 2014, after which the fifth volume of *Fantastic Four*—starting with the team in red outfits (!)—ran eighteen issues from April 2014 to June 2015 (the last four of them reverting to legacy numbering, issues #642-645).

At this point, the Marvel Universe ended, went through (the second) *Secret Wars*, and was reborn, but without the Fantastic Four or a comic to their name. While Reed and Sue were missing and presumed dead, Ben and Johnny served with various other teams and later starred in their own team-up book, *Marvel 2-in-One*, lasting twelve issues from February 2018 to January 2019. Near the end of that book, Reed and Sue returned, and the sixth volume of *Fantastic Four* began, lasting 48 issues from October 2018 to December 2022, followed by the seventh volume, which lasted 33 issues from January 2023 to August 2025, and the eighth volume, beginning in September 2025. This is to say nothing of the many other shorter ongoing series and mini-series that the team and the various members have enjoyed over the years…and don't get me started on Doctor Doom, who has enjoyed a number of featured titles outside of his regular focus in the *Fantastic Four* title!

References

All comics cited in this book are listed below with their publication dates, writers, and artists (pencillers, inkers, and colorists); story titles are given only when there are multiple stories in the comic. Most issues are available to buy digitally from Marvel.com or through Marvel Unlimited, and have been collected in either Epic Collections, Marvel Masterworks, or dedicated collections, with the most recent or convenient one listed with each issue.

4 #7 (September 2004). Roberto Aguirre-Sacasa (w), Steve McNiven, Mark Morales, and Morry Hollowell (a). Collected in *Marvel Knights Fantastic Four by Aguirre-Sacasa, McNiven & Muniz: The Complete Collection* (2019).

4 #9 (October 2004). Roberto Aguirre-Sacasa (w), Valentine De Landro, Matt Banning, and Dan Kemp (a). Collected as above.

4 #16 (May 2005). Roberto Aguirre-Sacasa (w), Jim Muniz, Jim Royal, Derek Fridolfs, and Brian Reber (a). Collected in *Marvel Knights 4: Divine Time* (2005).

4 #22 (November 2005). Roberto Aguirre-Sacasa (w), Jim Muniz, Cam Smith, Scott Hanna, and Brian Reber (a). Collected in *Marvel Knights 4: Impossible Things Happen Every Day* (2006).

Amazing Spider-Man, vol. 1, #3 (July 1963). Stan Lee and Steve Ditko (w) and Steve Ditko (a). Collected in *Amazing Spider-Man Epic Collection: Great Power* (2014).

Amazing Spider-Man, vol. 1, #18 (November 1964). Stan Lee (w) and Steve Ditko (a). Collected in *Amazing Spider-Man Epic Collection: Great Responsibility* (2016).

Amazing Spider-Man, vol. 2, #530 (May 2006). J. Michael Straczynski (w), Tyler Kirkham, Jay Leisten, and John Starr (a). Collected in *Civil War: The Road to Civil War* (2007).

Amazing Spider-Man, vol. 2, #533 (August 2006). J. Michael Straczynski (w), Ron Garney, Bill Reinhold, and Matt Milla (a). Collected in *Civil War: Amazing Spider-Man* (2007).

Amazing Spider-Man, vol. 2, #535 (November 2006). Same as above.

Amazing Spider-Man, vol. 2, #537 (February 2007). Same as above.

Amazing Spider-Man, vol. 2, #661 (July 2011), "The Substitute, Part One." Christos N. Gage (w), Reilly Brown, Victor Olazaba, and John Rauch (a). Collected in *Amazing Spider-Man: The Fantastic Spider-Man* (2012).

Annihilation: Silver Surfer #1 (June 2006). Keith Giffen (w), Renato Arlem and June Chung (a). Collected in *Annihilation Modern Era Epic Collection: Annihilation Day* (2025).

Annihilation: Silver Surfer #3 (August 2006). Same as above.

Annihilation: Silver Surfer #4 (September 2006). Same as above.

Avengers, vol. 1, #25 (February 1966). Stan Lee (w), Don Heck, Dick Ayers, and Stan Goldberg (a). Collected in *Avengers Epic Collection: Once an Avenger* (2014).

Avengers, vol. 1, #168 (February 1978). Jim Shooter (w), George Pérez, Pablo Marcos, and Phil Rache (a). Collected in *Avengers Epic Collection: The Yesterday Quest* (2023).

Avengers, vol. 1, #190 (December 1979). Roger Stern and Steven Grant (w), John Byrne, Dan Green, and Bean Sean (a). Collected in *Avengers Epic Collection: The Evil Reborn* (2024).

Avengers, vol. 7, #678 (March 2018). Mark Waid, Al Ewing, and Jim Zub (w), Pepe Larraz and David Curiel (a). Collected in *Avengers: No Surrender* (2018).

Avengers, vol. 8, #66 (May 2023). Jason Aaron (w), Javier Garrón, David Curiel, Morry Hollowell, Erick Arciniega, and Rachelle Rosenberg (a). Collected in *Avengers Assemble* (2023).

Avengers: The Children's Crusade #8 (January 2012). Allan Heinberg (w), Jim Cheung, Mark Morales, John Livesay, Justin Ponsor, and Paul Mounts (a). Collected in *Avengers: The Children's Crusade* (2012).

Avengers World #15 (January 2015). Nick Spencer and Frank Barbiere (w), Marco Checchetto and Andres Mossa (a). Collected in *Avengers World: The Complete Collection* 2019).

Avengers & X-Men: AXIS #3 (December 2014). Rick Remender (w), Leinil Francis Yu, Gerry Alanguilan, Matt Milla, Laura Martin, and Edgar Delgado (a). Collected in *Avengers & X-Men: AXIS* (2015).

Avengers & X-Men: AXIS #6 (January 2015). Rick Remender (w), Terry Dodson, Rachel Dodson, Edgar Delgado, and Jesus Aburtov (a). Collected as above.

Blood Hunt #5 (September 2024). Jed MacKay (w), Pepe Larraz, Marte Garcia, and Fer Sifuentes-Sujo (a). Collected in *Blood Hunt* (2024).

Books of Doom #1 (January 2006). Ed Brubaker (w), Pablo Raimondi, Mark Farmer, and Brian Reber (a). Collected in *Doctor Doom: Books of Doom* (2025).

Books of Doom #2 (February 2006). Same as above.

Books of Doom #3 (March 2006). Same as above.

Books of Doom #4 (April 2006). Same as above.

Books of Doom #5 (May 2006). Ed Brubaker (w), Pablo Raimondi, Andrew Hennessy, and Brian Reber (a). Collected as above.

Books of Doom #6 (June 2006). Same as above.

Captain America, vol. 1, #333 (September 1987). Mark Gruenwald (w), Tom Morgan, Dave Hunt, and Ken Feduniewicz (a). Collected in *Captain America Epic Collection: The Captain* (2021).

Civil War #1 (July 2006). Mark Millar (w), Steve McNiven, Dexter Vines, and Morry Hollowell (a). Collected in *Civil War* (2007).

Civil War #2 (August 2006). Same as above.

Civil War #3 (September 2006). Mark Millar (w), Steve McNiven, Dexter Vines, Mark Morales, and Morry Hollowell (a). Collected as above.

Civil War #4 (October 2006). Mark Millar (w), Steve McNiven, Dexter Vines, and Morry Hollowell (a). Collected as above.

Civil War #7 (January 2007). Mark Millar (w), Steve McNiven, Dexter Vines, John Dell, Tim Townsend, and Morry Hollowell (a). Collected as above.

Civil War: Choosing Sides #1, December 2006, "Choosing Sides." Ed Brubaker and Matt Fraction (w), David Aja and Matt Hollingsworth (a). Collected in *The Immortal Iron Fist: The Last Iron Fist Story* (2007).

Civil War II #1 (August 2016). Brian Michael Bendis (w), David Marquez and Justin Ponsor (a). Collected in *Civil War II* (2017).

Daredevil, vol. 1, #261 (December 1988). Ann Nocenti (w), John Romita, Jr., Al Williamson, and Gregory Wright (a). Collected in *Daredevil Epic Collection: A Touch of Typhoid* (2016).

Dark Reign: Fantastic Four #1 (May 2009). Jonathan Hickman (w), Sean Chen, Lorenzao Ruggiero, and John Rauch (a). Collected in *Dark Reign: Fantastic Four* (2009).

Dark Reign: Fantastic Four #4 (August 2009). Same as above.

Doctor Doom, vol. 1, #7 (November 2020). Christopher Cantwell (w), Salvador Larroca and Guru-eFX (a). Collected in *Doctor Doom by Cantwell & Larroca* (2024).

Doctor Doom, vol. 1, #9 (January 2021). Same as above.

Doctor Doom, vol. 1, #10 (February 2021). Same as above.

Doctor Strange and Doctor Doom: Triumph and Torment (July 1989). Roger Stern (w), Mike Mignola and Mark Badger (a). Collected in *Fantastic Four Epic Collection: The Dream Is Dead* (2023).

Doomwar #3 (June 2010). Jonathan Maberry (w), Scot Eaton, Andy Lanning, Robert Campanella, and Jean-François Beaulieu (a). Collected in *Black Panther: Doomwar* (2017).

Doomwar #4 (July 2010). Same as above.

Empyre #1 (September 2020). Al Ewing and Dan Slott (w), Valerio Schiti and Marte Gracia (a). Collected in *Empyre* (2020).

Empyre #3 (September 2020). Same as above.

Empyre #6 (November 2020). Same as above.

Empyre: Fantastic Four #0 (September 2020). Dan Slott (w), R.B. Silva, Sean Izaakse, Marte Gracia, and Marcio Menyz (a). Collected as above.

Fantastic Four, vol. 1, #1 (November 1961). Stan Lee (w), Jack Kirby, George Klein, Christopher Rule, and Stan Goldberg (a). Collected in *Fantastic Four Epic Collection: The World's Greatest Comic Magazine* (2014).

Fantastic Four, vol. 1, #2 (January 1962). Stan Lee (w), Jack Kirby, George Klein, and Stan Goldberg (a). Collected as above.

Fantastic Four, vol. 1, #3 (March 1962). Stan Lee (w), Jack Kirby, Sol Brodsky, and Stan Goldberg (a). Collected as above.

Fantastic Four, vol. 1, #5 (July 1962). Stan Lee (w), Jack Kirby, Joe Sinnott, and Stan Goldberg (a). Collected as above.

Fantastic Four, vol. 1, #6 (September 1962).). Stan Lee (w), Jack Kirby, Dick Ayers, Joe Sinnott, and Stan Goldberg (a). Collected as above.

Fantastic Four, vol. 1, #8 (November 1962). Stan Lee (w), Jack Kirby, Dick Ayers, and Stan Goldberg (a). Collected as above.

Fantastic Four, vol. 1, #9 (December 1962). Same as above.

Fantastic Four, vol. 1, #11 (February 1963), "A Visit with the Fantastic Four." Stan Lee (w), Jack Kirby, Dick Ayers, and Stan Goldberg (a). Collected as above.

Fantastic Four, vol. 1, #12 (March 1963). Same as above.

Fantastic Four, vol. 1, #13 (April 1963). Stan Lee (w), Jack Kirby, Steve Ditko, and Stan Goldberg (a). Collected as above.

Fantastic Four, vol. 1, #14 (May 1963). Same as above.

Fantastic Four, vol. 1, #16 (July 1983). Stan Lee (w), Jack Kirby, Dick Ayers, and Stan Goldberg (a). Collected as above.

Fantastic Four, vol. 1, #17 (August 1963). Same as above.

Fantastic Four, vol. 1, #22 (January 1964). Stan Lee (w), Jack Kirby and George Roussos (a). Collected in *Fantastic Four Epic Collection: The Master Plan of Doctor Doom* (2017).

Fantastic Four, vol. 1, #23 (February 1964). Same as above.

Fantastic Four, vol. 1, #24 (March 1964). Same as above.

Fantastic Four, vol. 1, #25 (April 1964). Same as above.

Fantastic Four, vol. 1, #28 (July 1964). Stan Lee (w), Jack Kirby and Chic Stone (a). Collected as above.

Fantastic Four, vol. 1, #29 (August 1964). Same as above.

Fantastic Four, vol. 1, #32 (November 1964). Same as above.

Fantastic Four, vol. 1, #37 (April 1965). Same creators as above. Collected in *Fantastic Four Epic Collection: The Coming of Galactus* (2018).

Fantastic Four, vol. 1, #38 (May 1965). Same as above.

Fantastic Four, vol. 1, #41 (August 1965). Stan Lee (w), Jack Kirby and Vince Colletta (a). Collected as above.

Fantastic Four, vol. 1, #42 (September 1965). Same as above.

Fantastic Four, vol. 1, #45 (December 1965). Stan Lee (w), Jack Kirby and Joe Sinnott (a). Collected as above.

Fantastic Four, vol. 1, #47 (February 1966). Same as above.

Fantastic Four, vol. 1, #48 (March 1966). Same as above.

Fantastic Four, vol. 1, #49 (April 1966). Same as above.

Fantastic Four, vol. 1, #50 (May 1966). Stan Lee (w), Jack Kirby, Joe Sinnott, and Stan Goldberg (a). Collected as above.

Fantastic Four, vol. 1, #52 (July 1966). Stan Lee and Jack Kirby (w), Jack Kirby, Joe Sinnott, and Stan Goldberg (a). Collected in *Fantastic Four Epic Collection: The Mystery of the Black Panther* (2019).

Fantastic Four, vol. 1, #56 (November 1966). Stan Lee (w), Jack Kirby and Joe Sinnott (a). Collected as above.

Fantastic Four, vol. 1, #57 (December 1966). Same as above.

Fantastic Four, vol. 1, #58 (January 1967). Same as above.

Fantastic Four, vol. 1, #60 (March 1967). Same as above.

Fantastic Four, vol. 1, #63 (June 1967). Same as above.

Fantastic Four, vol. 1, #65 (August 1967). Same as above.

Fantastic Four, vol. 1, #68 (November 1967). Same creators as above. Collected in *Fantastic Four Epic Collection: The Name Is Doom* (2020).

Fantastic Four, vol. 1, #75 (June 1968). Same as above.

Fantastic Four, vol. 1, #78 (September 1968). Same as above.

Fantastic Four, vol. 1, #79 (October 1968). Same as above.

Fantastic Four, vol. 1, #85 (April 1969). Same as above.

Fantastic Four, vol. 1, #87 (June 1969). Same as above.

Fantastic Four, vol. 1, #90 (September 1969). Same creators as above. Collected in *Fantastic Four Epic Collection: At War with Atlantis* (2020).

Fantastic Four, vol. 1, #94 (January 1970). Same as above.

Fantastic Four, vol. 1, #97 (April 1970). Stan Lee (w), Jack Kirby and Frank Giacoia (a). Collected as above.

Fantastic Four, vol. 1, #99 (June 1970). Stan Lee (w), Jack Kirby and Joe Sinnott (a). Collected as above.

Fantastic Four, vol. 1, #105 (December 1970). Stan Lee (w), John Romita, Sr., and John Verpotten (a). Collected in *Fantastic Four Epic Collection: Battle of the Behemoths* (2021).

Fantastic Four, vol. 1, #106 (January 1971). Stan Lee (w), John Romita, Sr., and Joe Sinnott (a). Collected as above.

Fantastic Four, vol. 1, #107 (February 1971). Stan Lee (w), John Buscema and Joe Sinnott (a). Collected as above.

Fantastic Four, vol. 1, #113 (August 1971). Same as above.

Fantastic Four, vol. 1, #123 (June 1972). Same as above.

Fantastic Four, vol. 1, #124 (July 1972). Same as above.

Fantastic Four, vol. 1, #125 (August 1972). Same as above.

Fantastic Four, vol. 1, #132 (March 1973). Roy Thomas (w), John Buscema, Joe Sinnott, and Petra Goldberg (a). Collected in *Fantastic Four Epic Collection: Annihilus Revealed* (2022).

Fantastic Four, vol. 1, #139 (October 1973). Gerry Conway (w), John Buscema, Joe Sinnott, and Stan Goldberg (a). Collected as above.

Fantastic Four, vol. 1, #141 (December 1973). Gerry Conway (w), John Buscema, Joe Sinnott, and George Roussos (a). Collected as above.

Fantastic Four, vol. 1, #142 (January 1974). Gerry Conway (w), Rich Buckler, Joe Sinnott, and Petra Goldberg (a). Collected as above.

Fantastic Four, vol. 1, #143 (February 1974). Gerry Conway (w), Rich Buckler, Frank Giacoia, and Petra Goldberg (a). Collected as above.

Fantastic Four, vol. 1, #149 (August 1974). Gerry Conway (w), Rich Buckler, Joe Sinnott, and Petra Goldberg (a). Collected in *Fantastic Four Epic Collection: The Crusader Syndrome* (2023).

Fantastic Four, vol. 1, #166 (January 1976). Roy Thomas (w), George Pérez, Vince Colletta, and Phil Rachelson (a). Collected as above.

Fantastic Four, vol. 1, #167 (February 1976). Roy Thomas (w), George Pérez, Joe Sinnott, and Phil Rachelson (a). Collected as above.

Fantastic Four, vol. 1, #168 (March 1976). Roy Thomas (w), Rich Buckler, Joe Sinnott, and Phil Rachelson (a). Collected in *Fantastic Four Epic Collection: Counter-Earth Must Due* (2024).

Fantastic Four, vol. 1, #169 (April 1976). Same as above.

Fantastic Four, vol. 1, #173 (August 1976). Roy Thomas (w), John Buscema, Joe Sinnott, and Phil Rachelson (a). Collected as above.

Fantastic Four, vol. 1, #175 (October 1976). Roy Thomas (w), John Buscema, and Janice Cohen (a). Collected as above.

Fantastic Four, vol. 1, #176 (November 1976). Roy Thomas (w), George Pérez, Joe Sinnott, and Michele Wolfman (a). Collected as above.

Fantastic Four, vol. 1, #197 (August 1978). Marv Wolfman (w), Keith Pollard, Joe Sinnott, and Barry Grossman (a). Collected in *Fantastic Four Epic Collection: Four No More* (2025).

Fantastic Four, vol. 1, #198 (September 1978). Marv Wolfman (w), Keith Pollard, Joe Sinnott, and Janice Cohen (a). Collected as above.

Fantastic Four, vol. 1, #199 (October 1978). Same as above.

Fantastic Four, vol. 1, #200 (November 1978). Marv Wolfman (w), Keith Pollard, Joe Sinnott, and Francoise Mouly (a). Collected as above.

Fantastic Four, vol. 1, #201 (December 1978). Same as above.

Fantastic Four, vol. 1, #205 (April 1979). Marv Wolfman (w), Keith Pollard, Joe Sinnott, and Glynis Wein (a). Collected as above.

Fantastic Four, vol.1, #208 (July 1979). Marv Wolfman (w), Sal Buscema, Al Milgrom, Frank Giacoia, Frank Springer, and Glynis Wein (a). Collected as above.

Fantastic Four, vol. 1, #211 (October 1979). Marv Wolfman (w), John Byrne, Joe Sinnott, and Ben Sean (a). Collected as above.

Fantastic Four, vol. 1, #214 (January 1980). Marv Wolfman (w), John Byrne, Joe Sinnott, and Carl Gafford (a). Collected as above.

Fantastic Four, vol. 1, #216 (March 1980). Marv Wolfman and Bill Mantlo (w), John Byrne, Pablo Marcos, and Carl Gafford (a). Collected in *Fantastic Four Epic Collection: The Possession of Franklin Richards* (2025).

Fantastic Four, vol. 1, #223 (October 1980). Doug Moench (w), Bill Sienkiewicz, Joe Sinnott, and Phil Rachelson (a). Collected as above.

Fantastic Four, vol. 1, #224 (November 1980). Doug Moench (w), Bill Sienkiewicz, Pablo Marcos, and George Roussos (a). Collected as above.

Fantastic Four, vol. 1, #225 (December 1980). Same as above.

Fantastic Four, vol. 1, #226 (January 1981). Doug Moench (w), Bill Sienkiewicz, Pablo Marcos, Bruce Patterson, and George Roussos (a). Collected as above.

Fantastic Four, vol. 1, #236 (November 1981), "Terror in a Tiny Town." John Byrne (w), John Byrne and Glynis Wein (a). Collected in *Fantastic Four by John Byrne Omnibus Vol. 1* (2011).

Fantastic Four, vol. 1, #238 (January 1982), "The More Things Change…" John Byrne (w), John Byrne, Terry Austin, and Bob Sharen (a). Collected as above.

Fantastic Four, vol. 1, #239 (February 1982). John Byrne (w), John Byrne and Glynis Wein (a). Collected as above.

Fantastic Four, vol. 1, #240 (March 1982). Same as above.

Fantastic Four, vol. 1, #243 (June 1982). Same as above.

Fantastic Four, vol. 1, #244 (July 1982). Same as above.

Fantastic Four, vol. 1, #245 (August 1982). John Byrne (w), John Byrne and Bob Sharen (a). Collected as above.

Fantastic Four, vol. 1, #246 (September 1982). John Byrne (w), John Byrne and Glynis Wein (a). Collected as above.

Fantastic Four, vol. 1, #247 (October 1982). Same as above.

Fantastic Four, vol. 1, #250 (January 1983). John Byrne (w), John Byrne and Christie Scheele (a). Collected as above.

Fantastic Four, vol. 1, #251 (February 1983). John Byrne (w), John Byrne and Glynis Wein (a). Collected as above.

Fantastic Four, vol. 1, #256 (July 1983). Same as above.

Fantastic Four, vol. 1, #257 (August 1983). Same as above.

Fantastic Four, vol. 1, #258 (September 1983). Same as above.

Fantastic Four, vol. 1, #261 (December 1983). Same creators as above. Collected in *Fantastic Four by John Byrne Omnibus Vol. 2* (2013).

Fantastic Four, vol. 1, #262 (January 1984). Same as above.

Fantastic Four, vol. 1, #267 (June 1984). Same as above.

Fantastic Four, vol. 1, #270 (September 1984). Same as above.

Fantastic Four, vol. 1, #271 (October 1984). Same as above.

Fantastic Four, vol. 1, #272 (November 1984). Same as above.

Fantastic Four, vol. 1, #274 (January 1985). John Byrne (w), John Byrne and Al Gordon (a). Collected as above.

Fantastic Four, vol. 1, #278 (May 1985). John Byrne (w), John Byrne, Jerry Ordway, and Glynis Oliver (a). Collected as above.

Fantastic Four, vol. 1, #280 (July 1985). Same as above.

Fantastic Four, vol. 1, #281 (August 1985). Same as above.

Fantastic Four, vol. 1, #283 (October 1985). Same as above.

Fantastic Four, vol. 1, #284 (November 1985). John Byrne (w), John Byrne, Al Gordon, and Glynis Oliver (a). Collected as above.

Fantastic Four, vol. 1, #285 (December 1985). Same as above.

Fantastic Four, vol. 1, #296 (November 1986). Stan Lee and Jim Shooter (w), Barry Windsor-Smith, Kerry Gammill, Ron Frenz, Al Milgrom, John Buscema, Marc Silvestri, Jerry Ordway, Vince Colletta, Bob Wiacek, Klaus Janson, Steve Leialoha, Joe Rubinstein, and Joe Sinnott (a). Collected in *Fantastic Four Epic Collection: All in the Family* (2014).

Fantastic Four, vol. 1, #298 (January 1987). Roger Stern (w), John Buscema, Sal Buscema, and Glynis Oliver (a). Collected as above.

Fantastic Four, vol. 1, #299 (February 1987). Same as above.

Fantastic Four, vol. 1, #300 (March 1987). Same as above.

Fantastic Four, vol. 1, #303 (June 1987). Roy Thomas (w), John Buscema, Romeo Tanghal, and Glynis Oliver (a). Collected as above.

Fantastic Four, vol. 1, #317 (August 1988). Steve Englehart (w), Keith Pollard, Romeo Tanghal, and George Roussos (a). Collected in *Fantastic Four Epic Collection: The More Things Change...* (2019).

Fantastic Four, vol. 1, #334 (December 1989). Walt Simonson (w), Rich Buckler, Romeo Tanghal, and George Roussos (a). Collected in *Fantastic Four Epic Collection: Into the Time Stream* (2014).

Fantastic Four, vol. 1, #335 (December 1989). Same as above.

Fantastic Four, vol. 1, #336 (January 1990). Walt Simonson (w), Ron Lim, Mike DeCarlo, and George Roussos (a). Collected as above.

Fantastic Four, vol. 1, #342 (July 1990). Danny Fingeroth (w), Rex Valve, Chris Ivy, and Nel Yomtov (a). Collected as above.

Fantastic Four, vol. 1, #350 (March 1991). Walt Simonson (w), Walt Simonson, Al Milgrom, and Brad Vancata (a). Collected in *Fantastic Four Epic Collection: The New Fantastic Four* (2018).

Fantastic Four, vol. 1, #351 (April 1991). Len Kaminski (w), Mark Bagley, Dan Panosian, and Max Scheele (a). Collected as above.

Fantastic Four, vol. 1, #357 (October 1991). Tom DeFalco (w), Paul Ryan, Danny Bulanadi, and Christie Scheele (a). Collected as above.

Fantastic Four, vol. 1, #358 (November 1991), "The Official Story." Tom DeFalco (w), Arthur Adams, Marie Javins, and Renee Witterstaetter (a). Collected as above.

Fantastic Four, vol. 1, #358 (November 1991), "Whatever Happened to Alicia?" Tom DeFalco (w), Paul Ryan, Danny Bulanadi, and Christie Scheele (a). Collected as above.

Fantastic Four, vol.1, #359 (December 1991). Same as above.

Fantastic Four, vol. 1, #364 (May 1992). Tom DeFalco (w), Paul Ryan, Danny Bulanadi, Max Scheele, and Paul Becton (a). Collected in *Fantastic Four Epic Collection: This Flame, This Fury* (2021).

Fantastic Four, vol. 1, #366 (July 1992). Tom DeFalco and Paul Ryan (w), Paul Ryan, Danny Bulanadi, and Gina Going (a). Collected as above.

Fantastic Four, vol. 1, #367 (August 1992). Tom DeFalco (w), Paul Ryan, Christopher Ivy, Raymond Kryssing, and Gina Going (a). Collected as above.

Fantastic Four, vol.1, #368 (September 1992). Tom DeFalco (w), Paul Ryan, Danny Bulanadi, and Gina Going (a). Collected as above.

Fantastic Four, vol. 1, #369 (October 1992). Same as above.

Fantastic Four, vol. 1, #370 (November 1992). Same as above.

Fantastic Four, vol. 1, #371 (December 1992). Same as above.

Fantastic Four, vol. 1, #372 (January 1993). Same as above.

Fantastic Four, vol. 1, #375 (April 1993). Tom DeFalco and Paul Ryan (w), Paul Ryan, Danny Bulanadi, and Gina Going (a). Collected as above.

Fantastic Four, vol. 1, #376 (May 1993). Same as above.

Fantastic Four, vol. 1, #378 (July 1993). Tom DeFalco (w), Paul Ryan, Danny Bulanadi, and Gina Going (a). Collected in *Fantastic Four Epic Collection: Nobody Gets Out Alive* (2022).

Fantastic Four, vol. 1, #379 (August 1993). Same as above.

Fantastic Four, vol. 1, #380 (September 1993). Same as above.

Fantastic Four, vol. 1, #381 (October 1993). Same as above.

Fantastic Four, vol. 1, #382 (November 1993). Same as above.

Fantastic Four, vol. 1, #383 (December 1993). Same as above.

Fantastic Four, vol. 1, #384 (January 1994). Same as above.

Fantastic Four, vol. 1, #386 (March 1994). Tom DeFalco (w), Paul Ryan, Danny Bulanadi, Mike Rockwitz, and Joe Andreani (a). Collected as above.

Fantastic Four, vol. 1, #391 (August 1994). Tom DeFalco (w), Paul Ryan, Danny Bulanadi, and John Kalisz (a). Collected as above.

Fantastic Four, vol. 1, #407 (December 1995). Same creators as above. Collected in *Fantastic Four Epic Collection: Strange Days* (2015).

Fantastic Four, vol. 1, #408 (January 1996). Same as above.

Fantastic Four, vol. 1, #409 (February 1996). Same as above.

Fantastic Four, vol. 1, #411 (April 1996). Same as above.

Fantastic Four, vol. 1, #416 (September 1996). Tom DeFalco (w), Carlos Pacheco, Bob Wiacek, Harry Candelario, P. Craig Russell, Al Milgrom, Ariane Lenshoek, Charlie Huston, and Ed Lazellari (a). Collected as above.

Fantastic Four, vol. 3, #½ (March 1998). Ralph Macchio (w), Ron Lim, Jon Sibal, and Tom Smith (a). Collected in *Fantastic Four: Heroes Return – The Complete Collection Vol. 1* (2019).

Fantastic Four, vol. 3, #1 (January 1998). Scott Lobdell (w), Alan Davis, Mark Farmer, and Liquid! (a). Collected in *Fantastic Four: Heroes Return – The Complete Collection Vol. 1* (2019).

Fantastic Four, vol. 3, #2 (February 1998). Same as above.

Fantastic Four, vol. 3, #4 (April 1998). Scott Lobdell and Chris Claremont (w), Salvador Larroca, Art Thibert, Steve Oliff, and Digital Chameleon (a). Collected as above.

Fantastic Four, vol. 3, #6 (June 1998). Chris Claremont (w), Salvador Larroca, Art Thibert, and Liquid! (a). Collected as above.

Fantastic Four, vol. 3, #7 (July 1998). Same as above.

Fantastic Four, vol. 3, #9 (September 1998). Same as above.

Fantastic Four, vol. 3, #11 (November 1998). Same as above.

Fantastic Four, vol. 3, #12 (December 1998). Chris Claremont (w), Salvador Larroca, Anthony Williams, Art Thibert, Andy Lanning, and Liquid! (a). Collected as above.

Fantastic Four, vol. 3, #13 (January 1999). Chris Claremont (w), Salvador Larroca, Art Thibert, and Liquid! (a). Collected as above.

Fantastic Four, vol. 3, #16 (April 1999). Chris Clarement (w), Salvador Larroca, Art Thibert, Erik Benson, and Liquid! (a). Collected in *Fantastic Four: Heroes Return – The Complete Collection Vol. 2* (2020).

Fantastic Four, vol. 3, #17 (May 1999). Chris Clarement (w), Salvador Larroca, Art Thibert, and Liquid! (a). Collected as above.

Fantastic Four, vol. 3, #19 (July 1999). Same as above.

Fantastic Four, vol. 3, #20 (August 1999). Same as above.

Fantastic Four, vol. 3, #24 (December 1999). Chris Clarement (w), Salvador Larroca, Art Thibert, Mark Pennington, and Liquid! (a). Collected as above.

Fantastic Four, vol. 3, #25 (January 1999). Chris Clarement (w), Salvador Larroca, Art Thibert, and Liquid! (a). Collected as above.

Fantastic Four, vol. 3, #27 (March 2000). Same as above.

Fantastic Four, vol. 3, #31 (July 2000). Same as above.

Fantastic Four, vol. 3, #32 (August 2000). Same as above.

Fantastic Four, vol. 3, #33 (September 2000). John Francis Moore (w), Salvador Larroca, Art Thibert, and Liquid! (a). Collected in *Fantastic Four: Heroes Return – The Complete Collection Vol. 3* (2021).

Fantastic Four, vol. 3, #44 (August 2001). Carlos Pacheco, Rafael Marin, and Jeph Loeb (w), Carlos Pacheco, Jesús Merino, and Liquid! (a). Collected as above.

Fantastic Four, vol. 3, #45 (September 2001). Carlos Pacheco, Rafael Marin, and Jeph Loeb (w), Jeff Johnson, Joe Weems, and Liquid! (a). Collected as above.

Fantastic Four, vol. 3, #49 (January 2002). Carlos Pacheco, Rafael Marin, and Jeph Loeb (w), Carlos Pacheco, Jesús Merino, and Liquid! (a). Collected as above.

Fantastic Four, vol. 3, #53 (May 2002). Carlos Pacheco, Rafael Marin, and Karl Kesel (w), Mark Bagley, Al Vey, and Liquid! (a). Collected as above.

Fantastic Four, vol. 3, #54 (June 2002), "A Choice of Dooms!" Carlos Pacheco, Rafael Marin, and Karl Kesel (w), Mark Bagley, Al Vey, Scott Koblish, and Liquid! (a). Collected as above.

Fantastic Four, vol. 3, #55 (July 2002). Karl Kesel (w), Stuart Immonen, Karl Kesel, and Liquid! (a). Collected as above.

Fantastic Four, vol. 3, #56 (August 2002). Karl Kesel (w), Stuart Immonen, Scott Koblish, and Liquid! (a). Collected as above.

Fantastic Four, vol. 3, #60 (October 2002). Mark Waid (w), Mike Wieringo, Karl Kesel, and Paul Mounts (a). Collected in *Fantastic Four by Waid & Wieringo: Imaginauts* (2025).

Fantastic Four, vol. 3, #61 (November 2002). Same as above.

Fantastic Four, vol. 3, #68 (June 2003). Same creators as above. Collected in *Fantastic Four by Waid & Wieringo: Unthinkable* (2025).

Fantastic Four, vol. 3, #69 (July 2003). Same as above.

Fantastic Four, vol. 3, #70 (August 2003). Mark Waid (w), Mike Wieringo, Larry Stucker, and Paul Mounts (a). Collected as above.

Fantastic Four, vol. 3, #500 (September 2003). Mark Waid (w), Mike Wieringo, Karl Kesel, and Paul Mounts (a). Collected as above.

Fantastic Four, vol. 3, #503 (November 2003). Mark Waid (w), Howard Porter, Norm Rapmund, and Matt Milla (a). Collected in *Fantastic Four by Waid & Wieringo Omnibus* (2018).

Fantastic Four, vol. 3, #504 (December 2003). Same as above.

Fantastic Four, vol. 3, #505 (December 2003). Same as above.

Fantastic Four, vol. 3, #507 (January 2004). Same as above.

Fantastic Four, vol. 3, #511 (May 2004). Mark Waid (w), Mike Wieringo, Karl Kesel, and Paul Mounts (a). Collected as above.

Fantastic Four, vol. 3, #518 (November 2004). Same as above.

Fantastic Four, vol. 3, #519 (December 2004). Same as above.

Fantastic Four, vol. 3, #520 (January 2005). Same as above.

Fantastic Four, vol. 3, #522 (March 2005). Same as above.

Fantastic Four, vol. 3, #523 (April 2005). Same as above.

Fantastic Four, vol. 3, #525 (June 2005). Karl Kesel (w), Tom Grummett, Lary Stucker, and Paul Mounts (a). Collected in *Fantastic Four: The Beginning of the End* (2008).

Fantastic Four, vol. 3, #526 (June 2005). Karl Kesel (w), Tom Grummett, Lary Stucker, Norm Rapmund, and Paul Mounts (a). Collected as above.

Fantastic Four, vol. 3, #528 (August 2005). J. Michael Straczynski (w), Mike McKone, Andy Lanning, and Paul Mounts (a). Collected in *Fantastic Four by J. Michael Stracynski Volume 1* (2006).

Fantastic Four, vol. 3, #530 (October 2005). Same as above.

Fantastic Four, vol. 3, #532 (December 2005). J. Michael Straczynski (w), Mike McKone, Andy Lanning, Kev Walker, Cam Smith, Kris Justice, and Paul Mounts (a). Collected as above.

Fantastic Four, vol. 3, #536 (May 2006). J. Michael Straczynski (w), Mike McKone, Andy Lanning, and Paul Mounts (a). Collected in *Civil War: The Road to Civil War* (2007).

Fantastic Four, vol. 3, #538 (August 2006). J. Michael Straczynski (w), Mike McKone, Andy Lanning, Kris Justice, Cam Smith, and Paul Mounts (a). Collected in *Fantastic Four: Civil War* (2007).

Fantastic Four, vol. 3, #539 (October 2006). Same as above.

Fantastic Four, vol. 3, #540 (December 2006). J. Michael Straczynski (w), Mike McKone, Andy Lanning, Cam Smith, and Paul Mounts (a). Collected as above.

Fantastic Four, vol. 3, #541 (February 2007). J. Michael Straczynski (w), Mike McKone, Andy Lanning, Kris Justice, Cam Smith, and Paul Mounts (a). Collected as above.

Fantastic Four, vol. 3, #542 (March 2007). Dwayne McDuffie (w), Mike McKone, Andy Lanning, Cam Smith, and Paul Mounts (a). Collected as above.

Fantastic Four, vol. 3, #543 (May 2007), "C'mon, Suzie, Don't Leave Us Hangin'." Same as above.

Fantastic Four, vol. 3, #545 (June 2007). Dwayne McDuffie (w), Paul Pelletier, Rick Magyar, and Paul Mounts (a). Collected in *Fantastic Four: The New Fantastic Four* (2008).

Fantastic Four, vol. 3, #546 (July 2007). Dwayne McDuffie (w), Paul Pelletier, Rick Magyar, Scott Hanna, and Paul Mounts (a). Collected as above.

Fantastic Four, vol. 3, #550 (November 2007). Dwayne McDuffie (w), Paul Pelletier, Rick Magyar, and Paul Mounts (a). Collected as above.

Fantastic Four, vol. 3, #552 (February 2008). Dwayne McDuffie (w), Paul Pelletier, Rick Magyar, and Wil Quintana (a). Collected in *Fantastic Four: The Beginning of the End* (2008).

Fantastic Four, vol. 3, #553 (March 2008). Same as above.

Fantastic Four, vol. 3, #554 (April 2008). Mark Millar (w), Bryan Hitch, Paul Neary, and Paul Mounts (a). Collected in *Fantastic Four by Millar & Hitch Omnibus* (2023).

Fantastic Four, vol. 3, #562 (February 2009). Mark Millar (w), Bryan Hitch, Cam Smith, Andrew Currie, and Paul Mounts (a). Collected as above.

Fantastic Four, vol. 3, #569 (September 2009). Mark Millar and Joe Ahearne (w), Stuart Immonen, Wade von Grawbadger, Scott Hanna, Paul Mounts, and Dean White (a). Collected as above.

Fantastic Four, vol. 3, #570 (October 2009). Jonathan Hickman (w), Dale Eaglesham and Paul Mounts (a). Collected in *Fantastic Four by Jonathan Hickman: The Complete Collection Vol. 1* (2018).

Fantastic Four, vol. 3, #575 (March 2010). Same as above.

Fantastic Four, vol. 3, #578 (June 2010). Same as above.

Fantastic Four, vol. 3, #579 (July 2010). Jonathan Hickman (w), Neil Edwards, Andrew Currie, and Paul Mounts (a). Collected in *Fantastic Four by Jonathan Hickman: The Complete Collection Vol. 2* (2019).

Fantastic Four, vol. 3, #583 (November 2010). Jonathan Hickman (w), Steve Epting and Paul Mounts (a). Collected as above.

Fantastic Four, vol. 3, #584 (December 2010). Same as above.

Fantastic Four, vol. 3, #585 (January 2011). Same as above.

Fantastic Four, vol. 3, #587 (March 2011). Jonathan Hickman (w), Steve Epting, Rick Magyar, Mike Perkins, and Paul Mounts (a). Collected as above.

Fantastic Four, vol. 3, #600 (January 2012), "Forever." Jonathan Hickman (w), Steve Epting, Rick Magyar, and Paul Mounts (a). Collected in *Fantastic Four by Jonathan Hickman: The Complete Collection Vol. 3* (2021).

Fantastic Four, vol. 3, #600 (January 2012), "Whatever Happened to Johnny Storm?" Jonathan Hickman (w), Carmine Di Giandomenico and Andy Troy (a). Collected as above.

Fantastic Four, vol. 4, #9 (August 2013). Matt Fraction (w), Mark Bagley, Mark Farmer, Paul Mounts, and Guru-eFX (a). Collected in *Fantastic Four: New Departure, New Arrivals* (2013).

Fantastic Four, vol. 4, #12 (November 2013). Matt Fraction and Christopher Sebela (w), Mark Bagley, Joe Rubinstein, and Paul Mounts (a). Collected in *Fantastic Four: Doomed* (2014).

Fantastic Four, vol. 5, #1 (April 2014). James Robinson (w), Leonard Kirk, Karl Kesel, and Jesus Aburtov (a). Collected in *Fantastic Four: The Fall of the Fantastic Four* (2014).

Fantastic Four, vol. 5, #3 (June 2014). Same as above.

Fantastic Four, vol. 5, #8 (October 2014). James Robinson (w), Leonard Kirk, Scott Hanna, and Jesus Aburtov (a). Collected in *Fantastic Four: Original Sin* (2014).

Fantastic Four, vol. 5, #12 (December 2014). James Robinson (w), Leonard Kirk, Karl Kesel, and Jesus Aburtov (a). Collected in *Fantastic Four: Back in Blue* (2015).

Fantastic Four, vol. 5, #642 (March 2015). Same creators as above. Collected in *Fantastic Four: The End Is Fourever* (2015).

Fantastic Four, vol. 5, #645 (June 2015). James Robinson (w), Leonard Kirk, Karl Kesel, Scott Hanna, Jesus Aburtov, and Israel Silva (a). Collected as above.

Fantastic Four, vol. 6, #1 (October 2018), "Our Day of Doom and Victory." Dan Slott (w), Simone Bianchi and Marco Russo (a). Collected in *Fantastic Four by Dan Slott Vol. 1* (2021).

Fantastic Four, vol. 6, #1 (October 2018), "Signal in the Sky." Dan Slott (w), Sara Pichelli, Elisabetta D'Amico, and Marte Garcia (a). Collected as above.

Fantastic Four, vol. 6, #3 (January 2019). Dan Slott (w), Sara Pichelli, Nico Leon, and Marte Garcia (a). Collected as above.

Fantastic Four, vol. 6, #5 (February 2019), "4-Minute Warning." Dan Slott (w), Aaron Kuder, Marte Gracia, and Erick Arciniega (a). Collected as above.

Fantastic Four, vol. 6, #7 (April 2019). Dan Slott (w), Aaron Kuder, John Lucas, Marte Gracia, and Rachelle Rosenberg (a). Collected as above.

Fantastic Four, vol. 6, #8 (May 2019). Dan Slott (w), Aaron Kuder, Stefano Caselli, Paco Medina, and Erick Arciniega (a). Collected as above.

Fantastic Four, vol. 6, #9 (June 2019). Dan Slott (w), Aaron Kuder, Stefano Caselli, David Marquez, Reilly Brown, and Matt Yackey (a). Collected as above.

Fantastic Four, vol. 6, #11 (August 2019). Dan Slott (w), Paco Medina, Kevin Libranda, Paolo Villanelli, Juanan Ramírez, and Jesus Aburtov (a). Collected as above.

Fantastic Four, vol. 6, #12 (September 2019), "Honeymoon Crasher." Dan Slott (w), Sean Izaakse and Marcio Menyz (a). Collected in *Fantastic Four by Dan Slott Vol. 2* (2022).

Fantastic Four, vol. 6, #13 (October 2019). Same as above.

Fantastic Four, vol. 6, #14 (November 2019). Dan Slott (w), Paco Medina and Jesus Aburtov (a). Collected as above.

Fantastic Four, vol. 6, #17 (February 2020). Dan Slott (w), Luciano Vecchio, Carlos Magno, Bob Quinn, and Sean Izaakse (a). Collected as above.

Fantastic Four, vol. 6, #20 (May 2020). Dan Slott (w), Paco Medina and Jesus Aburtov (a). Collected as above.

Fantastic Four, vol. 6, #32 (July 2021), "Duel Intentions." Dan Slott (w) and Javier Rodriguez (a). Collected in *Fantastic Four by Dan Slott Vol. 4* (2023).

Fantastic Four, vol. 6, #33 (August 2021). Dan Slott (w), R.B. Silva, Luca Maresca, and Jesus Aburtov (a). Collected as above.

Fantastic Four, vol. 6, #34 (September 2021). Dan Slott (w), R.B. Silva and Jesus Aburtov (a). Collected as above.

Fantastic Four, vol. 6, #35 (November 2021), "Death in Four Dimensions." Dan Slott (w), John Romita, Jr., JP Mayer, Scott Hanna, Cam Smith, Rafael Fonteriz, Mark Morales, Marte Garcia, and Erick Arciniega (a). Collected as above.

Fantastic Four, vol. 6, #35 (November 2021), "Stars." Mark Waid (w) and Paul Renaud (a). Collected as above.

Fantastic Four, vol. 6, #39 (March 2022). Dan Slott (w), Francesco Manna and Jesus Aburtov (a). Collected in *Fantastic Four by Dan Slott Vol. 4* (2023).

Fantastic Four, vol. 6, #40 (April 2022). Dan Slott (w), Rachael Stott and Jesus Aburtov (a). Collected in *Fantastic Four: Reckoning War* (2024).

Fantastic Four, vol. 6, #45 (September 2022). Dan Slott (w), Farid Karami and Jesus Aburtov (a). Collected as above.

Fantastic Four, vol. 6, #46 (October 2022). Dan Slott (w), CAFU and Jesus Aburtov (a). Collected as above.

Fantastic Four, vol. 6, #47 (November 2022). David Pepose (w), Juan Cabal and Jesus Aburtov (a). Collected in *A.X.E.: Judgment Day Companion* (2023).

Fantastic Four, vol. 6, #48 (December 2022). Same as above.

Fantastic Four, vol. 7, #1 (January 2023). Ryan North (w), Iban Coello and Jesus Aburtov (a). Collected in *Fantastic Four by Ryan North Vol. 1: Whatever Happened to the Fantastic Four?* (2023).

Fantastic Four, vol. 7, #6 (June 2023). Ryan North (w), Ivan Fiorelli and Jesus Aburtov (a). Collected as above.

Fantastic Four, vol. 7, #7 (July 2023). Ryan North (w), Iban Coello and Jesus Aburtov (a). Collected in *Fantastic Four by Ryan North Vol. 2: Four Stories about Hope* (2024).

Fantastic Four, vol. 7, #9 (September 2023). Ryan North (w), Ivan Fiorelli and Jesus Aburtov (a). Collected as above.

Fantastic Four, vol. 7, #11 (November 2023). Ryan North (w), Iban Coello and Jesus Aburtov (a). Collected as above.

Fantastic Four, vol. 7, #12 (December 2023). Same creators as above. Collected in *Fantastic Four by Ryan North Vol. 3: The Impossible Is Probable* (2024).

Fantastic Four, vol. 7, #18 (May 2024). Ryan North (w), Carlos Gómez and Jesus Aburtov (a). Collected in *Fantastic Four by Ryan North Vol. 4: Fortune Favors the Fantastic* (2024).

Fantastic Four, vol. 7, #25 (November 2024). Same creators as above (a). Collected in *Fantastic Four by Ryan North Vol. 5: Aliens, Ghosts and Alternate Earths* (2025).

Fantastic Four, vol. 7, #29 (April 2025). Ryan North (w), Cory Smith, Oren Junior, and Jesus Aburtov (a). Collected in *Fantastic Four by Ryan North Vol. 6: One World Under Doom* (2025).

Fantastic Four: 4 Yancy Street #1 (October 2019). Gerry Duggan (w), Greg Smallwood, Mark Bagley, Luciano Cecchio, Pere Pérez, and Erick Arciniega (a). Collected in *Fantastic Four by Dan Slott Vol. 2* (2022).

Fantastic Four Annual, vol. 1, #1 (1963), "Sub-Mariner Versus the Human Race!" Stan Lee (w), Jack Kirby, Dick Ayers, and Stan Goldberg (a). Collected in *Fantastic Four Epic Collection: The Master Plan of Doctor Doom* (2017).

Fantastic Four Annual, vol. 1, #2 (1964), "The Fantastic 'Origin of Doctor Doom!'" Stan Lee (w), Jack Kirby and Chic Stone (a). Collected as above.

Fantastic Four Annual, vol. 1, #2 (1964), "The Final Victory of Dr. Doom!" Same as above.

Fantastic Four Annual, vol. 1, #3 (1965), "Bedlam at the Baxter Building!" Stan Lee (w), Jack Kirby, Vince Colletta, and Stan Goldberg (a). Collected in *Fantastic Four Epic Collection: The Coming of Galactus* (2018).

Fantastic Four Annual, vol. 1, #15 (1980), "The Power of the People." Doug Moench (w), Tom Sutton and Ben Sean (a). Collected in *Fantastic Four Epic Collection: The Possession of Franklin Richards* (2025).

Fantastic Four Annual, vol. 1, #19 (1985). John Byrne (w), John Byrne, Joe Sinnott, and Glynis Wein (a). Collected in Collected in *Fantastic Four by John Byrne Omnibus Vol. 2* (2013).

Fantastic Four, vol. 1, #20 (1987). Steve Englehart (w), Paul Neary, Tony DeZuniga, and John Wellington (a). Collected in *Fantastic Four Epic Collection: All in the Family* (2014).

Fantastic Four Annual, vol. 3, #32 (2010). Joe Ahearne (w), Bryan Hitch, Andrew Currie, and Paul Mounts (a). Collected in *Fantastic Four by Millar & Hitch Omnibus* (2023).

Fantastic Four Annual, vol. 5, #1 (2014). James Robinson (w), Tom Grummett, Tom Palmer, and Jim Charalampidis (a). Collected in *Fantastic Four: Back in Blue* (2015).

Fantastic Four: Atlantis Rising #1 (June 1995). Tom DeFalco and Glenn Herdling (w), M.C. Wyman, Rey Garcia, Don Hudson, Goef Isherwood,

Kevin Yates, and Mike Rockwitz (a). Collected in *Fantastic Four Epic Collection: Atlantis Rising* (2024).

Fantastic Four: Foes #2 (April 2005). Robert Kirkman (w), Cliff Rathburn and Bille Crabtree (a). Collected in *Fantastic Four: Foes* (2005).

Fantastic Four: Grimm Noir #1 (April 2020). Gerry Duggan (w), Ron Garney and Matt Milla (a). Collected in Collected in *Fantastic Four by Dan Slott Vol. 4* (2023).

Fantastic Four: Reckoning War Alpha #1 (April 2022). Dan Slott (w), Carlos Pacheco, Rafael Fonteriz, Carlos Magno, and Guru-eFX (a). Collected in Collected in *Fantastic Four: Reckoning War* (2024).

Fantastic Four Special #1 (2005). Dwayne McDuffie (w), Casey Jones, Vince Russell, and Danimation (a). Collected in *Fantastic Four: The Life Fantastic* (2006).

Fantastic Four Unplugged #2 (October 1995). Mike Lackey (w), Adriana Melo, Tim Dzon, and Mike Rockwitz (a). Not yet collected.

Fantastic Four Unplugged #5 (May 1996). Mike Lackey (w), Adriana Melo, Tim Dzon, and Nel Yomtov (a). Not yet collected.

Fantastic Four: The Wedding Special #1 (2005), "The Life Fantastic." Karl Kesel (w), Drew Johnson, Karl Kesel, Drew Geraci, Drew Hennessy, and Morry Hollowell (a). Collected in *Fantastic Four: The Life Fantastic* (2006).

Fantastic Four: Wedding Special #1 (February 2019), "(Invisible) Girls Gone Wild." Gail Simone (w), Laura Braga and Jesus Aburtov (a). Collected in Collected in *Fantastic Four by Dan Slott Vol. 1* (2021).

Fantastic Four vs. the X-Men #2 (March 1987). Chris Claremont (w), Jon Bogdanove, Terry Austin, and Glynis Oliver (a). Collected in *Fantastic Four Epic Collection: All in the Family* (2014).

Fantastic Four vs. the X-Men #3 (April 1987). Same as above.

Fantastic Four vs. the X-Men #4 (June 1987). Same as above.

FF, vol. 1, #2 (June 2011). Jonathan Hickman (w), Steve Epting, Rick Magyar, and Paul Mounts (a). Collected in *Fantastic Four by Jonathan Hickman: The Complete Collection Vol. 2* (2019).

FF, vol. 1, #4 (July 2011). Jonathan Hickman (w), Barry Kitson and Paul Mounts (a). Collected as above.

FF, vol. 1, #12 (January 2012). Jonathan Hickman (w), Juan Bobillo, Marcela Sosa, and Chris Sotomayor (a). Collected in *Fantastic Four by Jonathan Hickman: The Complete Collection Vol. 3* (2020).

FF, vol. 2, #16 (March 2014). Matt Fraction and Lee Allred (w), Michael Allred and Laura Allred (a). Collected in *FF: Family Freakout* (2014).

Galactus the Devourer #6 (March 2000). Louise Simonson (w), John Buscema, Bill Sienkiewicz, and Christie Schelle (a). Collected in *Silver Surfer Epic Collection: Sun Rise and Shadow Fall* (2023).

The Incredible Hulk, vol. 1, #134 (September 1970). Roy Thomas (w), Herb Trimpe and Sal Buscema (a). Collected in *The Incredible Hulk Epic Collection: In the Hands of Hydra* (2019).

Infamous Iron Man #1 (December 2016). Brian Michael Bendis (w), Alex Maleev and Matt Hollingsworth (a). Collected in *Infamous Iron Man* (2023).

Infinity Countdown #3 (July 2018). Gerry Duggan (w), Mike Deodato, Jr., Mike Hawthorne, Aaron Kuder, Terry Pallot, Frank Martin, Jr., and Jordie Bellaire (a). Collected in *Infinity Countdown* (2018).

Infinity Countdown #4 (August 2018). Gerry Duggan (w), Mike Deodato, Jr., Mike Hawthorne, Aaron Kuder, Terry Pallot, José Marzan, Jr., Frank Martin, Jr., and Jordie Bellaire (a). Collected as above.

Infinity War #3 (August 1992). Jim Starlin (w), Ron Lim, Al Milgram, and Ian Laughlin (a). Collected in *Infinity War* (2012).

Invincible Iron Man, vol. 2, #600 (July 2018). Brian Michael Bendis (w), Stefano Caselli, Alex Maleev, David Marquez, Daniel Acuña, Leinil Francis Yu, Jim Cheung, Mike Deodato, Jr., Mark Bagley, Andrea Sorrentino, Gerry Alanguilan, Andrew Hennessy, Scott Hanna, Marte Garcia, Guru-eFX, Romula Fajardo, Jr., Marcelo Maiolo, and Rachelle Rosenberg (a). Collected in *Infamous Iron Man* (2023).

Invisible Woman #1 (September 2019). Mark Waid (w) and Mattia De Iulis (a). Collected in *Invisible Woman: Partners in Crime* (2020).

Invisible Woman #3 (November 2019). Same as above.

Invisible Woman #5 (January 2020). Same as above.

Iron Man, vol. 3, #14 (March 1999). Kurt Busiek and Roger Stern (w), Sean Chen, Larry Stucker, Eric Cannon, and Steve Oliff (a). *Fantastic Four: Heroes Return – The Complete Collection Vol. 1* (2019).

King in Black #2 (February 2021). Donny Cates (w), Ryan Stegman, JP Mayer, and Frank Martin (a). Collected in *King in Black* (2021).

Marvel 2-in-One #1 (February 2018). Chip Zdarsky (w), Jim Cheung, John Dell, Walden Wong, and Frank Martin, Jr. (a). Collected in *Fantastic Four: Fate of the Four* (2025).

Marvel 2-in-One #4 (May 2018). Chip Zdarsky (w), Valerio Schiti and Frank Martin, Jr. (a). Collected as above.

Marvel 2-in-One #11 (December 2018). Chip Zdarsky (w), Ramón Pérez and Federico Blee (a). Collected as above.

Marvel 2-in-One Annual #1 (2018). Chip Zdarsky (w), Declan Shalvey and Jordie Bellaire (a). Collected as above.

Marvel Fanfare, vol. 1, #2 (May 1982), "Annihilation." Roger McKenzie (w), Trevor von Eeden, Armando Gil, and Glynis Wein (a). Collected in *Marvel Masterworks: Fantastic Four Vol. 22* (2020).

Marvel Fanfare, vol. 1, #20 (May 1985). Jim Starlin (w), Jim Starlin, Al Milgrom, and Christie Scheele (a). Not yet collected.

Marvel Holiday Special 1994 (1994), "Losin' the Blues." Gregory Wright (w), Mike Manley and Gregory Wright (a). Not yet collected.

Marvel Super-Heroes #20 (May 1969), "This Man...This Demon!" Larry Lieber and Roy Thomas (w), Larry Lieber, Frank Giacoia, and Vince

Colletta (a). Collected in *Doctor Doom: The Book of Doom Omnibus* (2022).

Marvel Team-Up, vol. 1, #147 (November 1984). Cary Burkett (w), Greg LaRocque, Mike Esposito, and Julianna Ferriter (a). Collected in *Amazing Spider-Man: The Complete Alien Costume Saga Book 2* (2015).

Marvel Two-in-One #10 (July 1975). Chris Claremont (w), William Robert Brown and Klaus Janson (a). Collected in *Marvel Two-in-One Epic Collection: Cry Monster* (2018).

Marvel Two-in-One #11 (September 1975). Bill Mantlo and Roy Thomas (w), Williams Robert Brown and Klaus Janson (a). Collected as above.

Marvel Two-in-One #12 (November 1975). Bill Mantlo (w), Ron Wilson, Vince Colletta, and Janice Cohen (a). Collected as above.

Marvel Two-in-One #26 (April 1977). Marv Wolfman (w), Ron Wilson, Pablo Marcos, and Janice Cohen (a). Collected in *Marvel Two-in-One Epic Collection: Two Against Hydra* (2024).

Marvel Two-in-One #29 (July 1977). Marv Wolfman (w), Ron Wilson and Sam Grainger (a). Collected as above.

Marvel Two-in-One #30 (August 1977). Marv Wolfman (w), John Buscema, Pablo Marcos, and Janice Cohen (a). Collected as above.

Marvel Two-in-One #32 (October 1977). Same as above.

Marvel Two-in-One #42 (August 1978). Ralph Macchio (w), Sal Buscema, Alfredo Alcala, Sam Grainger, and Nel Yomtov (a). Collected in *Marvel Two-in-One Epic Collection: Remembrance of Things Past* (2025).

Marvel Two-in-One #60 (February 1980). Mark Gruenwald and Ralph Macchio (w), George Pérez, Gene Day, and Roger Silfer (a). Collected in *Marvel Masterworks: Marvel Two-in-One Volume 5* (2020).

Marvel Two-in-One #67 (September 1980). Mark Gruenwald and Ralph Macchio (w), Ron Wilson, Gene Day, and Frank Martin, Jr. (a). Collected in *Marvel Masterworks: Marvel Two-in-One Volume 6* (2022).

Marvel Two-in-One #70 (December 1980). Mark Gruenwald and Ralph Macchio (w), Mike Nasser, Gene Day, and George Roussos (a). Collected as above.

Marvel Two-in-One #71 (January 1981). Mark Gruenwald and Ralph Macchio (w), Ron Wilson, Gene Day, and George Roussos (a). Collected as above.

Marvel Two-in-One #77 (July 1981). Tom DeFalco (w), Ron Wilson, Chic Stone, and George Roussos (a). Collected in *Marvel Masterworks: Marvel Two-in-One Volume 7* (2024).

Marvel Two-in-One #80 (October 1981). Same as above.

Marvel Two-in-One #81 (November 1981). Same as above.

Marvel Two-in-One #92 (October 1982). Tom DeFalco (w), Ron Wilson, "A. Sorted," and Don Warfield (a). Collected (in black-and-white) in *Essential Marvel Two-in-One Volume 4* (2012).

Marvel Two-in-One #100 (June 1983). John Byrne (w), Ron Wilson, Frank Giacoia, Kevin Dzuban, and George Roussos (a). Collected as above.

New Avengers, vol. 3, #2 (March 2013). Jonathan Hickman (w), Steve Epting, Rick Magyar, and Frank D'Armata (a). Collected in *Avengers by Jonathan Hickman: The Complete Collection Volume 1* (2020).

New Avengers, vol. 3, #3 (April 2013). Jonathan Hickman (w), Steve Epting and Frank D'Armata (a). Collected as above.

New Avengers, vol. 3, #21 (September 2014). Jonathan Hickman (w), Valerio Schiti, Salvador Larroca, Frank Martin, Jr., and Paul Mounts (a). Collected in *Avengers by Jonathan Hickman: The Complete Collection Volume 4* (2021).

New Avengers, vol. 3, #22 (October 2014). Jonathan Hickman (w), Kev Walker and Frank Martin, Jr. (a). Collected as above.

New Avengers, vol. 3, #23 (October 2014). Same as above.

New Avengers, vol. 3, #27 (January 2015). Jonathan Hickman (w), Szymon Kudranski and Dono Sánchez-Almara. Collected in *Avengers by Jonathan Hickman: The Complete Collection Volume 5* (2022).

New Avengers, vol. 3, #33 (June 2015). Jonathan Hickman (w), Mike Deodato, Jr., and Frank Martin, Jr. (a). Collected as above.

New Avengers: Illuminati, vol. 1, #1 (May 2006). Brian Michael Bendis (w), Alex Maleev and Dave Stewart (a). Collected in *Civil War: The Road to Civil War* (2007).

One World Under Doom #1 (April 2025). Ryan North (w), R.B. Silva and David Curiel (a). Not yet collected.

Secret Invasion, vol. 1, #8 (January 2009). Brian Michael Bendis (w), Leinil Francis Yu, Mark Morales, and Laura Martin (a). Collected in *Secret Invasion* (2010).

Secret Invasion: Fantastic Four #1 (July 2008). Roberto Aguirre-Sacasa (w), Barry Kitson, Mick Gray, Scott Hanna, Paul Neary, and Chris Sotomayor (a). Collected in *Secret Invasion: Fantastic Four* (2009).

Secret Wars, vol. 1, #1 (May 1984). Jim Shooter (w), Mike Zeck, John Beatty, and Christie Scheele (a). Collected in *Secret Wars* (1992).

Secret Wars, vol. 1, #2 (June 1984). Same as above.

Secret Wars, vol. 1, #7 (November 1984). Jim Shooter (w), Mike Zeck, John Beatty, and Christie Scheele (a). Collected as above.

Secret Wars, vol. 1, #11 (March 1985). Jim Shooter (w), Mike Zeck, John Beatty, and Nelson Yomtov (a). Collected as above.

Secret Wars, vol. 1, #12 (April 1985). Jim Shooter (w), Mike Zeck, John Beatty, and Christie Scheele (a). Collected as above.

Secret Wars, vol. 2, #9 (March 2016). Jonathan Hickman (a), Esad Ribić and Ive Svorcina (a). Collected in *Secret Wars* (2016).

S.H.I.E.L.D., vol. 3, #4 (June 2015). Mark Waid (w), Chris Sprouse, Karl Story, and Dono Sánchez-Almara (a). Collected in *S.H.I.E.L.D.: Perfect Bullets* (2015).

Silver Surfer, vol. 1, #1 (May 1968), "The Origin of the Silver Surfer!" Stan Lee (w), John Buscema, Joe Sinnott, and Bill Everett (a). Collected in *Silver Surfer Omnibus* (2007).

Silver Surfer, vol. 3, #48 (April 1991). Jim Starlin (w), Ron Lim, Tom Christopher, and Tom Vincent (a). Collected in *Silver Surfer Epic Collection: Thanos Quest* (2018).

Silver Surfer, vol. 3, #123 (December 1996). George Pérez and J.M. DeMatteis (w), Ron Garney, Bob Wiacek, and Tom Smith (a). Collected in *Silver Surfer Epic Collection: Inner Demons* (2019).

Silver Surfer Annual, vol. 3, #3 (1990), "Shades of Guilt." Ron Marz (w), Ron Lim, Keith Williams, and Tom Vincent (a). Collected in *Silver Surfer Epic Collection: Thanos Quest* (2018).

Silver Surfer Annual, vol. 8, #1 (2018). Ethan Sacks (w), André Lima Araújo and Chris O'Halloran (a). Collected in *Marvel Universe: Time ana Again* (2019).

Spider-Man/Fantastic Four #2 (October 2010). Christos N. Gage (w) and Mario Alberti (a). Collected in *Spider-Man/Fantastic Four* (2011).

Spider-Man/Fantastic Four #3 (November 2010). Same as above.

Spider-Man/Fantastic Four #4 (December 2010). Same as above.

Strange Tales, vol. 1, #112 (September 1963), "The Human Torch Faces the Threat of 'The Living Bomb!'" Stan Lee and Joe Carter (w), Dick Ayers and Stan Goldberg (a). Collected in *The Human Torch & the Thing: Strange Tales – The Complete Collection* (2018).

Strange Tales, vol. 1, #115 (December 1963), "The Sandman Strikes!" Stan Lee and Dick Ayers (w), Dick Ayers and Stan Goldberg (a). Collected as above.

Super-Villain Classics #1 (May 1983). Stan Lee and Mark Gruenwald (w), Jack Kirby, John Byrne, Vince Colletta, George Klein, Ron Wilson, Jack Abel, and Andy Yanchus (a). Collected in *Silver Surfer Epic Collection: Freedom* (2015).

Super-Villain Team-Up #12 (June 1977). Bill Mantlo (w), Bob Hall, Don Perlin, and George Roussos (a). Collected in *Super-Villains Unite: The Complete Super-Villain Team-Up* (2015).

Super-Villain Team-Up #13 (August 1977). Bill Mantlo (w), Keith Giffen, Don Perlin, and Don Warfield (a). Collected as above.

Thing, vol. 1, #5 (November 1983). John Byrne (w), Ron Wilson, Hilary Barta, and Bob Sharen (a). Collected in *Thing Omnibus* (2022).

Thing, vol. 1, #10 (April 1984). John Byrne (w), Ron Wilson, Hilary Barta, and Julianna Ferriter (a). Collected as above.

Thing, vol. 1, #23 (May 1985). Mike Carlin (w), Ron Wilson, Bob Layton, and Bob Sharen (a). Collected as above.

Thing, vol. 2, #5 (May 2006). Dan Slott (w), Andrea Divito and Laura Villari (a). Collected in *The Thing: Idol of Millions* (2006).

Thing, vol. 2, #6 (June 2006). Dan Slott (w), Keiron Dwyer and Laura Villani (a). Collected as above.

Thing, vol. 2, #7 (July 2006). Same as above.

Thing, vol. 2, #8 (August 2006). Same as above.

Thor, vol. 6, #1 (March 2020). Donny Cates (w), Nic Klein and Matthew Wilson (a). Collected in *Thor: The Devourer King* (2020).

Thor, vol. 6, #6 (October 2020). Same as above.

The Ultimates, vol. 2, #2 (February 2016). Al Ewing (w), Kenneth Rocafort and Dan Brown (a). Collected in *The Ultimates: The Complete Collection* (2021).

The Ultimates 2, vol. 2, #2 (February 2017). Al Ewing (w), Travel Foreman and Dan Brown (a). Collected as above.

Uncanny Avengers, vol. 3, #1 (December 2015). Gerry Duggan (w), Ryan Stegman and Richard Isanove (a). Collected in *Uncanny Avengers: Lost Future* (2016).

Uncanny Avengers, vol. 3, #2 (January 2016). Same as above.

Uncanny Avengers, vol. 3, #17 (February 2017). Gerry Duggan (w), Pepe Larraz and David Curiel (a). Collected in *Uncanny Avengers: Civil War II* (2017).

Uncanny Avengers, vol. 3, #22 (June 2017). Same creators as above. Collected in *Uncanny Avengers: Red Skull* (2017).

Venom, vol. 5, #24 (October 2023). Al Ewing (w), Sergio Dávila, Sean Parsons, and Frank D'Armala. Collected in *Venom: Predestination* (2024).

War of the Realms: War Scrolls #3 (August 2019), "A Rose for Victor." Christopher Cantwell (w), Cian Tormey and Dan Brown (a). Collected in *Doctor Doom by Cantwell & Larroca* (2024).

World War Hulk #2 (September 2007). Greg Pak (w), John Romita, Jr., Klaus Janson, and Christina Strain (a). Collected in *Hulk: World War Hulk* (2019).

X-Men/Fantastic Four #1 (April 2020). Chip Zdarsky (w), Terry Dodson, Rachel Dodson, Dexter Vines, Karl Story, and Laura Martin (a). Collected in *X-Men/Fantastic Four: 4X* (2020).

X-Men/Fantastic Four #2 (April 2020). Chip Zdarsky (w), Terry Dodson, Rachel Dodson, Karl Story, Ransom Getty, and Laura Martin (a). Collected as above.

X-Men/Fantastic Four #3 (May 2020). Chip Zdarsky (w), Terry Dodson, Rachel Dodson, Ransom Getty, Laura Martin, Andrew Crossley, and Peter Pantazis (a). Collected as above.

Mark D. White is a professor in the Department of Philosophy at the College of Staten Island/CUNY, where he teaches courses in philosophy, economics, and law. He is the author of twelve books (including four in the *A Philosopher Reads...* series at Ockham Publishing), editor or co-editor of 19 more, and has written over 70 academic journal articles and book chapters in the intersections between economics, philosophy, and law.

You can find more information about Mark's books, articles, and blogs at:
http://www.profmdwhite.com and find him on social media as: @profmdwhite.

www.ingramcontent.com/pod-product-compliance
Lightning Source LLC
LaVergne TN
LVHW041212080426
835508LV00011B/922